COMISKEY PARK'S
LAST WORLD SERIES

COMISKEY PARK'S LAST WORLD SERIES

A History of the 1959 Chicago White Sox

Charles N. Billington

McFarland & Company, Inc., Publishers
Jefferson, North Carolina

All photographs are from the collection of
Tony Inzerillo and used with permission.

ISBN (print) 978-1-4766-7685-2
ISBN (ebook) 978-1-4766-3557-6

LIBRARY OF CONGRESS AND BRITISH LIBRARY
CATALOGUING DATA ARE AVAILABLE

LIBRARY OF CONGRESS CONTROL NUMBER: 2019942445

Front cover: Chicago White Sox shortstop Luis Aparicio
called safe after stealing second, avoiding the tag
of Boston Red Sox infielder Pumpsie Green

Manufactured in the United States of America

*McFarland & Company, Inc., Publishers
Box 611, Jefferson, North Carolina 28640
www.mcfarlandpub.com*

For all the fans of the Chicago White Sox ...
who put Mantle and Berra in their spokes
and Fox and Pierce under their pillows.
You know who you are.

Acknowledgments

I want to start out by thanking my wife Cynthia for her encouragement and support on this project, through its many ups and downs, and for being so helpful in its creation. A keen editor and linguist in her own right, Cynthia provided freely given and much needed technological assistance and suggestions. The enthusiasm and interest in this book that my son Matt, daughter Sarah, and son-in-law Matthew Norman shared were extremely helpful and important to me. Thanks so much for pushing me along!

I also owe a debt of gratitude to all the individuals who have come to my baseball lectures and presentations and exhorted me to write about the White Sox, and this team in particular. Sincere thanks to the staff of the Chicago History Museum, the Harold Washington Branch of the Chicago Public Library, the Glencoe Public Library, and the Skokie Public Library.

I also want to thank a group of gentlemen and acknowledge their support and encouragement of my writings, media appearances, and presentations over the years. I have been lucky enough to call them teammates for over a decade: Jim Doss, Dick Loescher, Jim Kapsa, Phil Shubitz, Dr. Joseph Ptasinski, the late Jeff Levens, Jim Hampson, the late Charlie Konkus, Steve Bradford, Perry Tasky, Bobby Berliner, Al Paveza, Jerry Tater, and George Vernier. Many of these fellows are rabid White Sox followers. All of them have an inextinguishable passion for baseball and still have the skill to play the game well. Each one of them has forgotten more baseball than I will ever know.

Lastly, there is not a day of writing in which the sage advice or imperative demands from a trio of professors at St. Olaf College does not cross my mind; my hope is that they read this without red pen in hand. Thank you, R. G. Peterson, Jack Schwandt, and David Wee. I think your lessons have lasted. I hope you agree.

Table of Contents

Preface

This book is about one of the most significant professional sports teams in Chicago's history, the 1959 Chicago White Sox. Their capture of the American League pennant was the crowning achievement of the team's most successful decade, when they were known nation-wide as the "Go-Go White Sox," an apt nickname. In an era when power hitting and home runs were becoming the norm, the 1959 Sox had more stolen bases than home runs. The customary thinking of the day was that you could not succeed in the modern baseball era without power hitting, that the days of winning it all with defense, pitching, and speed were long over—a feeling that even one of the team's owners had—but this collection of ballplayers proved them all wrong.

Led by Luis Aparicio, Nellie Fox, Sherman Lollar, Jim Landis, and Jim Rivera, the 1959 White Sox were one of the greatest defensive teams in history. During their careers, this corps of peerless glove men were selected to All-Star teams 39 times, and they earned 20 Gold Glove Awards. The team was so deep defensively that its two *backup* catchers, Earl Battey and John Romano, were All-Stars nine times and won three Gold Gloves during their careers.

Mentored by Ray Berres, one of the greatest pitching coaches of all time, the 1959 White Sox pitching staff was arguably the greatest of its era. Anchoring the staff was a great veteran later honored in baseball's Hall of Fame, Early "Gus" Wynn. Billy Pierce, one of the best left-handers in American League history who deserves to be enshrined in the Hall himself, was the fixture of the staff. In 1959, he started his 11th season for the South Siders. The other starters were Dick Donovan, Barry Latman, and Bob Shaw, while Rudy Arias, Turk Lown, Ray Moore, and Gerry Staley manned the best bullpen in either league.

At the same time the 1959 White Sox were elevating defensive play to an art form, they thrilled Chicagoans with a daring and exciting offense, the likes of which the baseball world had not seen for many years. Proving that you did not need power hitting to succeed, they won the American League pennant while stealing 113 bases and hitting only 97 home runs. Only two teams in the previous 25 years got to the World Series with more steals than homers. Thanks to Nellie Fox, perhaps the most patient but pesky number two hitter in baseball history, the Sox starting lineup walked *58 more times* than they struck out, an unheard-of achievement today. By contrast, the 2017 World Series Champion Houston Astros' starting lineup struck out *326 more times* than they walked. The White Sox offense excelled at putting the ball in play, sacrificing, stealing bases, and hitting in the clutch.

    I became interested in this team as an elementary school youngster. Back then, the loyalties of all the guys in the neighborhood were divided sharply between the Cubs and the Sox. Some followed one team simply because their dads did. Others chose one over the other perhaps because of neighborhood loyalties. If you had relatives in or came from Bridgeport, Canaryville, Chinatown, Hyde Park, Marshall Boulevard, Pilsen, or South Shore, you were undoubtedly a White Sox fan. However, if areas like Edgewater, the Gold Coast, Lakeview, North Park, Old Town, Ravenswood, or Rogers Park meant more to you, you were a Cubs fan. What about Wrigleyville, you ask? No place in Chicago was called Wrigleyville; there was a ballpark in Lakeview where Addison, Sheffield, and Clark Streets intersect, just like there is now.

    Growing up as a baby boomer in Chicago afforded one a unique perspective on baseball. We were fortunate enough to be one of only two cities that had a team in each league, and the only city with that distinction after 1957. In those years, all Cubs home games were afternoon affairs, and each one was televised. We would usually get home from school in time to listen to Jack Brickhouse announce the last two innings, and then fill the rest of the time slot with the inane but well-intentioned *Tenth Inning Show*. The problem with the Cubs in those days was three-fold: they had an apathetic owner, overseeing a weak organization, which never put a good product on the field. Other than that, and especially if you were a kid just learning about baseball, they were really entertaining. Once they foolishly got rid of Andy Pafko and Hank Sauer, the only Cub who generated any interest was Ernie Banks. When we could read well enough to digest the newspaper's sports section, it was always fun to turn the page with the standings upside down, just to get a feel for what it would be like to have the Cubs at the top and Pittsburgh or Philadelphia right behind them.

    The White Sox, on the other hand, were a very different story. In the 1950s, they had young, aggressive owners running a great organization that assembled teams perfectly suited for their huge, deadball-era stadium. Year after year, the only thing that kept them out of the World Series was the New York Yankees. While they played some day games, they heavily marketed their evening dates, and since only their day games were televised, those games were always more of an event than the Cubs telecasts were. Also, during the 1950s, a ticket to a Friday night game at Comiskey Park was perhaps the hottest entertainment venue in Chicagoland.

The book pays a great deal of attention to other aspects of this significant event that other books on the topic do not. Off the field and in the courtroom, a bitter family dispute over the team's ownership developed, causing a rift that played out very publicly. This issue is discussed in detail in the beginning of the book. Once the courts put the family feud to rest, the new owners soon discovered that they had to form a very difficult and uneasy alliance with the remaining family owner, which led to more ill will and continuing legal disputes. These are covered throughout the book, as the anger and rancor continued throughout the season and beyond. I offer a great deal of information about the nature of baseball in the 1950s as well, with significant historical anecdotes about other teams and how they fared during this era. The colorful contributions and departure of the White Sox's illustrious tenant, the NFL's

The 1959 Chicago White Sox pictured in July. 1st Row: Doby, Landis, Salas and Riosch (batboys), Smith, Simpson. 2nd Row: E. Colledge, Goodman, Cuccinello, Cooney, Gutteridge, Lopez. Beres, Staley, Lollar, Fox, A. Colledge. 3rd Row: Froelich, Snyderworth, Wynn, Arias, Moore, Lown, Romano, Shaw, Esposito, Rivera, Phillips. 4th Row: Torgeson, Pierce, Aparicio, Latman, Cash, Donovan, Heinman, Battey, McAnany.

Chicago Cardinals, is also covered in detail. The book ends with a discussion about why the White Sox were unable to repeat, making only one World Series appearance.

Along the way I delve into the economic, social, and community significance of the 1959 Fall Classic, the first pennant on Chicago's South Side in 40 years. In that year, the Chicago White Sox were finally able to lift the dark shadows of deceit that had hung over the organization for four decades, wiping away the smudge and shame of the infamous 1919 Black Sox. Since the Dodgers had abandoned Brooklyn the year before, the White Sox were also the last remaining "neighborhood" team in the majors, still playing where they were born in Bridgeport. There is an entire chapter on the effects and significance of the first American League pennant in four decades on this unique Chicago neighborhood.

All of my research was conducted at public libraries or the research library at the Chicago History Museum, where I reviewed old microfilm or donned latex gloves to protect 55-year-old newsprint. I was also fortunate enough to obtain photos from the collection of Tony Inzerillo, the official team photographer during that era.

To this day in Chicago, the White Sox still play second fiddle to the Cubs, and lately, more often than not, their fiddle has been quite out of tune. My hope is that this book will stir the memories of those who remember this fascinating team and educate and enlighten those too young to have experienced it. What follows is how it all unfolded.

Introduction

On Tuesday evening, September 22, 1959, 54,293 baseball fans gathered in Cleveland's massive Municipal Stadium to see the second-place Cleveland Indians host the first-place Chicago White Sox. In Chicago, 346 miles to the west, more than two million White Sox loyalists followed every moment of the game on their radios or televisions. At 9:42 p.m. Eastern Daylight Time, the game was in the last of the ninth, and the Sox were ahead, 4–2, but the Indians were making the most of their last opportunity. Reliever Gerry Staley was in a jam. His predecessor on the mound, Bob Shaw, had induced the Indians' first hitter to fly out but then yielded three consecutive singles. With only one away and the bases loaded, Cleveland slugger Vic Power strode to the plate. Staley threw a slider, spinning low and away from his wheelhouse. Power liked the pitch, swung over it, but still got enough wood on the ball to hit a sharp grounder back toward the mound, a blow that would tie the game if it got through the middle of the infield. As he had done so many times before, Luis Aparicio gracefully glided over from his shortstop position, stepped on second to force the sliding Jimmy Piersall, and fired a strike to a jubilant Ted Kluszewski at first base for the double play. The Sox had clinched their first pennant in 40 years.

Joy and jubilation broke out in Chicago, followed by a cacophony of car horns and fireworks, as 25,000 White Sox fans rushed to Midway Airport to greet their heroes. It did not matter that the plane would not land until 2:30 a.m. The crowd, including Mayor Richard Daley and his wife, would gladly wait. Like a lot of celebrations, this one would get out of control.

As the revelers celebrated, suddenly a frightening whine, one the public quickly recognized, pierced the night and silenced the crowd. In disbelief, fans stared at one another: Air Raid! Chicago Fire Department Commissioner Robert Quinn, carried away by the euphoria of the night, had taken it upon himself to activate Chicagoland's 110 air raid sirens at full volume.

Instantly the Bell Telephone Company's switchboards lit up; the company later reported that it handled the largest volume of calls since President Franklin Roosevelt's death. Hospital staffers called police stations and firehouses to ask if they should evacuate their patients. Individuals called newspaper offices to report that they were fleeing to Wisconsin or hiding in their basements. As local authorities scrambled to placate the jittery public, not even a ticker tape parade through Chicago's Loop the following day could completely calm the masses. For days afterward, newspapers ran letters to their editors, revealing the true measure of fear Quinn's celebratory endeavor created. The nation could tell that the South Side had waited a really, really long time for a baseball pennant.

1

February: See You in Court

Few years mean more to loyal followers of the Chicago White Sox than 1959. It was the year when achievement eclipsed potential, when 40 seasons of also-rans and utter failures were forgotten, when the dark sins of the Black Sox were washed away by the light of victory, and when that arrogant group of ballplayers from Gotham were finally put in their places. Forget about what happened in the World Series that followed. In 1959, the Sox won the American League pennant after 40 years of effort, the longest drought for any team in the major leagues at the time.

When the 1958 season ended, the White Sox offered no clues that 1959 would be remembered for generations. That year the South Siders finished a distant ten games behind the New York Yankees, once again playing bridesmaids to a foe they continually failed to conquer. They won 82 games in 1958, eight fewer than the previous year, and did not spend a single day in first place. By October, when the victorious New Yorkers were winning a dramatic World Series, faithful Sox followers bore a hopeless air of resignation toward their adversaries from the Bronx. During the 1958 season, the White Sox won only seven of their 22 contests against the Yanks. The team's inability to overtake New York was on the minds of the players as much as the fans. In a November 6 speech at the Illinois State Bar Association's booster club luncheon in Chicago's Sherman Hotel, star pitcher Billy Pierce gave an impassioned address, arguing that the White Sox "do not choke at the sight of a pinstriped Yankee uniform."

Optimists among the faithful had valid reasons for their positive outlook as they looked ahead to 1959. Sox standouts Luis Aparicio, Jim Rivera, and Jim Landis finished as the top three base stealers for 1958 in the American League, and the team as a whole tallied 101 steals. Meanwhile, their outstanding second baseman, Nellie Fox, led the league in hits, while veteran Early Wynn led all AL pitchers in strikeouts. Other contributors included Pierce, who went 17–11 with a 2.48 ERA, third-best in the majors, and Dick Donovan, who pitched 248 innings with pinpoint control. Nobody in the American League walked fewer batters per nine innings than the big right-hander. Even Sherman Lollar ended the season as one of the best clutch hitters in the majors. Sox optimists also pointed to a healthy Al Smith and youngsters like Johnny Callison and Barry Latman as evidence that the Sox might finally make it back to the post-season in 1959.

Pessimists—and through the years they were always well represented—could counter every argument. They would agree that the Sox could steal bases, but the lowly Cubs had a 23-year-old second baseman from Cuba, Tony Taylor, who stole as many bases as Rivera. The Sox might have led the majors with 101 stolen bases, naysayers argued, but they also had the exact same number of home runs, the worst in the majors. This sad lack of power, they added, completely negated Fox's leading the league in hits. Who was around to drive him in?

Wynn's strikeout pitch was working, but his ERA was a generous 4.13, and at 14–16, he had lost two more games than he had won. While the effectiveness of Pierce and Donovan could not be disputed, starting pitching on the South Side was thin after these two. Optimists would mention the promising young Barry Latman, but pessimists would point out that he had pitched only 60 innings in the majors. Al Smith had not had a good year since 1956, and Callison was all of 19 years old, too young to know how to use all the tools in his toolbox effectively at the big league level.

These were the ingredients simmering as the Hot Stove League warmed up in February 1959. Unfortunately it wasn't long before the team began generating as much ink in the business section of the newspapers as it normally did in the sports section. The situation that drew so much attention was unrelated to the caliber of players or speculation regarding the team's chances that year. Instead, it was the culmination of a long-running dispute among the heirs of the team's owners. Many observers felt the problem had started three years earlier, in 1956. Yet anybody who remembered what happened in 1956 would understand that the trouble had actually started 17 years earlier. The ownership conflicts of 1959 that ended in the sale of the White Sox were the result of a feud among the descendants of the franchise founder himself, the "Old Roman," Charles A. Comiskey, following the death of his son, J. Louis, in 1939.

Five individuals comprised the cast of characters in this family drama. The first was the Old Roman's son, J. Louis Comiskey, who died on July 18, 1939. Lou suffered from circulatory problems, the after-effects of his bout with rheumatic fever as a child. He also struggled with obesity and died of congestive heart failure at age 56. His widow, Grace Comiskey, his wife since 1913, died of a heart attack in her apartment at 3240 North Lake Shore Drive on December 10, 1956. Their first child, Dorothy, was born in 1917. Dorothy married John Rigney, a local boy from Oak Park, Illinois, who pitched for the White

Sox from 1937 to 1942 and again after World War II in 1946 and 1947. When his career in the majors was over, he worked in the White Sox front office. Dorothy's younger sister, Gracie, died of a heart attack in 1952 at age 31.

Louis' and Grace's son completed the cast. Charles A. Comiskey II was the youngest, most prominent, and ultimately perhaps the most tragic of all the family members. "Chuck" Comiskey, heir apparent and the apple of his long-deceased grandfather's eye, was born in 1926 and had worked in the Sox's front office since graduating from the College of St. Thomas in 1948. For as long as anyone could remember, Chuck was considered the obvious choice to follow in his grandfather's footsteps and run the team. But as things turned out, it would not be nearly that simple. Other people had other ideas, and the result was a protracted family dispute that revealed deep divisions in the internal workings of this very prominent, well-respected Chicago family. Taken together, the actions, desires, and wishes of Charles Comiskey and his five descendants created a climate of conflict and jealousy between the two remaining survivors, granddaughter Dorothy and grandson Chuck. As their acrimony intensified, even the Comiskey family's extensive Chicago connections could not keep the painful rift out of the public eye. As a result, 1959 became the most tumultuous year in the Chicago White Sox's long history.

When Lou died in 1939, he left an estate valued at $2.25 million, including 7,450 of the 7,500 outstanding shares of the White Sox.[1] As the only son of team founder Charles Comiskey, Lou had taken over the franchise when his father died in 1931. It was Lou's dying wish, and legend has it his father's as well, that young Chuck, barely a teenager in 1939, would someday run the team. For tax purposes, Lou's stock in the team was valued at $125 per share, and in accordance with the will, the First National Bank of Chicago was named executor. Lou's widow, Grace, received 4,000 shares of White Sox stock, about 53 percent of all outstanding shares. The remaining 3,450 shares were to be divided among the three children at a later time.

Less than two months after Lou's funeral, John Gleason, trustee of the estate at the First National Bank, told the Comiskeys that he intended to solicit bids for the White Sox franchise, as the trust department's analysis had found the team debt-ridden and unprofitable. Prior to his death, Lou Comiskey had borrowed against the team's equity to meet expenses and cover the cost of installing lights in the ballpark, a move he hoped would boost the flagging Depression-era attendance, since the franchise had lost over $675,000 over the previous 11 years. Lou's widow Grace was aghast. In her mind, the Comiskey name and the Chicago White Sox were synonymous, and selling the team was not an option. Accordingly, Grace renounced the will, claimed her dower rights, and sued First National to keep her baseball team. To almost everyone's surprise, on February 29, 1940, Cook County Probate Judge John F. O'Connell ruled in Grace's favor.

While her legal achievement was remarkable, the team's performance under her leadership, on the field and at the box office, was anything but. Between 1940 and 1949, the Sox managed only two winning seasons: 1940 and 1943. During those ten years, their winning percentage was .463. Between 1945 and 1949, the Cubs outdrew the White Sox by almost 1.9 million fans.

From her first days as the Sox's new owner, Grace feuded with manager Jimmy Dykes and general manager Harry Grabiner. Grabiner had started working for her father almost 40 years before, at age 14, and had risen through the ranks to become the Old Roman's most trusted executive.[2] It was Grabiner who convinced Lou to set up a farm system, and Grabiner who put forth the idea that installing lights for night games could save the franchise. As it turned out, he was correct on both counts. After lights were installed in 1939, the Sox posted only one year with an operating loss, the war-disrupted season of 1942, which they finished $55,000 in the red. The fruits of the farm system started to ripen after World War II, and by the 1950s, long after Grabiner's departure, the team realized a plentiful harvest. Grabiner had understood not only the business of baseball but all its economic eccentricities as well, and Lou Comiskey, like his father, valued his opinion. Lou's will stipulated that Grabiner would be retained for a period of ten years following his death, at a hefty annual salary of $25,000.[3]

In spite of his Lou's will, Grabiner was forced out in September 1945, at the end of a season in which Grace saw her team completely overshadowed by the pennant-winning Cubs. Grace did not trust Grabiner, thinking he might have had a hand in the First National's attempt to sell the team,[4] and she saw his generous compensation as a drain on the cash-strapped franchise. She also thought he was much too friendly with a young baseball executive named Bill Veeck, whom she did not trust because she thought he was conspiring against her to somehow take over the team's ownership. Five months following his departure, Grabiner went to Cleveland, joining Veeck's group of investors who had just purchased the Indians. He lived long enough to enjoy a World Series championship with the Indians in 1948, passing away three weeks after his team defeated the Boston Braves for the crown.

Nine months after dismissing Grabiner, Grace lost another South Side legend. On May 25, 1946, with the Sox sporting a 10–20 record following a listless 3–1 loss to the Detroit Tigers' Hal Newhouser, manager Jimmy Dykes quit, getting the final say in the last of his innumerable contract squabbles with Grace. For over 12 years, Dykes had provided the stability in the clubhouse and on the field that Grabiner had provided in the front office. Highly regarded in major league circles, Dykes went on to manage the Philadelphia Athletics, Baltimore Orioles, Cincinnati Reds, Detroit Tigers, and Cleveland Indians. With Grabiner and Dykes cast aside, the team's failures intensified.

Following Dykes' departure, White Sox pitching legend Ted Lyons removed himself from the active roster and took over as manager. Lyons did the best he could, and the White Sox went 35–22 that August and September. After that things simply fell apart. The Sox finished 27 games out of first in 1947, and when they lost 101 games the following year, Lyons lost his job. Grace made a second poor choice when she replaced Grabiner with Leslie O'Connor. O'Connor, who worked for years as one of Commissioner Landis' most trusted aides, was a business administrator, not a baseball executive, and had no experience with player procurement, contracts, talent evaluation, or personnel management. In 1948 he incensed Commissioner Happy Chandler when he defied a league edict barring teams from negotiating with a player still in high school by signing a young pitcher named George Zoeterman, a pitcher for Chicago Christian High School in Chicago's tough Private School League, to a contract.[5] When Chandler reminded O'Connor of the rule, O'Connor defied him and held his ground. Chandler responded by *suspending* the White Sox from the American League, barring the team from asking waivers on players, signing contracts with any player, or interacting in any fashion with any other major league club, and fining them $500 for good measure. These sanctions had never been applied before in major league history. Grace quietly paid the fine, and O'Connor's time was up. To make matters worse, Zoeterman signed with the Cubs as soon as he graduated from high school, but the Sox were spared further embarrassment when he never made it to the majors.

By this time, young Chuck Comiskey had become the newest member of the White Sox front office, and in October 1949, 52-year-old Frank Lane resigned as president of the American Association and took over as the Sox's general manager. In spite of the fresh blood and new ideas, things got worse before they got better. In the spring of 1949, the Sox's cash flow was so poorly managed that they had to take out a loan to finance spring training in Pasadena, California.[6] But Lane got right to work, and with Chuck's help, he changed the face of the franchise in less than two years.

Comiskey and Lane started the rebuild by putting every member of the team on waivers.[7] They discovered how much work they had in front of them when only one player—catcher Aaron Robinson—was claimed. As time went on, Comiskey and Lane engineered clever trades to bring in Nellie Fox from the Athletics, Billy Pierce from the Tigers, Chico Carrasquel from the Dodgers, and the first black Latino in major league history, Minnie Minoso, from the Indians. The engaging, multi-talented Minoso arrived in Chicago in May 1951, just as the sagging Chicago Cubs traded their most popular ballplayer, Andy Pafko, to Brooklyn, changing Chicago's baseball fortunes for the next 17 years. With Comiskey and Lane in charge, the "Go-Go Sox" were born, and nobody doubted that these two had been the midwives. From 1950 through 1966, 35th and Shields was the centerpiece for baseball in the City of Big

Shoulders. Yet despite their success, Grace Comiskey was never completely comfortable with her son Chuck running the franchise, as his father and grandfather had so fervently hoped.

Instead, Grace entrusted more and more responsibilities to her daughter Dorothy, and she occasionally went out of her way to show Chuck who was really in charge. Grace's skepticism toward her son seemed to be longstanding. During the 1940s, the Chicago press frequently referred to Chuck as the future "owner-president" of the team, the man who would "inherit the team on his 21st birthday." That the press would make such claims even though it was not stipulated in his father's or grandfather's will irked Grace. Chuck had also said that he hoped he'd be "ready to run the team" by the time he graduated from the College of St. Thomas in the Twin Cities because "being the president of a baseball team is no job for a woman, even my mother."[8] Chuck seemed to overlook the fact that older sister Dorothy had been helping their mother in the front office since 1940, when he was just starting prep school.

In 1948, soon after Chuck joined the Sox's front office, he went to spring training and declared that the Sox were a terrible team. Even though his assertion proved correct at the end of the season, his intemperate remarks earned him a very indignant calling-out by his mother. Another mishap occurred when Chuck attended the major leagues' winter meeting in Miami in 1950 and, in opposition to his mother's wishes, cast a vote against retaining Chandler as commissioner. For this, Grace gave him a public dressing down in the Chicago press, vowing to give him "a good talking to" when he returned.[9]

In 1952, Grace even went so far as to deny Chuck a raise. Miffed at being denied both more money and authority, Chuck left the family business and moved to Texas, taking a job with the Liberty Broadcasting Network, which was embarking on an ambitious expansion into sports broadcasting.[10] Six months later the venture failed, and Chuck was back in Chicago, returning to the White Sox "under the same circumstances and conditions that existed at the time of his resignation," as his mother quickly pointed out to reporters. What Grace left out of her statement was that to bury the hatchet, she had increased both his salary and authority. Two years later, in September 1954, mother and son disagreed about both the direction of the club and manager Paul Richards' contract extension, which led to Richards' resignation and subsequent departure for Baltimore.[11] His White Sox resume included one fourth- and three third-place finishes, with a record of 342–265. During his tenure on the South Side, only two other managers in the majors—Casey Stengel and Al Lopez—eclipsed Richards' success, and both of them piloted more veteran ball clubs.

In spite of his mother's indifference toward him, Chuck and Frank Lane put together a very respectable baseball organization, with winning seasons and first-division finishes becoming the norm. By 1955, however, Chuck's relationship with Lane had soured, and Lane had completely worn out his welcome. The last straw came during the evening of August 30, when a Sox victory over Boston vaulted the South Siders into first place. It should have been a joyous occasion, but Lane spoiled the proceedings when he exploded over home plate umpire Larry Napp's bad call and rushed to the private box of American League president William Harridge and launched a profanity-riddled tirade. Calvin Hubbard, the league's umpiring supervisor, was sitting with Harridge and heard the entire diatribe. Nobody in the organization sympathized with Lane, and commissioner Ford Frick fined him $500.

The episode elevated the bickering and disagreements between Comiskey and Lane to a new level of animosity, with the 59-year-old Lane deeply resenting a public rebuke from a man almost 30 years his junior. The following month Lane left the team, leaving Chuck and Dorothy's husband, John Rigney, to run the organization as co-general managers. Years after his departure, Lane had much to say about his relationship with Chuck Comiskey. Lane said he liked Chuck like a son and took it to heart when Mrs. Comiskey told him to be like a father to the young man. In spite of this, Comiskey often had no use for him, in spite of the fact that Lane turned a near-bankrupt franchise into one worth over $3 million that would eventually win a pennant after he was dismissed. Lane also mentioned that Comiskey's father-in-law, the lawyer Frank Curran, would chide him with questions about who was really in charge of the White Sox, and whether Chuck was misrepresenting his control and authority of the franchise to his wife and in-laws. Lane went so far as to say that Comiskey lied to them about becoming owner of the team, telling her it was in his father's will when it was not.[12]

Both Grace and Dorothy had wanted Lane, who was under contract until 1960, to remain with the team, and Grace complained to the press about her son's involvement when Lane resigned two months later in October 1955. In spite of her feelings, the Sox's success continued under her son and son-in-law, John Rigney. Comiskey, sensing that a young Luis Aparicio was ready for the big leagues and that the fleet-footed Jim Landis was not far behind, traded popular shortstop Chico Carrasquel and center field ball hawk Jim Busby to Cleveland for some badly needed offensive power in the form of Larry Doby. The move helped push the Sox to third place in 1956 and second in 1957. The following off-season, another bold move occurred when the beloved Minoso went to Cleveland for veteran pitcher Early Wynn and outfielder Al Smith. The move was met with skepticism, but in 1958 the Sox again finished second. During this period, Comiskey's and Rigney's farm system became the best in baseball. In short order, a rich crop of seven youngsters— Earl Battey, Johnny Callison, Norm Cash, Barry Latman, Jim McAnany, Gary Peters, and John Romano—launched successful careers in the majors. But in spite of Chuck's many contributions to the team's financial and on-field success, the schism between mother and son seemed irreparable. When she died of a heart attack on December 10, 1956, Grace's will surprised the baseball world by naming her daughter Dorothy the team's majority owner, bequeathing her 56 percent of the team, with Chuck getting the remaining 44 percent.

Grace's estate included 7,450 shares of White Sox stock, valued at $367 per share, making for a valuation of $2.73 million.[13] Grace willed her daughter 3,975 shares of stock and named her the executor of the estate. All shares, except those already in Chuck's and Dorothy's names, would continue to be held in the trust, which Dorothy, as executor, controlled. In settling her estate this way, Grace laid the foundation for bitter animosity between her son and daughter that would last for years. The first of many courtroom battles soon began.

In early 1957, Chuck went to Cook County Probate Court to force Dorothy as the executor to distribute the White Sox shares still held in trust by their mother's estate. Doing so would increase his level of complete control and ownership from about 14 percent, the amount he had prior to his mother's death, to 46 percent, since every share he *inherited* after Grace's death was still held in trust. Dorothy countered by asking the court to increase the membership on the board of directors from four to five. The four-person board consisted of Dorothy, her attorney Roy Egan, Chuck, and Chuck's attorney/father-in-law, Frank Curran. Under Illinois law, since Dorothy controlled almost 86 percent of the team (as most of the 46 percent in Chuck's name was still in the trust, which she controlled), if the number of directors were raised to five, she would control three of them, making it easier for her to oust Chuck from the board if she wished. Chuck answered the challenge by filing another suit to keep the board membership at four, and the court ruled in his favor. Afterwards he publicly criticized Egan, accusing him of giving his sister bad legal advice; Dorothy countered by declaring that her brother had "rule or ruin" ambitions.[14] A private issue between two privileged individuals was becoming an embarrassingly public spectacle.

Balance Sheet, Chicago White Sox, 1957

INCOME		EXPENSES (General Administrative)	
Home Games	1,574,642	Players, Coaches, Mgrs. Salaries	609,343
Road Games	344,052	Scouts Salaries	126,502
Spring Exhibitions	55,144	Scouts Expenses	53,071
World Series & All Star		Clubhouse Man & Bat Boys	5,886
Broadcast Revenue	207,584	Park Laborers & Janitors	95,376
Sold Player Contracts	17,801	Park Superintendent &	
		Custodians	30,820
Comiskey Park Rentals	49,565	Matrons & Scoreboard Men	5,681
Radio & TV Contracts	525,572	Ushers & Gatemen	69,377
Concessions	316,016	Ticket Sellers	61,267

INCOME		EXPENSES (General Administrative)	
Advertising	84,283	Watchmen	27,327
Parking	26,336	Social Security & Unemployment Compo	17,988
Interest on Gov't. Bonds	22,659	Player Contract Purchases	72,400
TOTAL INCOME:	$3,223,624	Uniforms	9,792
		Spring Training	75,377
		Minor League Salaries	101,902
		Minor League Travel & Expenses	172,646
		Players Insurance & Pension	152,501
		Travel Expenses	99,959
EXPENSES (Officers)		Balls, Bats, & Trainer Supplies	7,043
Officers Salaries	113,377	Building Repairs	121,884
Office Staff	42,833	Depreciation	42,171
Personal Property Tax	6,623	Real Estate Taxes	32,934
Telephone & Telegraph	13,885	Painting & Decorating	26,475
Advertising & Publicity	25,202	Electric, Power, & Heat	14,877
Travel & Entertainment	15,549	The Bard's Room	15,275
Stationery & Printing	25,095	Ticket Printing	9,418
Postage	3,193	Building & Liability Insurance	33,282
Legal Fees	15,592	Electric Service & Supply	28,866
Auditing Services	3,550	Laundry	5,018
Office Supplies	2,859	Medical & Hospital Expenses	2,047
Miscellaneous	4,725		
TOTAL OFFICERS EXPENSES:	$ 272,483	TOTAL GENERAL ADMINISTRATION COSTS:	$2,172,105

Provision for Federal Taxes:	$410,000
TOTAL, ALL INCOME:	$3,223,624
GRAND TOTAL, ALL EXPENSES:	$2,854,588
NET INCOME, 1957 SEASON:	$369,036

In spite of her determination to keep her brother away from any significant level of control, by late 1957 it became apparent that Dorothy, uncomfortable in the public eye, was losing interest in running the team. To free herself from the messy situation, she began very discreet negotiations to sell. On July 2, 1958, veteran sportswriter Leo Fischer of the *Chicago American* revealed that Bill Veeck and a group of investors had come to Chicago to discuss buying her out. Veeck had made inquiries about the team in the past, and Frank Lane recalled his rude rebuff from Grace, Dorothy's mother, after he sold the St. Louis Browns. "Mrs. [Grace] he said, 'This is no job for a woman. Why don't you sell me the club?' She said, 'You don't have two quarters to rub together. Get your ass out of here.'"[15]

Much to Dorothy's delight and Chuck's chagrin, this time Veeck had many quarters to rub together, thanks to the deep pockets of his partners, a group of eight investors he had assembled, referred to as the CBC Corporation. The group consisted of five Chicagoans, a New Yorker, and two former associates from his days in Cleveland. From the Chicago area were Veeck; Arthur C. Allyn, Sr., a prominent Chicago investor from Evanston, Illinois; Allyn's son, A. C. Allyn Jr.; J. Douglas Casey, an associate in Allyn's investment business; and Newton P. Frye, a Veeck acquaintance and Chicago attorney. The New Yorker was John Hilson, a prominent Manhattan investor and lifelong Yankees season ticket holder. In spite of his allegiance to the Yankees, he could not pass on the opportunity to buy into a major league team. Joining Veeck from his days with the Cleveland Indians were investment banker Andrew Baxter and baseball Hall of Famer Hank Greenberg. With these individuals joining him, Veeck saw to it that this time around, money would not be an issue.

When the startled Chuck Comiskey learned of Veeck's interest, he decided it was time to fulfill his life's ambition, and in the autumn of 1958, he made the first of three offers to buy his sister's shares of stock and take complete control of the franchise. Chuck's first offer angered Dorothy because it was so low. Still seeing his life's work as running the team his grandfather founded, he made two additional offers to buy her out, but was informed on December 11, 1958, by Dorothy's attorneys that she would never sell her share of the ball club to him, regardless of how much money he might offer her.[16] What Chuck did not know at the time was that one month earlier in November, Dorothy had agreed to Veeck's offer of a 90-day option to purchase her shares for $2.7 million. Dorothy was very content with this amount until Chicago insurance tycoon Charles O. Finley offered her even more. Enticed by Finley's figures, Dorothy tried to find a way to void Veeck's offer. She was now putting herself in a bad situation: refusing to sell to her own brother, who was successfully running the business; trying to back out on her purchase agreement with Veeck, which included a guaranteed sizable amount of cash, paid to her upfront with no strings attached, to guarantee his right to buy the team; and holding out for Finley's larger offer after telling her brother that no amount of money would matter to her. After the holidays, on January 2, 1959, Chuck Comiskey drove from his home in southwest suburban Hinsdale to Dorothy's residence in northwest suburban River Forest to hand deliver yet a fourth offer, which Dorothy ignored.

This sad tale of family dissention was the backdrop for the start of the 1959 Chicago White Sox season when spring training began the following month. As a means of jump-starting Chicago's interest in the upcoming season and distracting Sox fans from the legal wrangling surrounding their team, the *Chicago Tribune* found room among the college basketball and Golden Gloves boxing reports to print a positive piece about the South Siders in its February 1 edition. The article mentioned that during the second half of the 1958 season the Sox, at 46–33, had posted a better record for that period than any other American League team, three games better than the World Champion Yankees. Much of this success, the paper pointed out, was due to the big right-hander Dick Donovan, who went 3–10 with a 4.29 ERA in the first half of the season but did a positive about-face, going 12–4 with a 2.01 ERA for the second half. What the article did not point out was that the Sox were never really in the pennant race in 1958 because of their poor start; in fact, they were mired in last place as late as June 14. The Sox also led the major leagues in a dubious category, largely as a result of that start: a large drop in attendance, 30 percent from the 1,135,668 tickets sold in 1957. Although the Sox finished second in the league and played excellent, exciting ball for much of the year, their attendance decline between 1957 and 1958 was the worst in the major leagues.

With baseball revenues down at the start of the 1959 season, the *Associated Press* revealed that many of the game's biggest stars were facing significant pay cuts. In New York, the Yankees offered Mickey Mantle $70,000, $5,000 less than in 1958, even though his 42 homers were eclipsed only by the Cubs' Ernie Banks. Many other stars were also facing a salary reduction.[17] Despite winning the National League pennant and taking the World Series to seven games, the Milwaukee Braves were intent on cutting star pitcher Lew Burdette's salary. In Philadelphia, Richie Ashburn and Curt Simmons were also in line to be trimmed, as was Pittsburgh's Ted Kluszewski. Despite earning $100,000 and being one of the highest paid players in the game, Stan Musial was still unsigned, as were many other big names: New York's Whitey Ford, Boston's Jackie Jensen, Kansas City's Bob Cerv and Roger Maris, and Washington's Roy Sievers.

The South Siders were in the same boat as everyone else. By February 4, the Sox still had 17 unsigned players on the roster, and Chuck Comiskey, citing the huge loss in the previous season's ticket revenue, asked every player to take a pay cut. It did not matter to the Sox brass that over half the players were signed and in the fold, because many of those still unsigned—including Aparicio, Fox, and Landis, the heart of their great defense up the middle—could command the highest salaries.

The Sox worked diligently at inking every player before spring training, and by mid–February, Ray Boone, Romano, Landis, and Fox had all signed contracts for 1959. In spite of Chuck's singing the poor song, he gave Landis a 100 percent raise, doubling his salary from $7,000 to $14,000 on the strength of the swift, sure-handed center fielder's .277 average and 15 home runs.[18] The Sox front office knew that Landis, with his daily glove wizardry, extremely quick break on fly balls, and speed on the bases, deserved every cent of it. As for Fox, his lucrative $45,000 contract put him among the highest paid players in the game.[19] In 1958 he had led the team in batting and the American League in singles, fewest strikeouts, and most putouts for a second baseman. At the start of the 1959 season, he was acknowledged as one of the most accomplished players in baseball. Few could match his ability to wear out opposing pitchers by fouling off pitches at will, hitting behind a runner, pushing the ball to the opposite field, or coaxing a sacrifice fly at a game's most critical moment from his bottle-shaped Louisville Slugger. Fox consistently infuriated opposing hurlers with his penchant for staying alive in the batter's box. During the 1958 season, he struck out an average of only once every *14 games* as he furthered his reputation as one of the best number-two hitters in history.

On February 21, Fox's double play partner, Aparicio, ended his negotiations with the Sox and signed for $27,000, a handsome sum in those days for a fourth-year infielder. Aparicio had originally asked for $30,000, and the Sox had offered $6,000 less, with both sides agreeing to meet in the middle.[20] As in Fox's situation, it would have been difficult to pay the speedy 27-year-old Venezuelan any less. Nobody in the American League came close to matching Aparicio's fielding skills and speed, and the only other shortstop in the majors who was as valuable to his team was across town, the Cubs' Ernie Banks. While Banks' offensive gifts gave him tremendous power and run production, Aparicio possessed incredible speed, uncanny skill at reading a pitcher's delivery, and consistent dependability as a table-setter. When Chicagoans got involved in the inevitable comparisons between the two, Sox fans would simply bring up the old axiom that "speed never slumps." No knowledgeable Cubs fan failed to give the Magician from Maracaibo his due.

The encouraging news on the baseball front helped Chicagoans forget the continuing drama regarding the all-too-public struggle for the team's ownership. As if the three-way tug-of-war between the Comiskeys, Finley, and Veeck were not enough, *Chicago Tribune* columnist Herb Lyon revealed in his February 23 *Tower Ticker* column that a fourth party was interested in buying the team: radio personality Howard Miller and his business partner James Janek, owner of the famous Café Bohemia near Chicago's Union Station. Janek's restaurant, known for its exotic dishes—bear meat, elk, lion, and venison—and its proximity to the one of the busiest railway depots in the world made it a nationally-known destination for persons travelling to or through Chicago. Miller, who commanded a huge radio audience, lamented over the airwaves that a hallowed Chicago institution like the White Sox could be at the center of such a bitter and embarrassing family feud. To distinguish their bid from the others and remind the public that Veeck's reputation preceded him, Miller vowed that he and Janek would never move the team.

While nobody took this fourth offer seriously, suddenly the possibility that the Sox might be coming under new management cast a dark cloud. Could the slick-talking Veeck actually be thinking of moving the Sox? His track record made the possibility seem plausible. After buying the Browns, Veeck had lobbied hard to move them to Milwaukee or Baltimore. After he sold the St. Louis franchise, he was hired by Cubs owner Philip K. Wrigley to research the possibility of bringing a major league team to the West Coast. One of his partners in the CBC investment group, Hank Greenberg, was on the outs in Cleveland after some feared he was planning to uproot the franchise and move it the Twin Cities.

While all this was going on, Finley saw an opening and pursued it aggressively, reminding the public that he was a lifelong Sox fan and could never consider moving the team. Finley made Dorothy an offer that was both higher and simpler than Veeck's: a half-million in earnest money followed by a series of payments totaling $3.2 million. Finley's offer was a better deal than Veeck's $2.7 million, and it contained no other stock purchase contingencies requiring Chuck Comiskey's cooperation. Dorothy, who at this point saw Veeck's 90-day purchase option as an expensive impediment, offered him $100,000 to rescind it. Eager to get his hands on the team, and thinking Veeck had a weakness for quick cash, Finley then offered Veeck *another* $100,000 to void the purchase option. Suddenly Veeck's group was in the extremely enviable position of realizing $200,000 in less than 90 days for simply not buying a baseball team!

Veeck and his partners, however, wanted the White Sox more than the money. To thwart Finley's plan, Veeck went to court and got his 90-day stock purchase option declared legally binding. Meanwhile, Chuck fumed that he was running out of options to buy what he considered his legacy. In David Condon's *Wake of the News* column in the February 13, 1959, *Chicago Tribune,* Comiskey acknowledged that the team was slipping from his grasp. "This has been my life. The White Sox are a part of me. I know, of course, how Dorothy feels. She is a girl, and she is a wife and mother. She can't devote all her time to the family business. But she certainly knows how I feel about carrying on. This is what I want, and I am never going to sell."

On February 15, Chuck revealed to Edward Prell in the *Tribune* that his final bid, hand-delivered to his sister on January 2, had been for $3.35 million, almost $150,000 more than Finley's offer, and $650,000 more than Veeck's. In the article, he took his sister to task for initially declaring that the sale was "not about the money," then trying to renege on Veeck's offer when Finley offered more, all the while showing no interest in selling to the highest bidder, her own brother. "I have to think Dorothy has refused to sell to me out of … jealousy or spite," he fumed.[21] Meanwhile, the Veeck syndicate seemed in no particular hurry to consummate the deal, even though the 90-day purchase option would soon expire. It looked as if Veeck was either hoping to buy a portion of Chuck's stock so his group could gain complete control of the team, or persuade Chuck that his deal with Dorothy posed no threat to Chuck's interests.

The *Tribune* tried to put a sunnier spin on all things White Sox in its Sunday, February 15, edition, revealing that the team had called up 11 minor leaguers to report to spring training in Tampa the following week for a look-see at the major league level. The prospects included the young Gary Peters, who had gone 12–9 at Colorado Springs; his teammate, catcher Cam Carreon, a Californian who had blistered the ball at a .342 pace against Western League pitching; and Davenport first baseman Don Mincher, a .330 hitter with 23 homers in the Three I (Indiana, Illinois, and Iowa) League. Along with the pre-season pablum, the paper reported that the Las Vegas line for the Sox's chances at winning the World Series was 12–1, the same odds given for the lowly Cubs.

On the last Monday in February, the Sox officially opened spring training camp in Tampa, home of manager Al Lopez. The 39 reporting players included 19 pitchers, five catchers, nine infielders, and six outfielders.[22] Setting a starting date for the entire team instead of calling in pitchers and catchers early was a big change. Lopez's idea was that with everyone reporting at once, he could increase practice time and accelerate the pace of the team's preparation. Headquartered at the Tampa Terrace Hotel, the Sox practiced at Al Lopez Field, aptly named in honor of their skipper. Lopez, known throughout the Tampa area as "Mr. Baseball," got some good news the first day when he learned that Latman, the only player still unsigned, had inked his 1959 contract and would soon report to camp.

Meanwhile, Chuck Comiskey stepped away from the ownership crisis to announce that the Sox would be the first team in the majors to take credit card payments for tickets, explaining that any fan with a Diners' Club card could use it in person or by phone to purchase tickets to any upcoming home game.[23] This small bit of news served as yet another example of the many prudent changes and improvements the youngest Comiskey had made over the past decade. At the start of the 1950 season, he reconfigured the stadium layout, moving both bullpens from the sidelines to the vast outer reaches of center field. The following season, he replaced the tired, pedestrian-looking scoreboards on the left and right field walls with the dramatic new Chesterfield Cigarettes scoreboard, complete with the famous Longines clock. The huge new structure resembled a stately theater curtain, framed by the graceful symmetry of the outfield decks and their cathedral-arched back walls. In 1954, Chuck installed television sets at all concession stands so no patron would miss the action if he decided to nosh on one of Chef Ernie Carroll's culinary creations. And in October 1956, when a fire completely destroyed the press box, radio booths, and infield seating sections of the upper deck, he promptly rebuilt the entire section, replacing the antiquated press box with an air-conditioned, wide-windowed structure complete with shatter-proof glass. Sadly for Chuck, his catalogue of accomplishments could not delay the inevitable, as Veeck's lifelong dream of owning a team in his hometown was fast becoming a reality.

On Tuesday, February 17, the CBC Corporation called a press conference at the Blackstone Hotel on South Michigan Avenue and announced the deal.[24] The first item on Veeck's agenda was to introduce his partners. While the CBC Corporation comprised eight investors, a majority of the holdings were in the hands of three individuals: Greenberg, who owned 40 percent; Veeck, with a 30 percent stake, and Allyn Sr., with 24 percent. The remaining 6 percent was shared by Allyn Jr., Casey, Frye, Baxter, and Hilson. Veeck did not reveal the names of any bank or financial institution involved in the consultation or financing of the purchase.[25] To fend off any awkward questions about a moneyed syndicate taking over a beloved, 59-year-old community institution and family-owned business, Veeck offered three clarifications on some of the issues troubling the public.[26] First, he declared that under no circumstances would he move the Chicago White Sox. He added that he would never move *any* team under any circumstances to the West Coast. Bringing this point up first allowed Veeck to minimize the importance of Finley's claim that he was a "lifelong Chicago White Sox fan." It was also a way to deflate the only significant aspect of the Janek-Miller bid. Veeck's statement further served to soften the impact of his previous attempt to move the St. Louis Browns when they were under his control, and of the consulting work he did for Phillip Wrigley regarding baseball's westward expansion.

Veeck's second point was that he would have nothing to say and would answer no questions about the bitter and much publicized dispute between Dorothy and Chuck Comiskey. Lastly, he said he would have nothing to say about the team on the field until the final legal hurdle had been cleared and the CBC group controlled the majority of the White Sox stock. With Chuck, the chief architect of the team's most successful decade, still controlling 46 percent of the team, nothing good could have come from Veeck offering opinions about the successful product on the field his unchosen "partner" put together.

At the press conference, Veeck also gave a carefully worded treatise on his theory for success in a business as tricky as professional baseball. According to Veeck, there were three important aspects to running a profitable and successful franchise. The first was to sell as many tickets as possible as early as possible. To this end, Veeck vowed to work tirelessly 12 months a year promoting the team at banquets, church groups, community gatherings, and men's clubs. The second component in Veeck's strategy was to put the most competitive team possible on the field. Luckily for Veeck, the Sox's record in the 1950s spoke for itself. The third component was to make a point of entertaining the customers at every game. This was the showman side of Veeck that so many of the staid, silver-haired owners in baseball could never tolerate, and the side that made him so beloved by so many fans.[27]

Chuck Comiskey, needless to say a no-show at the CBC debut, was not about to take the loss of his team lying down. Instead, he fortified his legal resources, adding the descendants of the late Robert Emmett Cantwell I to his counsel. Cantwell had been one of his grandfather's closest friends and had served as president of the team's first fan club, the White Stockings Rooters Association, in the 1900s. Now the late Cantwell Sr.'s descendants, Robert Emmet Cantwell, Jr., Robert E. Cantwell III, and Louis Yager Cantwell, were all in Chuck's corner. They initiated a two-pronged legal attack.[28]

First, they returned to Judge Dunne and petitioned the court to nullify the sale between Dorothy and the Veeck syndicate. Among the legal rationales were the stated and implied wishes of the team's founder and the founder's successor, that someday Chuck would run the team as they themselves had. The second legal maneuver, more hardball than the first, sought to remove Dorothy as the executor of her mother Grace's estate. This was an aggressive and bold request. If it succeeded, the schism in the Comiskey family would deepen even further.

In response, although they felt sure they had an airtight case, Dorothy and her chief attorney Roy Egan added an up-and-coming young barrister to their table, Donald Reuben of Chicago's Kirkland, Ellis, Hodson, Chaffetz, and Masters. Their confidence came from knowing there was nothing nefarious or illegal about Dorothy's proposed sale to Veeck's group, and that to change an executor named by a decedent without just cause would be almost impossible to justify. The stage was set. The legal showdown would begin in Judge Dunne's courtroom on Thursday, March 5, 1959.

But no matter who owned the team, or how much of it they owned, the interested parties did not like what they read in the Chicago papers on February 27. The Chicago Cardinals, the city's "other" National Football League franchise that historically was relegated to the role of stepchild while the Chicago Bears were the city's favorite football sons, announced that their four decades of football in Comiskey Park were coming to an end.[29] The impact on the new owners was obvious: the Big Red's departure from 35th and Shields would cost the White Sox about $50,000 in annual revenue. This amount counted just the value of the lease; any splits from concessions, parking, or other sales would put the loss in the $70,000 range, and possibly more if by some miracle the Cardinals happened to do well at the gate. While these amounts were too insignificant to change the dollar value of the Sox franchise, the Cardinals' departure did not bode well for the Sox's cash flow and revenue stream. Both were already on the watch list due to the precipitous drop in ticket sales in 1958. All in all, February 1959 proved to be a harrowing month for the Bridgeport community: the Comiskey family out after 60 years, the Cardinals gone after 40. How much more bad news could a South Sider take in one winter?

2

March 1959:
"My Kingdom ... What Has Become of My Kingdom?"

After the unsettling ownership developments and disappointing news about their longtime autumnal tenants, the White Sox were glad to see March arrive. By the first of the month, they were well established in the Tampa Terrace Hotel and eager to leave its homey confines for Al Lopez Field. February ended with two days of rainstorms, cancelling all practices, but once the calendar flipped to March the weather followed suit, and training started in earnest. The team had 41 days to prepare for the season opener on Friday, April 10 in Detroit, and with the iffy weather, the Sox had to make the most of them.

Lopez was excited about the Sox's catching prospects. With his 19-year catching career in the majors—which included once catching the offerings of Walter Johnson in an exhibition—his feeling that Sherm Lollar, John Romano and Earl Battey were the strongest group of receivers in baseball was taken seriously.[1] With the 34-year-old Lollar behind the plate, the Sox had not only the league's best handler of pitchers, but also a backstop who just happened to hit 20 homers in 1958. If the pride of Durham, Arkansas, had a weakness, it would be his so-so throwing arm.

Earl Battey, ten years Lollar's junior, was one of the most coveted young players in the majors. The White Sox's super scout, Hollis Thurston, discovered Battey in Los Angeles. By the mid 1950s, Thurston, himself an effective starting pitcher for the South Siders 30 years earlier, was the team's supervisor of scouting for the West Coast. He could not help but notice the great potential that Battey, a three-sport athlete, flashed at Jordan High School in the heart of Watts. Young Earl, the oldest in a family of three brothers and seven sisters, was a shy and sensitive teen. His father was a construction worker,

and his mother worked as a domestic in a Los Angeles hotel. Chuck Comiskey signed Battey in 1953 to a minor league contract with a hefty $4,000 bonus and personally gave Mrs. Battey his word that he would care for and watch over her talented son. By 1955, Battey had proven that he had nothing else to accomplish for Colorado Springs in the Western League, so at the tender age of 20

Top: **The White Sox brain trust in 1959. Coaches Ray Berres, Tony Cuccinello, Don Gutteridge, and Johnny Cooney surround their seated boss, Al Lopez.** *Bottom:* **John "Honey" Romano, who caught 53 games for the 1959 White Sox. Two months after the World Series, he went to Cleveland as part of the Minnie Minoso trade.**

he was promoted to 35th and Shields to be Lollar's backup. Lopez said that all Battey needed to do was start hitting for average and get a little more experience handling pitchers, and then he could easily become the best catcher in the majors. In 1958, Battey hit eight home runs in only 168 at-bats, which projected close to 30 homers over a full season, huge numbers for any catcher. His throwing arm was one of the strongest in the majors, and his defensive abilities were getting better every season. While Lopez's predictions for Battey came true, unfortunately it did not occur in Chicago.[2]

Giving the Sox's skipper an even greater luxury of choice behind the plate was a 24-year-old, the pride of Hoboken's Demarest High School, John "Honey" Romano. Romano's success at Dubuque in the Midwest League resembled Battey's success in Colorado. Like Battey, Romano could hit for power and had a strong throwing arm. Unlike Battey and almost every other catcher in the majors at that time, Romano was swift afoot and knew how to use his speed correctly on the base paths. Chicago had not seen a catcher who could run as

Although overshadowed throughout the 1950s by Yogi Berra, Sherman Lollar became one of the most respected catchers of his era. An effective field general and great handler of pitchers, Lollar also led the team in home runs and RBI in 1958 and 1959.

well as Romano since the Cubs' speedy backstop, Len Rice, contributed to the city's last pennant in 1945. The only thing holding Romano back was his struggle to keep his weight down. In February 1959, however, the trimmed-down receiver showed up in Tampa 20 pounds lighter, spinning the scales to just a tad over 200, and reporting to camp in the best shape of his professional career. Like Battey, Romano would also become a star major league catcher, and also like Battey, it would not be in Chicago.[3] So the 1959 White Sox, already one of the two most pitching-rich teams in the American League, were just as formidable behind the plate for the upcoming season.

With spring training contests against other teams still a few weeks away, the players' time was occupied with drills, calisthenics, hitting and fielding practice, and, to break the monotony, the inevitable intra-squad games. For those contests, the roster was cut into two intramural squads. Team one, the "Cuccinellos," was managed by third base coach Tony Cuccinello, and team two, the "Gutteridges," had first base coach and infield mentor Don Gutteridge at the helm. To keep the sides even, each squad had the same number of rookies and veterans. Since these contests were not about to sell newspapers, the reporters covering spring training focused their attention on the fresh faces in the dugout, whetting Chicagoans' appetites for the farm system's hopefully bountiful harvest. The best appetizer the press served up to the hungry Sox fans was the handsome kid from California, John Wesley Callison.

Few players in Chicago baseball history endured a spring training camp with as much pre-season attention. The *Chicago Daily News* declared on Monday, March 2, that the team's entire fortunes would hinge on the young phenom's performance at the plate. Callison, born March 12, 1939, in Qualls, Oklahoma, was no stranger to challenges, having watched his parents eke out a hardscrabble existence before moving their two sons and daughters to California in search of a better life. As the years progressed, Callison's athletic talents brought him accolades in football and baseball at East Bakersfield High School. With the unabashed honesty of youth, Callison told David Condon in the Monday, March 2 edition of *Chicago Tribune*, that he had been such a good running back in high school that seven major universities offered him as full scholarship, but each one lost interest when they saw his grades.

Young "Johnny C," however, did not need the gridiron to gain recognition. Every West Coast baseball scout knew of him, and all marveled at his successes during his last two years of high school. As soon as he graduated in 1957, the White Sox signed him, adding a bonus of $10,000, $7,000 of which was within major league guidelines and another $3,000 that was slipped under the proverbial table. To ease the transition for the 18-year-old, the Sox assigned Callison to his hometown Bakersfield Bears in the Class C California League.[4]

California League pitching proved no more difficult for the 5'10", 175-pound outfielder than the high school pitching he had seen at East Bakersfield High the year before. In 86 games, Callison hit .340, with 41 extra-base hits and 31 steals. While few individuals hit at that clip in their first year of professional baseball, what impressed scouts the most was his phenomenal speed. Callison had enjoyed challenging his teammates to dashes, remarkably *running backwards* while his opponents sprinted forward, and usually winning the races. In 1957, Callison was named Outstanding Rookie in the California League, beating out future major leaguers like Vada Pinson and Chuck Estrada.

After the 1957 season, the Sox took a big risk with the still green young man, moving him up to their Triple A affiliate, the Indianapolis Indians. Once he arrived, Callison, 19 and newly married to his high school sweetheart, Diane Hammitt, began drawing comparisons to another native Oklahoman who could hit, run, and throw—Mickey Mantle. Callison was uncomfortable with the comparison, but the press could not resist. In spite of this pressure, he found his power stroke in Indianapolis and ended the year leading the league with 29 home runs, 93 RBI, and a .283 average. Callison grew up in a hurry off the field also, becoming a father when his daughter Lauri was born during the 1958 season. Meanwhile, the Sox were so pleased that they made him one of their late-season (September 9, 1958) call-ups. In the remaining weeks, Callison played in 18 games, hitting .297 in 64 at-bats and displaying the power and

Matinee idol and bobby-sox heart-throb Johnny Callison. After being traded at the end of the 1959 season, he went on to have a very successful 16-year career.

speed Sox fans had read about with his four doubles, two triples, and one home run. Lost among all these impressive statistics was the fact that he also had 12 RBI in those 18 contests. It was easy to see why so much rested on Callison's young shoulders. Hopes were so high that many ignored a critical fact: he would turn 20 just four weeks before Opening Day, 1959.

While the on-field prospects seemed bright for the 1959 Sox, developments for the team's erstwhile owner Chuck Comiskey seemed less promising. On Thursday, March 4, Judge Dunne was scheduled to establish the ownership of the team—or so it was hoped. Dunne, a former college gridiron star nicknamed "The Duke," was no stranger to sports issues. Dorothy did not bother to appear, but Chuck was in court with all members of his counsel. One of his attorneys, L. Yager Cantwell, approached the bench and addressed the court:

> Dorothy wants money, and doesn't want the team. Charley wants the team and doesn't care about money. Dorothy has proven by everything she has done that she is only interested in getting money for her stock. Charley has proven by everything he has done that he wants to own and manage the White Sox. He hired Frank Lane ... and trade by trade, year by year ... has built the most exciting "Go-Go" ball club in Chicago

his own way, a team which has yet to fulfill its destiny, which can still bring a World Championship to Chicago.

What will the Court do with these two heirs? They have compatible needs, compatible wants, and desires—with a perfect split of money and ball club. All the law books, all the decisions, all the logic in this universe cries out to this Court: "Give Charley what he wants, the White Sox. Give Dorothy what she wants, the money."

But now we come to a strange problem. Dorothy wants to take *less money* from Bill Veeck than what she has been offered by Charles Finley, and less money than what she has been offered by her own brother. Why? Greed cannot be the answer. If it were, she'd accept Charley's offer. She will not turn down Veeck, and she will turn down her own brother!!

Cantwell closed his argument with a Shakespearean flourish worthy of any summer stock thespian. "It is rumored that on some of our darker, stormy and rain swept nights, the Ghost of the Old Roman himself walks the halls and upper decks of the Baseball Palace of the World, and, like Hamlet's father, mourns and wails over what has happened to his kingdom."[5]

Dramatic as it was, the barrister's performance did not sway Judge Dunne. Instead, the judge rebuked the litigants for failing "to settle their disputes without any attendant publicity." He launched into his own speech, a judicial lecture aimed directly at the warring siblings:

This matter has been before the court a number of times and even more often in the newspapers. It is ordinarily neither the duty nor the privilege of the court to direct admonitions to litigants with respect to moral, social and family obligations. In this case, however, the court cannot refrain from comment that it is unfortunate that a family affair, such as this, has to be aired in the court and in the public press.

All too often children who have inherited property are willing to quarrel publicity about their inheritances, and, in so doing, drag into litigation the good names of their deceased parents or grandparent from whom they received the inheritances. The litigants here are merely enjoying the fruits of their parents' and grandparents' industry, who through their efforts and hard work built up a considerable fortune. In the interest of family unity and solidarity it is regrettable that the litigants here could not have seen fit to settle their disputes without any attendant publicity.[6]

Judge Dunne's lecture marked the beginning of the end of Chuck Comiskey's dream. In short order he granted a motion by Don Reuben dismissing Comiskey's petition to ban Dorothy's sale of her stock to Bill Veeck. The judge then quickly dismissed the petition to remove Dorothy as executrix of their mother Grace's estate, ruling out any notion of misconduct on Dorothy's part and labeling such a charge "mere opinion." Dunne gave Veeck until March 31 to put his $2.7 million bid on Dorothy's table. Meanwhile, Chuck's attorneys declared that they would return to court the following day to post an appeal bond, a prelude to moving the matter to Circuit Court.[7]

In spite of their energetic pronouncement to continue the good fight, at some level the Chuck Comiskey forces must have known it was over. Nothing had transpired in Judge Dunne's courtroom that could prevent Dorothy from completing her sale to Veeck's group. If it occurred before their appeal time, no court would reverse it, and as hard as they might try to make Dorothy's actions look like "misconduct of an executor," no number of slights toward her brother would validate such a charge. Was there misconduct toward her brother, the family, or the family's legacy? Perhaps, but the executor can interact only with the estate, and none of her "estate handling" since the time of her mother's death three years before could remotely be characterized as misconduct. As the *Chicago Daily News* declared in a March 5 headline, the ruling was the "End of a Baseball Dynasty."[8]

A thousand miles away from Judge Dunne's courtroom, the news was much more agreeable. Spring training's delicious baseball tidbits were being delivered by the press to a baseball-hungry populace every day. The Cincinnati Reds hired skeet shooting expert Lucky McDaniel to train their players in rifle marksmanship, which, management thought, would improve their depth perception. The Milwaukee Braves, still worried that veteran Red Schoendienst's injury might prevent him from taking the field, were moving into crisis mode over their lack of confidence in replacements Chuck Cottier, Felix Mantilla, and ex–Cub Casey Wise. The team's concerns were so significant they asked Hank Aaron if he would consider moving from right field to second base; Aaron politely declined. In Mesa, Arizona, National League MVP Ernie Banks of the Cubs picked up right where he had left off the year before, homering twice in the team's first intra-squad game. The Cubs also listened attentively to Rogers Hornsby praise the bat speed, power, and quick hands of an 18-year-old farmhand named Ron Santo.[9]

The Sox split two games with the Reds, losing 4–3 on Saturday, March 7, and won again the following Monday, 5–2. Battey and Landis notched two hits each, and Lopez got three decent innings each out of Wynn, Claude Raymond, and Gerry Staley. He also got a huge scare when Callison, chasing a pop-up, collided with Sammy Esposito. Callison's sunglasses left cuts on his nose and his eyelid, but the damage was minimal, and the team breathed a sigh of relief when the youngster stayed in the game.

Esposito was at third because Lopez did not have the luxury of a standout third sacker to pencil into the lineup every day. While the Yankees had Andy Carey, the Red Sox Frankie Malzone, and the Orioles a 22-year-old newcomer named Brooks Robinson, the Sox in 1958 boasted a trio of dependable third basemen: Billy Goodman, Bubba Phillips, and Esposito.

The veteran of the group, 33-year-old Goodman, was entering his 13th year in the majors, coming off a 116-game season in 1958, with a very respectable .299 average, 40 RBI, and a solid .355 on-base percentage. Throughout the 1950s, Goodman was one of the most consistent hitters in the majors; his crowning achievement was winning the AL batting title in

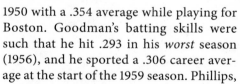

Left: **Bubba Phillips, a Little All-American halfback at Mississippi Southern, signed a contract with the Detroit Tigers while still in college. The versatile Phillips split third base starting assignments with Billy Goodman and played 23 games in the outfield.** *Right:* **Billy Goodman, 1950 American League batting champion. Goodman was an exceptional athlete who split the third base starting duties with Bubba Phillips in 1959.**

1950 with a .354 average while playing for Boston. Goodman's batting skills were such that he hit .293 in his *worst* season (1956), and he sported a .306 career average at the start of the 1959 season. Phillips, at 30 years younger than Goodman, hit a decent .273 in 84 games for the Sox in 1958, and because the Sox were desperate for more power at the plate, Lopez earmarked him to start at third in 1959. While Phillips had only five homers in 1958, that was five more than the combined total of Goodman and Esposito. The Sox skipper felt that if given time, the West Point, Mississippi, native could blossom into a 15–20-homer corner infielder. Esposito presented a different athletic profile. He was a versatile, play-anywhere fielder with great baseball instincts but a chronically weak hitter. He started 1959 with experience in 276 games, a career batting average of .220, five home runs and 41 RBI.

In spite of Esposito's offensive weakness, Lopez loved him because he was a skilled jack-of-all-trades utility man. Originally Esposito had visions of making the majors as a shortstop or second baseman, and had honed those skills at Waterloo, but he was stuck in an organization with Chico Carrasquel and Nellie Fox in the big show and a promising young Luis Aparicio on the way up. After a stint in the military, Esposito's focus shifted to third base. His value as an adequate third baseman who could fill in at either short or second—and even play the outfield in a pinch—was something Lopez could not ignore. For these and many other reasons, Sox fans loved Esposito.

The amiable, dark-haired ballplayer epitomized the feel-good story about a local boy who made good. A native of Chicago's far South Side Roseland community, Esposito had led Fenger High School to the Mayor's Football

Sammy Esposito, jack of all trades, the local boy who made good. A native of Chicago's Roseland neighborhood, he led Fenger High School to a city football championship before starring as a Big Ten point guard at Indiana. Esposito was a fan favorite at Comiskey Park for ten years.

Championship Prep Bowl in 1948, where the 5'8", 129-pound senior had quarter-backed his team to a tie against Lindbloom High for the city co-championship. That winter, Esposito set a Chicago Public High School record, scoring 81 points in a single basketball game. The staff at Indiana University, 200 miles away, took notice.

Not only did he win a full basketball scholarship to IU, but during his brief collegiate career, he developed into one of the shiftiest point guards in the Big Ten. Veteran White Sox scout Doug Minor was equally impressed with Esposito's baseball skills and signed him to a contract after his sophomore year, with the Sox calling him up in September 1952. A stint in the military followed, but by 1955, Esposito was in the majors for good. The brown-eyed, brown-haired Esposito was still single during the 1959 season and was a favorite among the female fans. True to his Jack Armstrong similarities, he still lived with his parents in Chicago's Roseland community at the start of the 1959 season.[10]

The Sox's next contest yielded their second spring training victory, an inartistic 7–5 win over the Pirates. While Lopez was pleased with his two prized Johnnies—both Callison and Romano hit homers—Donovan looked terrible on the mound, and the newly acquired Tommy Qualters was not much better. It took Pittsburgh only three innings to nick Donovan for three runs, and Qualters, an off-season pick-up from the Philadelphia Phillies, gave up two runs in the ninth. Qualters was one of seven pitchers competing for a spot in the back of the bullpen, and with 26 appearances in the National League in 1958, he was expected to have a big advantage.

Playing a team like Pittsburgh early in spring training was just what the Sox pitching staff needed. Perennial National League doormats since World War II, the Pirates were the most improved team in baseball in 1957 after Danny Murtaugh replaced the beleaguered Bobby Bragan. Before Bragan's departure, the Pirates were 31 wins under .500 at 36–67, but under Murtaugh's direction went 26–25 in their last 51 games for a 62–92 finish. In 1958, the stocky little skipper followed up one of the most remarkable turn-arounds in baseball history, leading the franchise to second place with an 84–70 record, a 22-game improvement, only eight games behind the pennant-winning Milwaukee Braves. With a lineup that included Bill Mazeroski, Dick Groat, Frank Thomas, Roberto Clemente, Bill Virdon, and Bob Skinner, Pittsburgh was quite a challenge for Ray Berres' pitching staff, but the Sox won because the Pirates committed six errors, three by their huge, young, power-hitting first baseman, Dick Stuart. The Pirates organization was intent on weighing the risks a player like Stuart posed, and the only way to do so was to give him playing time in the Grapefruit League, however hard on the eyes that might be at times. They thought so much of the tall, slugging San Franciscan and his 16 homers in only 67 games during 1958 that they traded veteran first baseman Dee Fondy and moved proven slugger Ted Kluszewski to the bench. As the 1958 season progressed, however, the Pirates learned that all that raw power came at a cost. Stuart was as much a liability at first base as he was an asset at the plate. His miscues as a first sacker earned him one of the best nicknames in the history of the game: Dr. Strangeglove.

Lopez broke up the early part of the Sox spring training schedule with a Gulf of Mexico fishing trip for the entire squad. Frequent rains cancelled many practices and drove the team indoors for others. Callison, hitless in 22 at-bats, needed the rain-induced time off. A Grapefruit League game against the St. Louis Cardinals foreshadowed events that would occur in October, when Chuck Essegian, a husky ex–Stanford fullback hoping to win a reserve outfield role, slugged two homers off Dick Donovan, whose weak spring training outings were becoming a concern.

Overshadowing Donovan's poor performance was the appearance of Hank Greenberg and Bill Veeck in the stands. Veeck was cordial to the press but had little to say about his new majority ownership, other than that he had invited Chuck Comiskey to the game.[11] Chuck declined the invitation, claiming a prior golf commitment in Clearwater.

The following day, Detroit's aging Gus Zernial hit a two-run homer off Bob Shaw. Zernial, a broad-shouldered, 36-year-old native of Beaumont, Texas, was one of the best pinch-hitters of his era. Sox followers remembered him fondly for two things: setting the team's single season home run mark of 29 in 1950, and posing provocatively as Marilyn Monroe's batting instructor, with the picture drawing national attention and enraging Joe DiMaggio no end.

Back in Chicago, the much-anticipated summit between Chuck, Dorothy, and Veeck finally occurred Thursday, March 12. The *Tribune* ran a picture of the trio with forced smiles sharing a "coffee toast" to the team's good fortune. Chuck was the only one to speak after the gathering, and his evasiveness spoke volumes: "I talked to him and he [Veeck] talked to me. It was a mutual conversation, with two people talking. We talked about everything, I guess, and solved all the problems of baseball, football, and basketball. The picture hasn't changed from two days ago."[12] Gossip columnist Herb Lyon wrote in the Wednesday, March 18, *Chicago Tribune* that Chuck would only make peace with Veeck if he received assurances that John Rigney (still with the organization even after his wife Dorothy sold out) severed all ties to the team.

Meanwhile, in Florida, Callison finally broke out of his slump with two singles against the Reds, one off the highly touted 22-year-old Chicagoan, Jim O'Toole, and the other at the expense of veteran Brooks Lawrence.

With two weeks gone and three weeks of spring training remaining, the Sox defense looked solid. Their pitching staff, with the exception of Donovan, was up to expectations, but their offense still lacked consistency and power.

At home, however, South Siders were focused on a much more significant development for the team, one that would change Bridgeport's autumns forever.

That same Thursday, March 18, the White Sox front office learned that the football Cardinals, their longtime Comiskey Park tenants, had signed an agreement with the Chicago Park District to play four of their six 1959 home games in Soldier Field.[13] Walter Wolfner, the team's managing director, and James H. Gately, president of the Chicago Park District, made the announcement. Wolfner had a curious history with the Cardinals and their ownership. He was the Bidwills' family attorney in 1947 when Cardinals owner and horse-racing tycoon Charles "Stormy" Bidwill died. Wolfner eventually married Violet Bidwill, Charles' widow, who took control of the team at the time of her husband's passing; the bitterness and rancor between Wolfner and Violet's two adult sons made for much bad publicity.

From a financial standpoint, the White Sox could lose at least $50,000, about 2 percent of the Sox's gross income, because of the Cardinals' departure, but the loss to Chicago's South Side community would be immeasurably greater. It brought an end to the Cardinals' colorful 40-year history at Comiskey Park, a sad occasion for the shrinking but fiercely loyal Cardinals fan base who steadfastly refused to give the cross-town Bears the time of day. After the 1958 NFL season ended and the Cardinals attendance figures came out, the handwriting was on the wall. The Big Red sold only 99,203 tickets for the five home games.[14]

To shore up their dismal attendance, Wolfner wanted to move the franchise to Evanston, Illinois, a large university suburb immediately north of Chicago, so that the Cardinals could play at Northwestern's Dyche Stadium. Bears owner George Halas made sure that this was not going to occur without a stamp of approval by NFL Commissioner Bert Bell and an appearance by all parties in the Superior Court of Cook County. Halas dusted off an old contract he had signed in 1931 with Dr. David Jones, the owner of the Cardinals before Charles Bidwill bought the team the following year for $50,000. He also submitted a reaffirmation of the contract signed by Bidwill himself in 1937 and 1939. The contract divided the city of Chicago in half to establish which team could play where: the Cardinals south of Madison Avenue, and Bears north, with just two exceptions. Both teams could play at Soldier Field, and both could share a new stadium if it were ever built. Wolfner felt that since Dyche Stadium was outside the Chicago city limits, the contract did not apply.[15] Halas, of course, felt the agreement was based strictly on geographical limitations. The last thing he wanted was the Cardinals playing in an area surrounded by prosperous communities, in a stadium with ample parking and 7,000 more seats than Wrigley Field. Dyche's capacity in 1959 was 55,000, and the stadium was just three blocks east of the busy Chicago

& North Western Railroad's Central Street Station and one block west of the Chicago Transit Authority's ground-level station at Isabella Street, which was a four-minute walk to the Dyche Stadium's north end zone.

The crafty Halas thought the lawsuit could be his big opportunity to get the Cardinals out of the Chicago area once and for all. He had actually been good friends with the late Bidwill, who helped Halas in the earlier years with loans and other financial favors, and even became an investor in the Bears when Halas fell on hard times in 1932. Halas' feelings were nowhere near as warm, however, toward Wolfner. To limit the Cardinals' public appeal and exposure, the sly Bears owner had seen to it that the Cardinals almost never received any television exposure in Chicago. He did so by engineering the NFL policy that dictated a blackout in any city hosting an NFL game that was occurring at the same time. Since the Bears were home when the Cardinals were on the road, Wolfner's team could never get any television exposure unless they moved their game to a Saturday. Since Chicago for most of the 1950s was the only city in the NFL with two teams, this unique set-up severely limited the Cardinals' media exposure. That suited Halas just fine. Compounding these troubles for the Cards, the NFL was pressuring them to do *something* to become more profitable. The league claimed that almost all teams lost money when they came to play the Cardinals in Chicago. Since the Big Red were consistently last in attendance, their visitors' share of the gate was very small.

Commissioner Bell wasted no time closing the door on the Cardinals' move to the leafy northern suburbs, declaring that the contract relegating the Cards to the area south of Madison Street was legal and binding. Stung by the decision, Wolfner hinted that the Cardinals might pursue the matter in Appeals Court, but he quickly dropped the idea.[16] Bell's decision surprised nobody; he was closely aligned with Halas throughout his term as NFL commissioner.[17] By the end of February, Wolfner's talks with the Park District were well under way, and now, three weeks later, an agreement had been cobbled together. The Park District agreed to move the gridiron in Soldier Field about 90 feet south and to install 3,200 box seats in the first 20 rows between the 20-yard lines.[18] These would be the first seats with backrests in the historic old stadium. Meanwhile, the north end of the cavernous arena would be blocked off by approximately 25 rows of bleacher seats. This move reduced available seating from roughly 101,000 to 52,300, with sight lines greatly improved from every location. With future revenue projected at a conservative rate of $3.50 per paying customer, the Cardinals' front office envisioned filling the stadium to capacity, which would generate gross receipts of over $180,000 per game. Apparently they forgot that in 1958 the team averaged just over 19,000 fans for each home game.

Total stadium capacity when the Cardinals were playing, however, was really a moot point. During their last nine seasons at Comiskey, the Big Red drew more than 30,000 fans only nine times, and six of those dates were against the Bears. On those dates, Comiskey Park was swollen with Bears fans eager for the novelty of a field trip to 35th and Shields, once they figured out how to access the Wentworth Avenue streetcar. Bears home game tickets were often hard to come by in the 1950s, and traipsing to Comiskey meant a chance to see their oversized navy-and-orange-clad heroes in person. Wolfner openly expressed how pleased he was with the terms of the Park District lease. Unlike the arrangement he had had at Comiskey Park, rent at Soldier Field was contingent on paid attendance, increasing the team's changes of growing their slim profit margin.

Many felt that a huge loss with this sad development was a huge loss for Chicago. Like the White Sox and Brooklyn Dodgers, the Chicago Cardinals were very much a *neighborhood* professional team, with origins dating to the turn of the century. Their absence meant that part of the South Side's cultural identity would be lost. Few images in the city's sports scrapbook were as unforgettable as a field-level camera shot of Ollie Matson or Charlie Trippi tearing a hole in the opponent's line, with Comiskey Park's stately cathedral arches framing the massive scoreboard, and the catwalk connecting the stands suspended under the giant board like a graceful necklace. For those sitting in the outfield upper deck or anywhere along the third base line, Comiskey Park was a fantastic place to watch football, like so many of the old major league baseball stadiums, especially when compared to the faceless, uninspiring "multi-purpose" urban bowls of later decades.

The Cardinals' rich history as Chicago's first professional football team dated to 1898 in the Morgan Park neighborhood, three years before the White Sox even existed. Founder Christopher O'Brien had christened his gridiron group the Morgan Athletic Club, later changing the name to the Racine Cardinals, named for Racine Avenue, which bordered their home at the Chicago Park District's old Normal Field. Their signature color, "Cardinal Red," was actually a faded crimson, the result of frequent washings at the University of Chicago when the originally dark maroon uniforms were worn by the collegians. At the turn of the century, these hand-me-downs were all the budget-strapped Cardinals could afford. The Cards brought pro football to Comiskey Park, the Baseball Palace of the World, in 1922.

While never approaching the financial or on-field success of their hated cross-town rivals, over the years the Big Red faithful thrilled to the exploits of gridiron greats like Ernie Nevers, Marshall Goldberg, Paul Christman, and Pat Harder. They would gaze with pride at the local boys who made good, like Elmer Angsman, from the 8000 block of South Paulina Street; Don Engels, a Fighting Dragon from Evanston's historic St. George High School and the quarterback of the victorious 1952 University of Illinois Rose Bowl team; or

Don Stonesifer, a kid from Logan Square who starred at Carl Schurz High School and Northwestern. Every now and then, fans would marvel at some little guy every other team had ignored, guys about the size of the White Sox batboys, like the amazing Billy Cross. Cross, barely five and a half feet tall and taken as an afterthought in the 24th round of the 1950 draft, often proved simply impossible to tackle. He had more moves than a newly minted Swiss watch and thrived in his role as backfield yin to the immortal Charlie Trippi's yang. It did not matter that the team rarely met with success; the Cardinals were part of the old neighborhood. A beloved and unforgettable piece of Chicago's cultural landscape disappeared when the Chicago Cardinals left 35th and Shields.

Meanwhile, the rocky relationship between the Sox owners did not show any signs of changing in the near future. Even though Chuck, Dorothy, and Veeck had met and tried to appear friendly for the press the week before, Chuck went back to Cook County Probate Court on Tuesday, March 17, to "enjoin William Veeck from holding a stockholders' meeting Friday, March 20, for the announced purpose of electing one director to fill out the four-member board."[19] While this move tied Veeck's hands by preventing him from holding the scheduled meeting, Chuck was not happy with Judge Dunne's activities two days later. On Thursday, March 19, Dunne ordered the distribution of the 1,541 shares of stock left in Grace's estate to Dorothy. He also denied Chuck's request that those same shares be offered for private sale. If Judge Dunne had ruled that they could be sold instead of transferred to Dorothy, Chuck would have had an opportunity to purchase them, increasing his White Sox holdings. Chuck's lawyers, as expected, announced that they would appeal this latest defeat as well.

Down in Florida, young Bob Shaw caused some smiles in the Sox dugout with a very successful outing against the hard-hitting Kansas City Athletics. Shaw, whom the Sox got from the Tigers in 1958, was beginning to open some eyes with his varied repertoire of pitches and consistent performance. After an uneventful but much-publicized matchup against the Yankees—in front of a huge crowd for those days of 4,600 in Miami's pink-seated Marlin Stadium—Dick Donovan finally got on track the following day with his best outing of the spring, pitching the last four innings against the Pirates for a 4–2 win. Equally encouraging was the White Sox hitters' ability to get the better of two of the best pitchers in the National League, Bob Friend and Elroy Face. After putting away two of the Senior Circuit's best the day before, the same Sox hitters were completely befuddled by a pair of lesser lights throwing against them the following day. Uneventful victories over Kansas City and St. Louis, coupled with a tie against the Yankees, closed out the team's Florida spring training experiences.

With March coming to an end, Lopez, Cuccinello, and Berres put their heads together to make the league-mandated roster cuts by Wednesday, April 1. By March 29, they were down to 36 players, when pitchers Jim Derrington and Hal Trosky, Jr., and infielder Don Prohovich were sent to Indianapolis. Derrington, who saw some time with the Sox in both 1956 and 1957, would not play again in the major leagues. Trosky, whose father played first base for the Indians and White Sox for over a decade in the 1930s and 1940s, had appeared in two games for the Sox in 1958 and closed out his professional career in the minors. To get down to 33 players on April 1, the Sox optioned Joe Hicks, Chuck Lindstrom, and Jim McAnany to the team's Hollywood, Florida, training facility. Hicks would be called up to the South Side during the 1959 season, and McAnany was destined to play a huge role for the Sox later on. Lindstrom, the son of New York Giants Hall of Famer Fred Lindstrom, had appeared in one game for the Sox in 1958, which turned out to be his only major league action.

Norm Cash in 1959. Cash went with John Romano to Cleveland after the 1959 World Series and won the AL batting title in 1961 while playing for Detroit, where he became one of the most productive power hitters in Tigers history.

The organization felt very good about their prospects for the coming season as long as nobody brought up the subject of scoring runs. They desperately needed some power and had valid concerns about whether Callison was ready. On the positive side, the veterans started to hit consistently in Florida, and Romano proved to be a nice surprise. With Romano developing some of his great potential, Lopez could put him behind the plate and keep Lollar's bat in the lineup by playing him at first base. Nobody had paid much attention to another youngster who was seen as a long shot at best to make the team, but who was having the hottest bat all spring—Norm Cash. Before Opening Day, he would be the talk of the team.

3

April: Play Ball,
but Try to Play Nice

The Sox finished Grapefruit League spring training commitments with contests against the Milwaukee Braves, Cincinnati Reds, St. Louis Cardinals and Pittsburgh Pirates, closing their 1959 Sunshine State experience with an 11–9 record. Before they broke camp, Gabe Paul, owner of the Cincinnati Reds, told the press he thought the Chicagoans would be better off leaving the Tampa spring training site for good, saying there was not enough room for both the Reds and the Sox to train there. Three other cities—Sarasota, Florida, and two Arizona towns, Chandler and Yuma—expressed interest, but the Sox organization made no comment.[1] As they moved north to start the season, the Sox's itinerary included exhibition games in Charlotte against the Senators; in Nashville, home of Cincinnati's best minor league team; and in Indianapolis, home of the Sox's best minor league squad, again against the Reds.

Lopez and pitching coach Ray Berres revealed their starting rotation for the upcoming season: Pierce, Wynn, Donovan, Moore, and Latman. If rainouts or scheduling issues warranted going to a four-man rotation, Latman or Moore would be moved to the bullpen. Lopez also tried to convince the press that he was not concerned about Callison's hitting. While the much-ballyhooed rookie could barely keep his batting average above his weight, Lopez blamed Callison's .200 average on his penchant for swinging at high pitches and said that all he needed was more exposure to major league pitching. Lopez noted that Callison had been a slow starter the previous year at Indianapolis, striking out twice as often during the first half of the season as he had in the second half. The Sox manager believed his bat would come around and that during the wait, the Sox would be stronger because of the youngster's great defensive skills. However, Callison's statistics included very few extra-base hits, and the lack of power hitting throughout the White Sox lineup remained a concern.

The meaningless game against the Senators in Charlotte proved to be a good one for Norm Cash, who tripled and homered, driving in four runs. In 1958, the 24-year-old appeared as a late-season call-up in 13 games, pinch-hitting in five of his eight at-bats. For the 1959 season, Lopez had already named veteran Earl Torgeson to start at first, and Cash had remained on the roster only because as a returning military reservist, his presence did not count against the roster limit. In spite of his limited appearances, the stocky young Texan had become the leading Sox hitter in the pre-season with a .471 average featuring two doubles, two triples, and two homers. Cash was a gifted athlete, and the Sox were not the first professional team in Chicago to want him. In 1954 he gained 1,500 yards as a running back at Sul Ross State College in Texas, and George Halas drafted him for the Bears in the 13th round as a futures pick. Since baseball's career opportunities and earning potential far eclipsed those of pro football in the 1950s, Cash followed the money and decided to concentrate on baseball.

The victory over the Reds in Indianapolis completed the final chapter of the 1959 spring training campaign. The Sox drew 27,854 customers for their 12 games in Tampa and the Charlotte-Nashville-Indianapolis swing, with more than half of the customers appearing at the last three games on their way home to Chicago. Since the revenues in Tampa were worse than expected, those three games went a long way toward paying the $80,000 cost of spring training. To boost future pre-season revenues, on Monday, April 6, the Sox announced that they would leave Tampa and move their spring training base to Sarasota in 1960.

The Sox completed four objectives during spring training: tune up their already solid defense; get Latman established as a starting pitcher; expose Callison to more big-league pitching; and, as Lopez announced after the Indianapolis game on the plane en route to the season opener in Detroit, start a new first baseman. Lopez surprised everyone by announcing that Cash would start at first base. Cash's performance gave El Senor no choice but to relegate Torgeson to a back-up role, at least for the start of the season, since Cash had legitimately emerged as the most promising hitter on the team. The Sox needed some heavy lumber, and if Cash could continue to provide it, there would be less pressure on Callison.

In Chicago, Sox loyalists looked forward to Bob Elson and Don Wells describing Opening Day action on WCFL (the *Voice of Labor*) radio, and to watching the Tuesday, April 14, home opener on WGN TV with Jack Brickhouse and Vince Lloyd at the microphones.

By the late 1950s, baseball executives saw television as a critical component of their revenue stream.[2] While the fears that radio broadcasting would cut into gate receipts had been laid to rest two decades ago, major league teams were divided on whether television was a financial friend or foe. In

1959, the Sox received about $300,000 from WCFL for radio rights to broadcast the entire season and about $250,000 from WGN TV for the broadcast rights to 55 home games. In the 1950s, WGN televised every home day game at Comiskey Park, but none of the night games.[3] The broadcasting money represented a sizeable portion of their $3,223,624 operating income. Radio and television revenue ($550,000) almost matched concessions ($316,016) and road games ($344,052) combined.[4] By the late 1950s, two variables determined how lucrative a team's television contract could be: whether the team was a pennant contender, and the size of the team's broadcast media market. The Yankees were a good example. In 1959, they had $825,000 in television revenue, the highest amount in baseball, befitting a team with a huge market and the winningest tradition in the game. They had 144 of their 154 games televised. While their television contract was the highest in the majors, it was far from the best in revenue-per-game, paling in comparison to the Detroit Tigers' deal. In 1959, the Tigers received $9,100 for each of the 55 games they agreed to broadcast, over $3,300 more than the Yankees' revenue per game. Baseball executives, however, consistently worried that television might be reducing attendance, and the goal of maximizing broadcast revenue while not cutting into the gate led to some novel arrangements, like the Cleveland Indians' innovative plan. For the 1959 season, the Indians would broadcast 56 games for about $6,250 per game, totaling $350,000. To protect attendance at huge Municipal Stadium, none of the home Sunday doubleheaders would be on TV, hopefully assuring crowds in the neighborhood of 75,000 on those afternoons if the team were doing well. By the mid–1950s, the Indians were the only American League team in Ohio and Pennsylvania, and for many teams, the wider the geographic draw, the wiser it was not to broadcast all the games. The Tigers, playing in a large city, still drew a good percentage of their fans from western Michigan, the Upper Peninsula, northern Indiana, and the Toledo, Ohio, area. Their thinking was that if more than 55 games were on television, out-of-towners might be less likely to travel to a game.

In Chicago, WGN would also broadcast every 1959 Cubs home game, but the perennial non-contenders would receive only $200,000, $2,600 per game. Since Cubs and Sox home stands almost never coincided, the two Chicago teams struck an agreement with WGN not to broadcast road games, to protect the gate of the team playing at home. The Milwaukee Braves, on the other hand, intentionally negotiated a smaller and less lucrative television contact than almost every other team. This was in spite of their perennial success in the 1950s and their wide following in Wisconsin, Minnesota, Upper Michigan, Iowa, and the Dakotas. The purpose of this limited television exposure was to protect the gate, since a large number of Braves followers drove long distances to see the team.[5]

The pre–Opening Day prognostications in the Chicago media started

Monday, April 5, five days before the debut in Detroit. Richard Dozer, in the Sunday, April 5, *Chicago Tribune*, went out on a limb and picked the Sox to win the pennant, expecting great things from Callison and Romano and citing the advancing years of Yankees stalwarts like Whitey Ford, Hank Bauer, and Yogi Berra. WGN's broadcast team of Jack Brickhouse, Vince Lloyd, and Lloyd Petit picked the Sox for second, while their colleagues Jack Quinlan and Lou Boudreau picked them for third. John Kuenster, in the Thursday, April 9, *Chicago Daily News*, also picked the Sox for third, reasoning that the aging Yankees had one more year left, the Detroit Tigers were vastly improved, and the Sox's bats were just too feeble.

On Thursday, April 8, Lopez trimmed his roster to the final count by releasing pitcher Bill Dufour (in spite of his nifty 18–11 record and 2.94 ERA the year before at Charlotte) and veteran catcher Les Moss. Moss was at the end of a successful 13-year major league career, his departure hastened by Romano and Battey. Widely respected in the baseball world, within the next ten years Moss would manage both the Sox and the Tigers.

The front office ownership strife surfaced again on the eve of the season opener in Detroit. Circuit Judge William J. Tuohy listened to five hours of testimony on April 8 regarding two issues: Chuck's request to force Dorothy to sell him more stock out of his mother's estate and his request to declare Dorothy's sale to Veeck's syndicate null and void. Tuohy promised a ruling on the matter by April 29.[5]

When Opening Day finally arrived, the Chicago print media went all-out to trumpet the news. The *Tribune* ran a full-page panoramic shot of Wrigley Field with the outfield turf still showing the ravages of the Bears season which ended four months before. It mattered little that an early-morning snowstorm cancelled the Cubs' opener against the Los Angeles Dodgers— baseball was in the air.[6] Bill Furlong of the *Chicago Daily News* paid tribute to the start of the season with a poetic offering:

> At the moment of impact, cynicism dies and hope is born.
> Here is the Great American Religion. Its chapel is a bleacher seat;
> Its spire is a maze of lights. It lives on faith; reality is its hearsay.
> The faithful line their pews and munch their peanuts and await the words,
> At last it comes…. "Play Ball!!"[7]

For the season opener in Detroit, Lopez posted the following lineup. The players' 1958 statistics appear in parenthesis:

Luis Aparicio, ss	(.266, 2HR, 40 RBI)
Nellie Fox 2b	(.300, 0, 49)
Jim Landis, cf	(.277, 15, 64)
Sherm Lollar, c	(.273, 20, 84)
Norm Cash, 1b	(.250, 0, 0)
Al Smith, rf	(.252, 12, 58)

Johnny Callison, lf	(.297, 1, 12)
Bubba Phillips, 3b	(.273, 5, 30)
Billy Pierce, p	(17–11, 2.68 ERA)

With Aparicio and Fox at the top of the lineup, the Sox boasted the most effective one-two punch in the majors. Landis, Lollar, and Smith could hold their own in the middle of the order. The bottom of the lineup, however, was a huge question mark, and if Callison stumbled or Cash could not continue his spring training success at the plate, veterans like Jungle Jim Rivera and Earl Torgeson would have to step in and be effective.

Thanks to a series of late-autumn trades, the Tigers, the Sox's Opening Day opponent, were widely regarded as the most improved team in baseball. They had one of the most successful and profitable runs in the majors between 1934 and 1950, winning two World Series, appearing in two others, and finishing second six times. Their performance in the 1950s, however, was unspectacular, and they entered the 1959 campaign with a .477 winning percentage for the previous nine seasons. The same biases that impaired the progress of other teams in the 1950s held the Tigers back, as the Briggs family was reluctant to pursue talented minority ballplayers.[8] Every team in the majors had integrated except the Boston Red Sox when the Tigers finally signed Ossie Virgil, a Dominican-born third baseman, in 1958. In the front office, when owner Walter Briggs, Sr., died, his son Spike offered to buy out his two sisters. Foreshadowing the conflicts the Comiskey family would have, his offer was turned down, and in 1956 radio tycoon John Fetzer purchased the team for a whopping $5.5 million. Changes on the field soon followed. In the autumn of 1958, the Tigers significantly changed their roster, upgrading three starting positions and strengthening the pitching staff. They first traded troubled shortstop Billy Martin and throw-in Al Cicotte to Cleveland for pitchers Don Mossi and Ray Narleski, and reserve shortstop Ossie Alvarez. They fortified the catching position, getting Lou Berberet from the Red Sox for little-used righty hurler Herb Moford. Four days later, they sent starting third baseman Reno Bertoia, shortstop Ron Samford, and outfielder Jim Delsing to the Senators for shortstop Rocky Bridges, third baseman Ed Yost, and minor leaguer Ned Chisley.

The Tigers' potent Opening Day lineup:

Ed Yost, 3b	(.224, 8 HR, 37 RBI)
Harvey Kuenn, cf	(.319, 8, 54)
Al Kaline, rf	(.313, 16, 85)
Gail Harris, 1b	(.273, 20, 82)
Frank Bolling, 2b	(.269, 14, 75)
Larry Doby, lf	(.283 13, 45)
Rocky Bridges, ss	(.263, 5 28)
Red Wilson, c	(.299, 3, 29)
Jim Bunning, p	(14–12, 3.52 ERA)

From the second through the sixth spots in the batting order, the Tigers had one of the most formidable lineups in the majors. Their offensive firepower, coupled with a starting staff of Jim Bunning, Paul Foytack, Frank Lary, and the newly acquired Don Mossi, gave the Tigers their most legitimate shot at the American League pennant in many years. While Kaline started the game in right field, as the 1959 season progressed he spent most of his time in center field. The Tigers' biggest star started 122 games in center (and only 15 in right field) in 1959.[9]

A large crowd was expected in Tiger Stadium for the Friday opener, and in spite of cloudy skies and a 37-degree temperature reading, 38,332 warmly clad spectators showed up to cheer on their heroes. Few thought they would still be there four hours and 25 minutes later, but that was how long it took the White Sox to dust off their Opening Day hosts with a 9–7, 14-inning victory. All told, 43 players—23 Sox and 20 Tigers—saw action in the game. Starting pitchers Bunning and Pierce were long forgotten by the time Nellie Fox (of all people) hit a two-run homer in the top of the 14th to give Sox reliever Gerry Staley the win and Mossi the loss. Fox, who hit no home runs during the entire 1958 campaign, paced the Sox 17-hit attack, going 5-for-7, while Lollar got three safeties and young Cash went 2-for-4. Callison, the Sox's other rookie hopeful, went hitless and was replaced in the late innings by local boy Lou Skizas. Newcomer Rocky Bridges and Al Kaline combined for six of the Tigers' 14 hits.

While this first victory was certainly an exhilarating win, it was not without its seamier side. Callison was hit on the side of the head with an empty pint bottle thrown from the stands, and later on a whiskey bottle and other debris littered the field. American League President Joe Cronin assured the press after the game that nothing like this would occur again at Tiger Stadium.[10]

Much to the delight of their baseball-hungry fans back in Chicago, the White Sox managed to sweep the Tigers in this season-opening series with a pair of 5–3 victories on Saturday and Sunday, April 11 and 12. In Saturday's matchup, Wynn earned the 250th win of his career and Aparicio hit a seventh-inning home run to break a 3–3 tie, so in the first two games of the season, two game-deciding, critical home runs came from two most unexpected sources, Fox and Aparicio. On Sunday, April 12, Dick Donovan, who had developed a cadre of skeptics with his weak spring training performance, outpitched Tigers ace Frank Lary. Cash's first homer of the year proved to be the difference, with Arias and Shaw coming out of the bullpen to preserve the win. With three wins under their belt, the trip to Chicago to play on Tuesday, April 14, against Kansas City could not have gone better.

The Chicago media was abuzz regarding the Sox's home opener, greatly anticipating the creativity and innovation Veeck might display. He had made headlines the week before on Thursday, April 9, when he put hundreds of laborers on a temporary payroll to completely scrub Comiskey Park, from the upper deck ceilings to the cement floor in the main concourse below the stands. Veeck's picture appeared in the *Chicago Tribune*, bucket in hand, cleaning some of the 50,000 seats.[11] He made more news the next day when he announced that he was extending an official invitation to Cuba's Prime Minister Fidel Castro, who was visiting the United States, to the Sox's first game.[12] In April 1959, the American public still viewed Castro as a curiosity instead of a symbol of communist expansion, and Veeck reasoned that with Castro's significant baseball background, why not invite him? Some applauded Veeck's innovation, while others saw it as just another one of his PR moves. The new owner boasted to *Tribune* columnist David Condon that the Sox's home debut would be the hottest thing in Chicago since Mrs. O'Leary's cow.[13] The gossip columnists loved having Veeck in town. He was rumored to bring Harlem Globetrotters owner Abe Saperstein in as a partner.[14] There were whispers that Joe DiMaggio was on his way to the Windy City to help Veeck and Greenberg in the front office. A column also came out claiming that he already made plans to move the team to New Orleans.[15]

Meanwhile, Veeck's unwanted partner and business adversary, Chuck Comiskey, draped a wet blanket on the happy start of the season when he filed a petition with Judge Tuohy seeking to prevent a meeting of the team's stockholders. Comiskey asked the court for the election of a new board of directors, giving both Veeck *and* himself control of two seats, which would, of course, create a potential deadlock. Veeck's attorneys claimed that, as the majority shareholder, the Veeck group was entitled to elect one director to fill the vacancy created by Grace Comiskey's death in 1956, which had gone unfilled. Under this scenario, Veeck would control three votes and Chuck only one. Tuohy gave Chuck's lawyer Yager Cantwell one week to submit additional information and announced that he would give his opinion April 29—the same day he would render a decision about Chuck's request to force Dorothy to sell him more stock and declare Dorothy's sale to Veeck null and void. While the entire South Side got ready to play ball, it looked like the new owners could still not get themselves to play nice.[16]

The players' ritual of getting established in Chicago for the six-month season did not change very much in the 1950s. Almost all the players lived on the southeast side of Chicago, in the Hyde Park neighborhood near 55th Street and Lake Shore Drive. The team's presence in this area went back many years. Prior to his death, Lou Comiskey lived at Jackson Towers, overlooking Lake Michigan and the Museum of Science and Industry, at 5555 South Everett. Three apartment hotels, the Flamingo-on-the-Lake (5500 South Shore Drive), the Picadilly (Hyde Park and Blackstone Boulevards) and the Shoreland (54th and South Shore Drive) together housed almost three-quarters of the team.

The Veeck family's temporary quarters at the start of the season was nearby, a suite in the Hotel Sherry.

In 1959 there were only two ticket prices for all regular season Sox games, $2.50 for a box seat and $2.00 for the grandstand. Tickets for children under 12 were 90 cents less. Grandstand seats were reserved on Sundays, holidays, and night games, but unreserved at all other dates. Fans had a choice of the following beverages:

Milk	.20
Hot Chocolate	.25
Small Coffee	.15
Large Coffee	.25
Orange drink	.15
Lemonade	.25
Pepsi Cola	.15
Hamms Beer	.40

Hamms was a major sponsor of the Sox and Cubs games on WGN TV and was the only beer sold at Comiskey Park. It was the main product of the Theodore Hamm's Brewing Company, located in the Swede Hollow section of St. Paul, Minnesota. The brewery dated back to the end of the Civil War and became famous for its innovative advertising. They used a turn-of-the-century love song for their trademark radio jingle, *From the Land of Sky Blue Waters,* and cleverly developed the Hamm's Bear as their buffoonish, cartoon mascot. Marhoefer hot dogs were 30 cents, while a Lazar's Kosher Red Hot was 35, the same price as a pack of regular or king size cigarettes.

The Sox also had a novel way of handling ticket scalpers. On page three of the Official 1959 White Sox Program, a small warning appeared in bold print:

For your own protection: buy your Sox tickets
from only authorized Sox outlets.
DO NOT PAY MORE THAN THE PRINTED
PRICE ON THE FACE OF THE TICKET.
Help us eliminate scalpers. If you secure tickets from any source other
than the official Sox outlets, bring the stub to our office at 35th & Shields.
Report the name of the source and we will take them from the season ticket
holder and allocate the same seats to you the following year, if you desire them.

The Sox's opponent for their home opener was the Kansas City Athletics, a team whose futility during the 1950s was eclipsed only by the Washington Senators. The A's, preparing for their fifth season in Kansas City after moving from Philadelphia in 1955, had tallied a disappointing .403 winning percentage over the previous nine seasons, with 558 wins and 827 losses. Their only winning year was 1952, when they finished fourth with a record of 79–75, 16 games behind the pennant-winning Yankees. In the autumn of 1954, a heartbroken Connie Mack, by then 93 years old, sold the team to Arnold Johnson of Kansas City for $3.5 million. Mack, who lost a fortune during the Depression,[17] was unable to muster the financial resources to turn the Athletics into a winner again. To make ends meet after that, he consistently sold off the team's most promising or successful players, dooming the Athletics' chance of consistent success. By the 1950s, after years of consistently small attendance, Mack had no alternative other than to sell his life's work. The team's sale and move to Kansas City was greeted by many observers with a great deal of skepticism; some thought that after the novelty of being home to a major league team wore off, a small market like Kansas City would never be able to support a major league franchise. The grand old man died just two years later.[18]

The Athletics had averaged only 413,831 fans in Philadelphia from 1950 through 1954, drawing a paltry 304,666, less than 4,000 per game, during their last year in the City of Brotherly Love. Through it all, Mack had worked hard to put a quality product on the field. To his credit, he was also one of the first owners in the American League to sign and play African American ballplayers, most notably Bob Trice, who debuted for the A's on September 13, 1953, and became one of their starting pitchers in 1954.

Johnson was an extremely successful Kansas City businessman whose fortune came from real estate, vending machines, and manufacturing. Before the sale was complete, he openly discussed moving the A's out of Philadelphia, and in spite of losing 91 games in 1955, the Athletics drew over 1.3 million fans the first season in Kansas City, eclipsing their biggest draw in Philadelphia over their entire 54 years there by 400,000. To prove that the novelty of major league baseball could linger for more than one year, the A's lost an abysmal 102 games in 1956 but still drew over a million customers, better than half of all major league teams that year.

The organization might have been able to play a level of baseball worthy of all that attention if Johnson did not have such a strange, entangled alliance with the New York Yankees. Astute observers in the 1950s came to recognize Johnson's franchise as a high-level feeder team for the Bronx Bombers, and indeed, between 1956 and 1960, no fewer than 11 top-level players migrated from the Athletics or their minor league subsidiaries to the Yankees. The list includes many individuals with very successful careers: Hall of Famer Enos Slaughter, traded to the Yankees in August 1956; Art Ditmar, Bobby Shantz, and Clete Boyer, all departing in February 1957; Ryne Duren and Harry "Suitcase" Simpson, shipped east by the Athletics in June 1957; Hector Lopez and Ralph Terry, May 1959; Joe DeMaestri and Roger Maris, December 1959; lastly, Bob Cerv in May 1960. There were at least two others curious connections between the two teams. The construction contract to refurbish Kansas City's Municipal Stadium went to Yankees co-owner Del Webb's construction company, and Daniel Topping, the other Yankees principal, was on the Board of Directors of Johnson's corporations.

Nobody in baseball was too excited about the Kansas City roster in 1959, even though some of the young A's were destined to have significant moments of greatness when they moved to other teams. Manager Harry Craft listed the following lineup for the April 14, Comiskey Park opener:

Bill Tuttle, cf	(.231, 11 HR, 51 RBI)
Roger Maris, rf	(.247, 19, 53)
Hector Lopez, 2b	(.261, 17, 73)
Bob Cerv, lf	(.305, 38, 104)
Hal Smith, 3b	(.273, 5, 46)
Dick Williams, 1b	(.276, 4, 32)
Harry Chiti, c	(.268, 9, 44)
Joe DeMaestri, ss	(.219, 6, 38)
Ralph Terry, p	(11–13, 4.24)

The Sox, behind Billy Pierce's 32nd career shutout, won, 2–0, in front of a disappointingly small crowd of 19,303. Aparicio drove in both runs with a single in the bottom of the fifth inning, and the crowd enthused over Callison's first hit in the majors, a bunt single, raising his average to .083 (1-for-12). The Sox got eight hits, seven off A's starter Ralph Terry and the other off reliever Bud Daley. Only Joe DeMaestri got more than one hit off Pierce, who held Kansas City's long-ball threats, Maris and Cerv, hitless.

The White Sox win, however, was not the only big hit of the day. True to form, Veeck and his charges wowed the crowd with an onslaught of hoopla and promotions. Before the game, he presented Early Wynn with 250 silver dollars, along with a check for the same amount, to commemorate his 250 career victories. Fox and Aparicio, for no particular reason, received what was billed as the world's largest loaf of bread, measuring 20 feet and weighing 200 pounds. To demonstrate to the fans that all factions of top management were on the same page (tsk, tsk), Veeck, his shirtsleeves flapping in the breeze, threw the opening pitch to Chuck Comiskey, who positioned himself in a half-crouch behind the plate. Chuck, dapper in his blue business suit, looked like a youngster stopping off on his way home from church who in his eagerness to play did not change clothes. When fans rose for the National Anthem, two cannon shots rang out from Armour Square Park, just outside the left field stands. This did not go as planned, since the prevailing north wind blew the smoke and cannon ball debris all over the field, at one point interfering with Pierce's concentration on the mound. Finally, as a magnanimous gesture to show that with Veeck the fans always come first, patrons were treated to free liquid refreshments from the seventh inning until the end of the game. Premier Castro did not make it to 35th and Shields and offered no reason for his absence. By game time, he had left the United States and was in Havana, where he threw out the first ball to inaugurate the 1959 International League season.

The Sox's baseball magic came to an end on Wednesday, April 15, when the Athletics demonstrated what kind of offensive power they could generate with a 10–8 victory, and the Athletics won the series the following day when catcher Frank House and Cerv both homered off Wynn to pave the way to an easy 6–0 victory. During the series, rumors started that Veeck was intent on getting his old standby, Larry Doby, from the Tigers, and also sign the ancient Satchel Paige to a contract. Both had starred for him in Cleveland, and Paige, who had also spent time with the St. Louis Browns when Veeck owned the team, was currently pitching for the minor league Miami Marlins. Why Veeck wanted Doby was unclear. The Sox outfield was set, Doby was older than any of the starters, and given his age, his ability to bolster the supposedly anemic Sox offense seemed doubtful.

While many Chicagoans spent the spring speculating about what kind of an owner Veeck would be, Norma Lee Browning, in the April 15 *Chicago Tribune* Magazine Section, wrote about the woman behind the man, Veeck's second wife, Mary Frances. They met when Veeck owned the Cleveland Indians and Mary Francis was working as the press agent for the Ice Capades. A drama major and graduate of the Carnegie Institute of Technology, she previously worked as a fashion model. Browning wrote that the petite brunette's graceful figure and simple beauty brought Rosalind Russell or Audrey Hepburn to mind. The couple got off to a stormy start. Mary Francis was irked that Veeck's World Series–winning Indians were upstaging her ice show's tour dates in Cleveland. Veeck was so smitten, however, that he proposed to her after their first date. Mary Frances would not accept his proposal unless Veeck agreed to wait at least one year and convert to Roman Catholicism. By 1959, the couple had four children, ages eight months to eight years, and Mary Frances effortlessly adapted to the rigors of being the wife of a flamboyant baseball team owner. While Mary Frances was temporarily making the best of it with a family of six living in a suite at the Sherry Hotel, she pointed out that she and Bill were looking for a permanent home on Chicago's South Side close to the ballpark. In the early years of her marriage, when Veeck owned the St. Louis Browns and she could not find a home suitable to their needs, Mary Frances simply redecorated part of the Browns' office suite in ancient Sportsman's Park and turned it into a ten-room apartment. While in St. Louis, she put her press agent acumen to good use, combing through the newspapers' vital statistics section and sending the parents of every newborn boy two tickets to a Browns game and an unsigned contract for the infant to join the team at age 16. Gender roles being what they were in the early 1950s, the parents of a newborn girl would receive no contract but instead two Browns tickets and a poem about their new daughter, written by Mary Frances herself. Browning, presenting a model of 1950s marital stratification, ended the article by pointing out that Mary Frances drank in every bit of information about baseball that she could, through television, radio, newspapers, and trade publications, but that she "would never open [my] mouth to offer an opinion. If I did I would probably sound either like a 'little expert' or an idiot. It's still a man's game. I just listen."

The White Sox's first weekend series at 35th and Shields began Friday, April 17, with the Detroit Tigers coming to visit. Winless after five games, Detroit was off to its worst start in seven years. After the Sox surprised them with a sweep of the opening series in Detroit, the Tigers lost two more games at Cleveland. Lary and Donovan pitched in the Friday series opener, but neither could get through six innings. In the sixth, ex–Yankee hurler Tom "Plowboy" Morgan came in for Lary, and Rudy Arias took over for Donovan. Something more significant, however, had occurred in the top of the sixth, when Lopez pinch-hit the veteran Earl Torgeson for the struggling Callison. Torgeson came through with a single, scoring Cash, who was on base after his second hit of the day. Lopez sent fan favorite Jungle Jim Rivera in to pinch run for Torgeson. Callison sat down, Torgeson came through, and Rivera doubled in the eighth inning, driving in two runs to put the Sox up by two. After Arias surrendered a Detroit run in the ninth, Turk Lown came in to preserve a nifty 6–5 victory. This game served as an early-season example of the managerial acumen Lopez would display throughout the year. Cash's hitting (two hits, three RBI), Lopez's managing, and Rivera's clutch theatrics sent the tiny crowd of 2,656 home happy, but more importantly took the negative spotlight off the slow-starting Callison, who already seemed weary in this young season from carrying such great expectations on his shoulders.

The Tigers had no problems with Sox starter Ray Moore on Saturday, solving him for seven hits and five walks in 6⅓ innings as the Tigers evened the series with a 5–2 victory. Just as disappointing to management as the loss was the small gate for the first Saturday home game of the season—7,159. Any chances the Sox had of winning the series or increasing the gate the following day were eliminated by Mother Nature. When home plate umpire Bill Summers saw that the temperature was 37 degrees with about 500 people in the stands, he cancelled the game. The Sox left Comiskey Park early and started packing for a trip to Kansas City.

After arriving on Monday, April 20, the Sox were guests of the Athletics in Municipal Stadium for a two-game series starting Tuesday evening, April 21. In the first game, they lost a lackluster affair to Bob Grim, 8–3. A third loss in four games to Kansas City was bad enough, but the way the Sox gave it away was unsettling. It marked another milestone in the Sox fans' disenchantment with Al Smith, who played his worst game to date in a Sox uniform. Smith made four blunders that directly affected the outcome of the game. In the bottom of the second, a routine fly ball from the Athletics' Hector Lopez perplexed him and Lopez reached first on the error. In the fourth,

Smith let Frank House's catchable pop-up drop in front of him for an undeserved hit and run. Hector Lopez victimized him again in the seventh inning with a deep fly ball to right that Smith completely misjudged into a double. In the ninth, Smith became Grim's fifth strikeout victim, ending the game as he watched a fat pitch cross the middle of the plate. By the end of the game, Smith's batting average had fallen to .167, and he had just one hit in his last 15 at-bats. After this game, Veeck and general manager Hank Greenberg conferred about their team's anemic batting order. Veeck, desperate for a power hitter, called Washington Senators owner Clark Griffith and offered him three unnamed players and $250,000 if Griffith would part with slugger Roy Sievers, pitcher Pedro Ramos, and catcher Clint Courtney. Sievers was a favorite of Veeck's going back to his time owning the St. Louis Browns. Establishing himself as one of the more consistent power hitters in the American League, Sievers had 39 homers, 108 RBI, and nearly 300 total bases in 1958. Griffith turned Veeck's offer down, explaining that he would not gut his team of its stars for any amount of money.

In the next game on April 22, the White Sox demonstrated the kind of "hitless wonder" team they could be. Facing veteran A's hurler Tom Gorman in the seventh inning with an 8–6 lead, the Pale Hose scored an amazing 11 runs on just one hit en route to a stunning 20–6 victory. Catcher Ray Boone led off the historic seventh and reached first on an error by A's shortstop Joe DeMaestri. Smith sacrificed Boone to second and reached first when catcher Hal Smith juggled the bunted ball. Callison singled to right, scoring Boone as Maris misplayed the ball, allowing Smith to score from first and the sprinting Callison to get all the way to third base. A rattled Gorman then walked Aparicio and allowed the speedy Venezuelan to steal second while he fumed on the mound. Pitcher Bob Shaw batted for himself and walked, loading the bases. At that point, A's manager Harry Craft had seen enough of Gorman and brought in Mark Freeman, who fell under the same spell as his frazzled predecessor, walking Torgeson and Fox to force in two more runs. Landis followed with a weak bouncer back to the mound, and Freeman forced Shaw out with a toss to the plate. With Lollar up and the bases still loaded, Freeman pitched tentatively, wary of Lollar's power, and walked him. A red-faced, enraged Craft stormed out of the Kansas City dugout, yanked Freeman, and summoned George Brunet to the mound. Brunet walked Boone and Smith to force in two more runs. This time Craft stayed in the dugout and remained there even after Brunet hit Callison with a pitch (driving in a run) and then walked Aparicio to force in another run. At this point, the Sox had nine tallies with only one away. Shaw batted again and struck out. Bubba Phillips pinch-hit for Torgeson and drew another walk, as did Fox. Both of these free passes forced in runs; the Sox's run total for the inning was now up to 11. Landis came to the plate and had the ignominy of making two of the inning's three outs when he grounded out to shortstop to retire the side. The top of the seventh inning summary in Kansas City of April 22, 1959: White Sox, 11 runs, one hit, aided by ten walks, three errors, and one hit batsman. This lucky turn of events made the flight to Cleveland on Thursday, April 23, a very pleasant one.

The Indians team awaiting the Sox in cavernous Municipal Stadium on the shores of Lake Erie had been the biggest surprise of the young 1959 season. The Tribe entered the Friday night contest with a 10–1 record, 3.5 games in first place, with a one-run loss to Kansas City the only blemish on their record. While few prognosticators thought a great deal of the Indians' chances at the start of the season, Cleveland boasted a strong roster and was closing out the most successful decade in the team's history.

The only team in the American League to eclipse the success of the Indians between 1950 and 1958 was the New York Yankees. During those years, the Indians tallied 815 wins and 570 losses for an overall winning percentage of .588. They won more than 90 games six consecutive seasons (1950–1955), winning 111 games in 1954 before they were unexpectedly swept in four games by the New York Giants in the World Series. The Indians also finished second to the Yankees five times—1951–1953, 1955, and 1956. Heading up their success on the field were hitters like Al Rosen, Luke Easter, Larry Doby, and Rocky Colavito. Rosen was the only one of the four to play for the Indians for his entire career. Remembered today more as a baseball executive than a player, the "Hebrew Hammer" drove in 100 runs five years in a row, led the American League in home runs twice, and made four All-Star teams. In 1953, Rosen was the unanimous choice for the American League MVP award, winning the home run title with 43 round-trippers, leading the league in runs batted in (145), and missing the batting title by one percentage point to Washington's Mickey Vernon. He also became a hero in America's Jewish community. Rosen was a skilled boxer in his youth whose leadership skills emerged during World War II, and bench jockeys around the league learned that Rosen would physically challenge anyone who belittled or dismissed him because of his Jewish faith. Rosen also declined to take the field on religious holidays. The accomplished slugger had a big following and seemed to engender the jealousy of his boss, general manager Hank Greenberg. Greenberg and Rosen had several bitter contract negotiations which Rosen never forgot.

Cleveland's pitching staff was equally strong, with Bob Feller, Early Wynn, Bob Lemon, Mike Garcia, and the tragic Herb Score. Score was referred to as a left-handed Bob Feller after he became the first rookie in history to average more than one strikeout per inning and had a record of 36–19 in his first two seasons. On May 7, 1957, Gil McDougald of the Yankees hit Score in the face with a line drive, breaking his cheekbone and damaging his vision. Score came back to pitch late in the 1958 season but was never the same. He suffered another setback when he tore a tendon pitching on a damp night against the Washington Senators.

The Indians' success at the turnstiles matched their success on the field.[19] From 1950 through 1958, Cleveland averaged almost 1.2 million fans per season, trailing only the perennial champion Yankees at the gate over that period. The majority owner in the late 1950s was William R. Daley, who bought the team from Myron H. Wilson in 1956 for $3.9 million, believed to be the highest amount paid for any major league team up to that time. Daley's partners were Ignatius A. O'Shaughnessy, scion of St. Paul society, and Greenberg, the general manager. In two short years, however, Daley had soured on Greenberg and forced him to relinquish his partnership. Cleveland fans were often upset with the way Greenberg ran the team, and when Daley learned that Greenberg was one of the individuals behind a plot to move the Indians to Minneapolis-St. Paul, his days in Ohio were numbered. While the organization could look back on the early 1950s with a great deal of pride, by the late 1950s they started trending downward, finishing in sixth place (one game under .500) in 1957 and fourth (one game over) in 1958. General Manager Frank Lane's history of aggressive trades, however, seemed destined to pay dividends. Cleveland's surprising start during the spring of 1959 instilled some badly needed enthusiasm among their many fans.

For the Friday night match-up, Indians manager Joe Gordon penciled in the following lineup:

Jimmy Piersall, cf	(.237, 8 HR, 48 RBI)
Vic Power, 1b	(.312, 16, 80)
Minnie Minoso, lf	(.302, 24, 80)
Rocky Colavito, rf	(.303, 41, 113)
Russ Nixon, c	(.301, 9, 46)
George Strickland, ss	(in minor leagues)
George Leek 3b	(in minor leagues)
Billy Martin, 2b	(.255, 7, 42)
Herb Score, p	(2–3, 3.95 ERA)

The Indians featured a powerful batting order and were stronger at five positions in 1959 than they were at the end of the 1958 season. At first base, Power was a big upgrade from the aging Mickey Vernon. During the 1958 season, while splitting time between Kansas City and Cleveland, Power finished first in the American League in triples, second in doubles, third in hits, and fifth in batting average. In right field, Colavito, a matinee idol among Cleveland's bobbysoxers, was in a class with Bob Cerv, Jackie Jensen, Mickey Mantle, and Roy Sievers during the 1958 campaign. The tall, 26-year-old Adonis from New York City led the American League in slugging and home run percentage, was second in homers and RBI (behind Mantle and Jensen), and third in total bases and runs scored. Irascible Jimmy Piersall won a Gold Glove Award patrolling center field in 1958 and was younger and more energetic than the player he replaced, Larry Doby. Over at second, fiery Billy Martin, obtained in a trade with the Detroit Tigers, replaced the aging Bobby Avila. George Leek, a promising rookie third baseman, replaced the weak-hitting Billy Harrell. One reason the Indians had only one loss in their first 11 games at the start of 1959 was the hitting of Power (.409) and Strickland (.385). If Cleveland's pitching could remain consistent, they could be just as much a threat to the Yankees as the Tigers and White Sox.

After dropping the series opener Friday night in front of a healthy crowd of 28,498, the Sox gambled in Saturday's game by penciling in young Barry Latman to start against the ace of the Indians' staff, Cal McLish. Calvin Coolidge Julius Caesar Tuskahoma McLish had an interesting baseball career.[20] He debuted with the Brooklyn Dodgers in 1944 when they were desperate for pitching. At the time, he was one of the few ambidextrous hurlers in professional baseball history, but the Dodgers would have none of his bi-laterality and had McLish establish himself as a right-hander. He moved to the Pittsburgh Pirates in 1947, the Chicago Cubs in 1949, and then to Cleveland in 1956. At the start of the 1957 season, McLish's undistinguished career statistics included a 10–25 record with a career 5.64 ERA. Yet with the Indians he went 9–7 in 1957, continuing his improvement in 1958 with a 16–8 record and 2.99 ERA.

The Sox prevailed in the Saturday contest much as they had the previous Wednesday in Kansas City, winning the game late with a five-run, one-hit outburst. Both Latman and McLish pitched well through five innings. In the top of the seventh, Callison, sporting a .133 batting average, belted his second home run of the season, a long fly that settled in the outer reaches of the cavernous right field grandstand; with Rivera on base; the blast put the Sox up, 3–1. Cleveland got to Latman and his replacement, Turk Lown, for four runs in the bottom of the seventh, the big blow being Colavito's round-tripper off Lown; Indians 5, Sox 3. In the top of the ninth, however, with Dick Brodowski relieving for the Indians, the Sox answered with another burst of "hitless wonder" excitement. Lollar walked, and Lopez sent Bubba Phillips in to run for him. Ray Boone reached on Strickland's throwing error from shortstop and Phillips, off with the pitch, scored all the way from first. After Rivera popped out, Callison returned to the plate, and Lopez put the faster Al Smith in to run for Boone. Callison grounded to first but was safe when Brodowski mishandled the throw from Power, allowing Smith to score the tying run. Aparicio walked, and Lopez called on Earl Torgeson to pinch-hit for Lown. With Callison on second and Aparicio on first, Torgeson broke the tie with a home run into the right field stands. A badly shaken Brodowski retired Billy Goodman and Nellie Fox, but the damage was done. The Sox's line score for the bottom of the ninth: five runs, one hit, three Cleveland errors, no Sox runners left on base. Shaw pitched as the closer, struck out Piersall, and yielded a single to Power, who raced to third when Shaw threw a wild pitch. Minoso grounded out, scoring Power, but Colavito ended the game by grounding out to Phillips at third. Sox win, 8 -6, in what would become typical "go-go Sox" style.

The Sox made it three out of four by sweeping the Sunday doubleheader, 6–5 and 5–2. Billy Pierce did it all in the second game, spreading eight Indians hits with his mound mastery and leading the Sox's offense by going 3-for-4. The little lefty doubled off Gary Bell in the second inning and tripled in the ninth, when the Sox added two insurance runs off Indians reliever Humberto Robinson. As this important weekend ended, the South Siders had every reason to feel good about themselves. They had arrived in Cleveland three games behind their weekend hosts and left town only one game out, raising their own record to 9–5 and bringing the Indians a little closer to earth with a 10–4 mark.

Upon their return, the Sox began preparing for the arrival of the 1958 World Champion New York Yankees, the New Yorkers' first visit to Chicago in the young season. The level of the Yankees' athletic and financial success in the 1950s was matched only by the contempt many fans in the seven other American League cities felt for them. From 1950 through 1958, they boasted a phenomenal winning percentage of .633, with 876 victories and 507 defeats. The Yanks won the pennant every year during that period except in 1954, finishing second behind the Indians in spite of winning 103 games. Owners Dan Topping and Del Webb purchased the Yankees in 1945 from the estate of beer baron Jacob Ruppert, who died in 1939, for $2.8 million. The reason for the sale six years after his passing was because his three nieces needed liquidity to pay the estate taxes.[21] Topping's fortune came from manufacturing, while Webb was a Phoenix-based builder and land developer pioneering in planned communities. The Yankees were not only the most successful team on the field in the 1950s but also the most profitable at the box office. They drew over a million fans every year from 1950 to 1958, the only baseball team to do so, averaging 1.62 million per season. No other franchise could come close to this level of support. The Cleveland Indians were a distant second, averaging almost a half-million less per season. The team's success made Topping and Webb the most influential and powerful executives in baseball. Set in their ways, the Yankees refused to have any minority players until they called up catcher Elston Howard in 1955. Webb was quoted as saying that if the team had integrated, it would offend all the season ticket holders from Westchester County.

For the Wednesday, April 29 contest, manager Casey Stengel's championship lineup was as follows:

Hank Bauer, rf	(.268, 12 HR, 50 RBI)
Norm Siebern, lf	(.300, 14, 55)
Mickey Mantle, cf	(.304, 42, 97)
Bill Skowron, 1b	(.273, 14, 73)
Yogi Berra, c	(.266, 22, 90)
Gil McDougald, 2b	(.250, 14, 65)
Andy Carey, 3b	(.286, 12, 45)
Bobby Richardson, ss	(.247, 0, 14)
Bob Turley, p	(21–7, 2.97 ERA)

In 1958, Mantle's offensive domination of American League pitching had continued. He was first in total bases (307), runs scored (127), and home runs (42); second in home run percentage (8.1); third in slugging percentage (.592); and fifth in RBI (97). As a testimonial to his rare athletic gifts, he was also fourth in stolen bases (18), in spite of a chronically injured knee. Year in and year out, the Yankees could also count on Berra to be among the best-hitting catchers in the game. And with stars like Turley, Whitey Ford, and Ryne Duren on the mound, their pitching superiority was on a par with their offensive power. Turley led the American League in victories (21), tied with Billy Pierce for first in complete games (19), and led in fewest hits per nine innings (6.5); was second in shutouts (6); and third in total strikeouts (168). Ford was first in ERA (2.01) and shutouts (seven), and third in fewest hits per nine innings (7.14). The bespectacled fire-baller Ryne Duren led all American League relievers by saving 19 games. With all this talent, the Bronx Bombers remained the class of the major leagues.

For the two-game series, Stengel arranged his pitching rotation so that the Sox would have to beat the Yankees' two best, Turley and Ford. With Al Lopez and six players out with influenza, substitute manager Tony Cuccinello had his hands full, especially since Turley's mound opponent would be the Sox's fifth starter, Ray Moore. In the first inning, Mantle homered with Norm Siebern on base, giving the Yanks an early lead. They never looked back, earning an easy 5–2 victory.

While fewer than 10,000 fans showed up for Wednesday's loss, a throng of 26,944 came to the "Baseball Palace of the World" for the Thursday, April 30 encounter, a classic match-up between the two best American League lefties of the era, Whitey Ford and Billy Pierce. Mantle did not appear in the Yankees' lineup. He broke a finger in batting practice, causing Stengel to write in Tony Kubek to bat third and play center field. While this development helped the Sox's chances, the Yankees took control in the top of the third inning. Ford coaxed a walk out of Pierce, who retired leadoff man Bauer but yielded a bunt single to McDougald. Bill Skowron doubled to deep right center, pushing two runs across to give the Yanks a 2–0 lead. The Sox started pecking away, getting a run back in the bottom of the third and tying things up in the sixth when Sherm Lollar blasted his third home run of the season deep into the left field seats off a tiring Ford. Phillips followed with a single, scoring when Pierce and Aparicio did the same, giving the Sox a one-run lead, 3–2. Stengel sent aging Enos Slaughter to the plate to pinch-hit for Ford in the top of the seventh, so the Sox did not have to worry about facing the tough lefty for the rest of the game. But the Yankees clawed their way back to tie the score when Berra crossed the plate on a wild pitch by Pierce. Duren came in for Ford, and the Sox found him unhittable, while the Yankees were getting nowhere with Pierce remaining on the mound. With the game still tied in the bottom of the 11th, Duren, as he was known to do, developed a bad streak of wildness, walking Fox, intentionally walking Lollar after a sacrifice, and then walking Goodman. With the bases full of White Sox, Al Smith delivered a single to ring up an 11-inning, 4–3 victory over the hated Yankees. Smith badly needed the walk-off hit to repair his standing with the fans and was fortunate that such a big turnout was on hand to witness it. Meanwhile, the Yankees could only shake their heads, thinking about Pierce's masterful performance: 11 innings pitched, nine hits, two walks, and only three runs allowed. They were also shaking their heads over their dismal 7–8 record and seventh-place standing in the American League after the first month of the season:

Cleveland	10–4
Chicago	10–6
Baltimore	9–7
Kansas City	9–7
Washington	8–9
Boston	6–7
New York	7–8
Detroit	2–13

Although the Sox were off to a good start, there were still weaknesses that needed to be addressed. With one month of the season under their belts, only four players were hitting above .250: Fox (.423), Rivera (.381), Goodman (.357), and Aparicio (.317). The remaining starters were not bringing any offense whatsoever. Lollar's average was .241, Phillips' was .216, and Landis' a poor .210. Three players—Smith (.179), Cash (.167), and Callison (.133)—were not hitting their weight. Lopez had little in his managerial cupboard to replace them, with Boone hitting .238 and Torgeson, in spite of some clutch pinch-hits, at only .167. Lou Skizas, whom Lopez had inexplicably chosen over Rivera to replace Callison when the rookie's bat consistently failed, sported an abysmal .077 average. Many observers felt Veeck might have been impulsive earlier in the month when he wanted to give up the store for Sievers, questioning what the addition of one home run hitter would do for a lineup that included nobody to consistently protect him, yet the Sox's offense would lead anybody to the same conclusion.

While April ended with Veeck unable to help his team at the plate, he was pleased with his good fortune in Cook County Circuit Court. As expected, the mid–April decision between Comiskey and Veeck to settle their differences out of court went nowhere. Judge Tuohy concluded the April 9 hearing by reconvening all sides in the dispute on April 29. He denied Chuck's request to force Dorothy to sell him 300 shares of White Sox stock from their mother's estate and paved the way for a complete transfer of Dorothy's interests in the White Sox to Veeck's syndicate. Even though knowledgeable observers felt this was a death knell for Chuck's chances to gain control of the team, none of the followers of the White Sox legal soap opera thought he would take this lying down. Soon afterward, Veeck announced the formation of the new board of directors. It was also revealed in court that Veeck had put all his shares of White Sox stock in his wife Mary Frances' name. With this latest legal development, Veeck's new hope was to direct all his attention to the team on the field.[22]

Outside of baseball, it was an interesting spring, on both local and national levels, with developments that would have far-reaching effects on Chicago and the nation for many years to come. In Chicago, the horrific aftermath of the previous December's Our Lady of Angels parochial school fire lingered over Chicago like the smoke from the blaze itself. By spring, hearings into the deaths of the 99 victims, most of them children, were completed, along with the demolition of the charred school building's remains. Interestingly, there was no talk of any lawsuits; perhaps the esteem the victims' families had for the Chicago archdiocese, or the psychic grip the church had at that time on Chicago's fabled "old neighborhoods," was the reason.

On a lighter note, Chicago was in the midst of a golden age in nightclub entertainment, with Martin Denny appearing at the London House, Luis Prima and Keely Smith heating up the Chez Paree, and cool jazz trumpet virtuoso Miles Davis filling tables and chairs at the Empire Room. Elsewhere Mattel introduced the Barbie Doll, and Japan exported the first Toyotas and Datsuns. Perhaps the most significant artifact, however, was a technological development from the Southwest that would dwarf all the Barbie Dolls, Datsuns, and Toyotas combined. A company called Texas Instruments quietly introduced the microchip.

4

May: Win Some, Lose Some

The Sox woke up to some bad news on Friday, May 1, when they learned that outfielder Jim Rivera broke a rib while making a tumbling catch in Yankee Stadium the night before. This occurred right when Lopez realized that Rivera, sporting a .384 batting average in limited play, could be an answer to the White Sox's outfield woes. In spite of all the hype and publicity that preceded Callison, now that the season was well underway, it was apparent that he was not ready for major league pitching. Lopez was also reluctant to continue using local boy Lou Skizas, who had only one single in 13 at-bats. Veeck and Greenberg moved quickly and made a trade.

They found a willing partner in the Cincinnati Reds. The Reds finished April with an 8–7 mark and would have done better with more pitching help. Manager Mayo Smith started Jerry Lynch, Vada Pinson, and Gus Bell in the Reds outfield, a trio that produced 57 home runs and 197 RBI during the 1958 campaign. Smith had Del Ennis on the bench as a fourth outfielder, an established power hitter in his 14th season in the big leagues. The Philadelphia native's offensive resume included 286 homers in 13 seasons and seven seasons with more than 100 RBI. Ennis also had World Series experience with the Philadelphia Phillies. In 1950, he was the key slugger for the pennant-winning "Whiz Kids." Ennis was available for two reasons. The muscular Reds lineup was loaded with hitters, and he was now 34 years old. Smith had traded Ennis once before, in 1956, when he sent him to the St. Louis Cardinals in exchange for the pride of Sauk Rapids, Minnesota, Eldon "Rip" Repulski. So Ennis came to the White Sox, and the Reds got the light-hitting, Chicago native Lou Skizas and left-handed reliever Don Rudolph. Cincinnati's eagerness to get rid of Ennis became apparent after they arranged their expanded roster following the trade. They sent Skizas to the International League to play for the Havana Sugar Kings and assigned Rudolph to split the rest of the season between Havana and the Seattle Rainiers of the Pacific Coast League, essentially burying the players they received in the minors just to move Ennis' salary.

While Rudolph appeared in only 16 games for the Sox during his two-year stay, he brought a certain something to the locker room that would be difficult to replace. Well liked but considered a flake, Rudolph added a clause in his Sox contract stating that the team had to correct his biography in the programs. Rudolph was sensitive about his height, and the program said he was 5'11". Rudolph insisted he had "grown taller" in the off-season, in spite of the fact that he was 28 years old. Rudolph's theories about warming up confounded pitching coach Ray Berres. He insisted upon throwing only slow lobs in the bullpen, claiming he was saving his "hard stuff" for when he entered the game. By 1959, Rudolph was established enough for the Topps Company to issue his baseball card. Card #179 that year had a cartoon panel on the back that said "Don's wife is a professional dancer."[1] Innocent enough; why corrupt the youth of Cold War America, the old boy network at Topps must have reasoned, with more information than that? Indeed, she was a dancer, and their careers intermingled.

On an off-night in 1954 when Rudolph was with the Colorado Springs Sky Sox in the Western League, he went to a gentlemen's club. Much to his delight, Patricia Artae Brownell, a former coed from California's Chico State College, was performing. Her stage name was Patti Waggin,' and she billed herself as "The Coed with the Educated Torso."[2] Ms. Waggin' at that time had quite a following in burlesque circles, and the young left-hander stayed for three performances, later admitting that it was "love at third sight." Unfortunately for Rudolph, Ms. Waggin' ignored his advances after the show.

As fate would have it, Patti had a performance in Baltimore, Rudolph's hometown, during the off-season. Rudolph arrived well before the show began. When it was over, he once again mustered the courage to request the pleasure of her company. This time Ms. Waggin' agreed, and 12 months later they were married.

Patti's field of expertise led to some interesting wrinkles in Don's career. Cynics in the media sometimes mentioned that Rudolph could be the only pitcher in the majors whose wife's curves were better than the ones he threw, and that her charms were more impressive than Don's changeup. Rudolph did not take offense at such statements, but welcomed them, thinking that any publicity about himself and his wife would be good publicity. In the off-season, he managed Patti's engagements and dreamed of opening a nightclub with a mock law enforcement theme, and naming it "Don Rudolph's Patti Waggin.'"[3] It was evident from an off-field perspective that Mr. and Mrs. Del Ennis had big shoes to fill, indeed.

Unfortunately Ennis did not arrive early enough on Friday, May 1, to participate in one of the more historic days in White Sox history. Their opponents, the Red Sox, came to the South Side sporting a disappointing 6–8 record in the young 1959 season. Between 1950 and 1958, the Red Sox had been fairly successful, with three third- and four fourth-place finishes and a decent .533 winning percentage (739–646). In spite of winning a majority of their contests, however, Boston's success was somewhat misleading. The only year they were in a pennant race after Labor Day was 1950, when they won 94 games but still finished a game behind the Tigers and four games behind the pennant-winning Yankees. In 1954, the Red Sox finished fourth, in the first division, with an improbable record of 69–85, 42 games behind the first-place Indians. Whether they won or lost, however, participation in pennant races did not affect their popularity or profitability. New Englanders loved their Red Sox, and between 1950 and 1958 they averaged well over a million paid customers, in spite of Fenway Park being one of the smallest stadiums in the majors. The only teams with a better gate during this period of time were the Yankees, Indians, and Tigers.

Their owner, Thomas Yawkey, purchased the team in 1933 from Mid-westerner Robert Quinn, the former general manager of the St. Louis Browns.[4] Quinn's Red Sox fared poorly on the field, and when they went 43–111 in 1932 and drew 172,000 fans (less than 2,300 per game), he was financially doomed. Quinn borrowed against his life insurance to meet payroll when the 1933 season opened, and the 30-year-old Yawkey had just inherited $7 million, which was burning a hole in his pocket. Quinn jumped at the chance to unload the Red Sox to Yawkey for $1 million.

By the 1950s, one of the major problems holding the Red Sox back from consistently competing with New York, Cleveland, and Chicago was their refusal to sign minority ballplayers. As the 1959 season began, the Red Sox were the only team in the majors not to have a minority player on their roster, and some in the press privately snickered about how fitting it was that manager Mike Higgins' nickname was "Pinky." Higgins put together the following lineup for the May 1 matchup against the White Sox:

Don Buddin, ss	(.237, 12 HR, 43 RBI)
Pete Runnels, 2b	(.322, 8, 59)
Gene Stephens, cf	(.219, 9, 25)
Vic Wertz, 1b	(.279, 3, 12)
Jackie Jensen, rf	(.286, 35, 122)
Frank Malzone, 3b	(.295, 15, 87)
Bill Renna, lf	(.268, 4, 18)
Sammy White, c	(.259, 6, 35)
Tom Brewer, p	(12–12, 3.72 ERA)

The frequent absence of the ailing Ted Williams was a major reason the Red Sox arrived in Chicago with a losing record. In 1958, Williams hit .328, homered 26 times, drove in 85 runs, drew 98 walks, and slugged at a .584 clip. His $125,000 salary was the highest in baseball, eclipsing Stan Musial's by $25,000.[5] Pete Runnels' .322 average in 1958 was second only to Williams', and Jackie Jensen led the Junior Circuit in RBI while finishing fifth in both homers and total bases (293). Jensen won the American League's Most Valuable Player award in 1958, and as a consequence the Red Sox raised his salary to $38,000. The addition of the hard-hitting Vic Wertz at first base further solidified Boston as one of the best offensive teams in baseball at the start of the 1959 season.

All the headlines Williams made with the Red Sox during the 1950s overshadowed Jackie Jensen's unique story. Jensen was a 32-year-old of Danish extraction from San Francisco. He was an All-American fullback at the University of California in 1948, nicknamed the "Golden Boy," and married Olympic diving medalist Zoe Ann Olsen in 1949. That same year, the Oakland Oaks of the Pacific Coast League, figuring that his baseball talents eclipsed his gridiron skills, signed him to a $75,000 contract, out-bidding several major league teams, and made a tidy profit the following year when they sold that contract (along with that of infielder Billy Martin) to the Yankees for $100,000. In Jensen, the Yankees thought they had found the aging Joe DiMaggio's successor, but they quickly changed their minds after he hit only .171 in 1950. By 1952, the Yankees committed to another blond bomber, this one from Oklahoma: Mickey Mantle. Jensen, now expendable, was traded to the lowly Washington Senators. Another trade the following year dispatched him to Boston for Mickey McDermott, and the pride of Scotland Neck, North Carolina, Tommy Umphlett.

After the trade, Jensen became so discouraged with baseball that Red Sox general manager Joe Cronin had to talk him out of quitting. Cronin convinced Jensen that Fenway Park would reawaken his hitting prowess and also helped the husky slugger with his fear of airplane travel. For a while it worked. Jensen established himself in Boston, driving in 100 or more runs in five of six seasons and becoming one of the most feared sluggers in the game. In their 1953 baseball guide, *The Sporting News* listed model trains as Jensen's hobby.[6] At the time, nobody picked up that this trivial note about one of his avocations grew out of a phobia that would cost him his baseball career.

Jensen loved trains, traumatized by air travel, and never mastered his fear of flying. In 1960, yearning for the placidity of railway travel and unable to cope with the anxiety that airplanes caused him, Jensen chose to stay home for the entire season. The following season, with American League teams scheduled to fly even more with the addition of the Los Angeles Angels, Jensen quit baseball entirely.

On May 1, a crowd of 13,022 came to Comiskey Park, experiencing not only the game but Bill Veeck's much-publicized "Fan Promotion Day." For all the hoopla surrounding this event, the Sox hoped for a bigger turnout, since one outrageous gift would be awarded to some dubiously lucky fan every inning. Coupons were taped under nine seats, and the awards were as follows:

1st Inning: 1,000 hot dogs
2nd Inning: 1,000 tickets to the May 2 game
3rd Inning: 1,000 cigars
4th Inning: 1,000 tickets to the May 9 game
5th Inning: 1,000 cans of beer
6th Inning: 150 cans of motor oil
7th Inning: A year's supply of bread
8th Inning: 1,000 cans of soda pop
9th Inning: Two season passes

With Veeck it did not matter if the awards were outlandish; the more outrageous the offerings, he reasoned, the greater the publicity.

While all the promotional commotion occurred in the stands, Wynn had the game of his life on the field. Locking up in a classic pitchers' duel with Boston's Tom Brewer, Wynn threw a complete-game one-hitter and struck out 14. His eighth-inning homer was the only tally of the game. Like Pierce the week before against the Yankees, Wynn did literally everything to win the game, a 1–0 masterpiece.

Early "Gus" Wynn's story was a remarkable one. He was born January 6, 1920, in Hartford, Alabama, a rural area known for cotton and peanuts. His father was Scotch-Irish and his mother Native American. His father played semipro ball and worked as an auto mechanic. Young Early built his strength carrying cotton bales for ten cents an hour. After he broke his leg in a football game, baseball became his only sport. In 1937 Wynn heard about an open tryout sponsored by the Washington Senators in Sanford, Florida. Wynn, who did not own a baseball uniform, showed up in his coveralls. The Senators were impressed with the 6'2", 200-pound 17-year-old's fastball and signed him to a contract. Wynn immediately quit high school and pitched for Sanford in the Florida State League, going 16–11 with a 3.41 ERA his first season. He spent 1938 and 1939 with Charlotte in the Piedmont League, going 25–24 against much tougher competition. The Senators, languishing in sixth place near the end of the 1939 season, called Wynn up; his debut was September 13, 1939. Pitching 20⅓ innings over three games, the promising youngster went 0–2 with a 5.75 ERA. During the off-season, he married Mabel Allman, from Morgantown, North Carolina. Wynn returned to Charlotte for all of 1940 and got promoted to Springfield (Massachusetts) in 1941, coming into his own with a 16–12 record and a 2.56 ERA. In 1941, he was a September call-up once more, proving he belonged in the big leagues with a 3–1 record in five games and a sparkling 1.58 ERA. He started 1942 as the Senators' third starter, starting 28 games with a 10–16 record.

His wife Mabel died in December 1942. Suddenly cast in the role of being a 22-year-old widower with an infant son, he left the baby with relatives during the next two seasons. Wynn missed the 1945 season completely due to military service. He was assigned to the Tank Corps and shipped overseas, serving in MacArthur's Philippine "I Shall Return" engagement until the summer of 1946. Once discharged, Wynn appeared in only 17 games, going 8–5 with a 3.11 ERA, in 107 innings. During his time in the service, he married Lorraine Follin, who would be his wife of 50 years.

When Bill Veeck gained control of the Cleveland Indians, he yearned for Wynn's services, but Senators owner Clark Griffith would not part with the hurler after his 17–15 showing in 1947. The crafty Veeck, however, had a plan. In November 1948, he worked out a trade with the White Sox to obtain veteran hurler Joe Haynes. He had no interest in adding Haynes to the Indians' World Champion pitching staff but used him as bait to get Wynn. Haynes was Griffith's son-in-law, and Griffith supposedly got tired hearing hints from his better half about how nice it would be if their daughter's husband was together in Washington with the rest of the family. Finally on December 14, Veeck got the Christmas gift he wanted, sending Haynes, pitcher Ed Klieman, and first baseman Eddie Robinson to Washington for Wynn and Mickey Vernon. Indians pitching coach Mel Harder helped Wynn improve his curveball, develop a slider, and use a knuckler as his changeup pitch, creating a future Hall of Famer in the process.

Wynn was a fixture in the great Cleveland starting rotations from 1949 through 1957. Over that nine-year stretch, the ornery right-hander won 163 games while losing only 100, an average of over 18 victories a season, and firmly established himself as one of the top pitchers in the majors. The Sox got him in December 1957, when Greenberg, then the general manager of the Indians, soured on the 37-year-old hurler and eagerly acquired Minnie Minoso and infielder Fred Hatfield for Wynn and Al Smith. The trade at first was an unpopular one with South Siders because of the departure of the legendary Minoso. While they were slow to accept Smith, Sox fans eventually changed their minds about the trade when they saw what Wynn could still do on the mound. His off-season pursuits also fascinated the fans. Aside from power boating around his home in Nokomis, Florida, Wynn was one of the few ballplayers flying his own airplane, cruising Florida's coast in a Cessna 170.[7]

On Saturday, May 2, the Red Sox earned a split in the two-game series when Latman, starting for the Sox, put them in a hole early, giving up a run in the first inning and two more in the third. Just as frustrating was the Sox's inability to solve the offerings of Red Sox starter Ike DeLock. Ennis started, batted cleanup, and went 1-for-5; Cash's average fell to .154, and after the game Landis was under .200. The front office once again intervened to get some offense.

The Athletics proved a willing trading partner, agreeing to take Ray

Early Wynn warms up at Comiskey Park under the watchful eye of a "1950s Casual"-attired admirer. Wynn won 300 games in his 23-year, Hall of Fame career.

Boone, the veteran infielder, in exchange for 34-year-old outfielder Harry "Suitcase" Simpson. Simpson, playing behind Bob Cerv, Bill Tuttle, and Roger Maris, was hitting a solid .286 for the A's at the time of the trade, while Boone, a versatile infielder with a solid offensive reputation, was at the tail end of his career, hobbled by knee problems and bursitis. Boone was unhappy with the trade and threatened to retire. Veeck personally intervened and convinced him to give Kansas City, one of baseball's graveyards all through the 1950s, a chance. The Athletics' desperate need for infield help was their only justification for the trade.

Simpson had a colorful baseball career, characterized by a lot of promise and potential that was never completely realized. He hit a measly .224 in 1946 for the Philadelphia Stars in the Negro National League after his discharge from the army, but followed that debut season up with a respectable .286 in 1947. During the spring of 1948, he caught the eye of one Eddie Gottlieb, who spent his summers as a bird-dog baseball scout. His primary occupation was coach and general manager of the American Basketball Association's Phila - delphia Warriors. Gottlieb wrote a glowing report on the 6'1", 180-pound out- fielder, referring to him as the "tan Ted Williams" in a report for the Cleveland Indians. Simpson was a potential five-tool All-Star, and Gottlieb believed in him to the extent that he paid Simpson's travel expenses to the Indians' spring training out of his own pocket. At the time, the Indians had just acquired the first black player to play in the American League, Larry Doby. They signed Simpson to a contract and sent him to Wilkes-Barre in the Eastern League, where he hit 31 home runs. Encouraged with their lucky find, the Indians promoted Simpson to the San Diego Padres in the Pacific Coast League, the best minor league in the country. Simpson toyed with PCL pitching, hitting. 323 while slugging 31 homers. The lithe, grace - ful outfielder made the majors for good in 1951, and the Indians were ecstatic.

Harry "Suitcase" Simpson, a highly- touted Negro League star who broke into the American League with Cleveland in 1951. In 1959, Simpson had only 14 hits during his four months with the White Sox, but had one of the most clutch sea- sons in history; four of those hits were game-winners, and he drove in 13 runs.

In actuality they were a little too ecstatic, putting a lot of pressure on the 26-year-old at the start of the 1951 season, declaring him to be one of the best prospects in Indians his- tory. They played him in 122 games, even though in many of those contests he showed he was not ready for major league pitching, hitting only .229 with seven home runs. He fell short of expectations the next two seasons as well. In late March 1954 he broke his wrist while sliding at the plate. The Indians sent him to Indianapolis to rehab and never called him up in 1954. As a consequence Simpson missed the Indians' World Series appearance. The following year, after they acquired the slugging Ralph Kiner, the Indians no longer needed his services and sold him to Kansas City. Greenberg offered a different reason for Simpson's departure in his autobiography, blaming the atmosphere created by the Cleveland press for Simpson's situation: "Another thing [the press] were wont to do was criticize when we had too many black players. I think at one time we had five blacks on the team. One of them was … Harry Simpson, a good ballplayer, and he had to compete against Bob Kennedy, who was more or less a favorite, a nice Catholic boy who really wasn't as good a ballplayer as Simpson, but that didn't make any difference to the press."[8]

Kansas City manager Lou Boudreau tinkered with Simpson's batting stance, and he responded by hitting .301 in 1955 and .293 in 1956 with 21 homers. The rangy outfielder was lucky enough to be one of the A's traded to the Yankees the following season, thanks in part to Billy Martin.

Some in the press said Martin's bad behavior in 1957 became Simpson's ticket to Manhattan. On May 17, six Yankees—Hank Bauer, Yogi Berra, Whitey Ford, Johnny Kucks, Mickey Mantle, and Martin—went to celebrate Martin's birthday by seeing Rat Packer Sammy Davis, Jr., perform at the Copacabana Night Club. During the performance, a huge brawl ensued, resulting in a lot of negative publicity for the team. As a consequence of the Copacabana Riot, as it came to be known, Bauer was sued for assault, and a month later the team gave up on the seemingly incorrigible Martin. Simpson, fireballing Ryne Duren, and outfielder Jim Pisoni left Kansas City for Yankee Stadium, while Martin, Ralph Terry, the promising Woody Held, and outfielder Bob Martyn were exiled to the A's. In June 1958, Simpson boarded the New York–Kansas City shuttle again, returning to the A's with pitcher Bob Grim, while the Yanks received Duke Maas and the aging Virgil Trucks in return. Eleven months later, Simpson found himself in Chicago.

Aside from symbolizing the ludicrous trades between the hapless A's and the peerless Yankees in the 1950s, people thought Simpson got his nickname because he seemed to epitomize the capable ballplayer whose underappreciated abilities and contributions were always overshadowed by frequent moves to different teams. The real history behind the moniker, however, had to do with his anatomy. While Simpson was playing with Philadelphia in the Negro Leagues, a sportswriter commented on his size 13 shoes and used the nickname "Suitcase" in a column, taken from the character in the *Toonerville Folks* cartoon strip. It stayed with him throughout his career.[9]

The Baltimore Orioles, now in their sixth season on the East Coast, followed the Red Sox into Comiskey Park for a single game on Sunday, May 3.
One of the newer entries in the American League, the Orioles came to being
in 1954 when Jerrold C. Hoffberger, the chief executive of Maryland's National
Brewery Company, bought the St. Louis Browns from Bill Veeck for $2.5 mil-
lion. Hoffberger insisted on getting American League approval to move the
Browns east prior to consummating the sale. Veeck had asked for the same
favor before he put the Browns up for sale but was rebuffed, largely because
several American League owners wanted him out. The move transformed
the most moribund franchise in baseball history into a profitable entity that
improved the next four seasons on the field. The Browns' average annual gate
was an abysmal 339,239 customers between 1950 and 1953. They almost
tripled their attendance, averaging 960,933 fans in their first four years in
Maryland. On the field, they lost 100 games in three of their last five years in
St. Louis, with three seventh- and two eighth-places finishes to show for their
efforts. After losing 100 games their first year in Baltimore, the Orioles eventually improved to a fifth-place finish in 1957, 21 games behind the Yankees,
and a sixth-place finish in 1958 when they were 17½ games out. For the young
1959 season, Baltimore was 10–8, in third place, one game behind the Sox.
They were managed by Paul Richards, who moved east after growing weary
of Frank Lane's interference and the bickering among the Comiskeys while
he managed the White Sox. Richards penciled in the following lineup for the
Sunday matinee affair:

Chico Carrasquel, ss	(.234, 4 HR, 34 RBI)
Bobby Boyd, 1b	(.309, 7, 36)
Gene Woodling, lf	(.276, 15, 65)
Gus Triandos, c	(.245, 30, 79)
Willie Tasby, cf	(.200, 1, 1)
Billy Klaus, 3b	(.159, 1, 7)
Al Pilarcik, rf	(.243, 1, 24)
Billy Gardner, 2b	(.225, 3, 33)
Billy O'Dell, p	(14–11, 2.97 ERA)

The Orioles' biggest shortcoming was generating an offense. In 1958,
their team ERA (3.40) was second only to New York's 3.22. Weaknesses at
the plate plagued them all season. They hit only 108 home runs, with only
the White Sox (101) doing worse in that category. Their team batting average
of .241 was one point better than that of the Senators, who were worst in the
majors. First baseman Bobby Boyd, however, had established himself as one
of the most consistent hitters in the majors, and Gus Triandos was emerging
as one of the best offensive catchers in the game. Triandos' 30 home runs in
1958 topped all catchers in the majors. The big, 28-year-old San Franciscan
joined some elite company, since only four other catchers had hit 30 or more

homers in one season in the previous 20 years: Yogi Berra (1952 and 1956), the Phillies' Stan Lopata (32 in 1956), Roy Campanella (31 in 1950, 33 in 1951, 41 in 1953, and 32 in 1955), and the Giants' Walker Cooper (35 in 1947).

In this single game against the Orioles, the Sox wasted a solid eight-inning performance by Dick Donovan when Turk Lown gave up home runs to two unlikely candidates, Billy Gardner and ex–White Sox Chico Carrasquel, for a 4–2, ten-inning loss. Sox fans hoped for better results in the two-game match-up against the Senators on May 5 and 6, especially since Wynn and Pierce were slated to pitch. The old saying that Washington was "first in war, first in peace, and last in the American League" certainly held true in the 1950s. The Senators had finished in last place the previous two seasons, going 55–99 in 1957 and 61–93 in 1958. Since 1950 their winning percentage was .416 (577–809)—bad. During that period, only the Athletics and the Browns/Orioles fared worse. What set the Washington club apart from those other two was that they rarely showed potential for improvement, and they had no chance to improve their revenue by moving to another city. Between 1950 and 1958, they averaged a little over 550,000 in paid attendance each season, by far the lowest total in the American League. The team was the sole source of income for its owners, Calvin Griffith and his sister, Thelma. They had each inherited 50 percent of the team stock when their uncle and adoptive father, venerable baseball legend Clark Griffith, died in 1955.[11] Clark's penurious ways led to the Senators' long history of futility on the field, and it was apparent to his niece and nephew that the team could not survive if it stayed in Washington. During the 1958 season, rumors of a secret deal to move to Minneapolis–St. Paul and play in a new Metropolitan Stadium located in suburban Bloomington, near the Twin Cities' new airport, began to spread. The politicians in the Nation's Capital, however, would have none of it, and throughout 1958 and 1959, Washington power brokers threatened to reexamine baseball's anti-trust exemption should the Senators attempt to move. Manager Cookie Lavagetto's lineup for Tuesday, May 5:

Reno Bertoia, 2b	(.233, 6 HR, 27 RBI)
Bob Allison, cf	(.200, 0, 0)
Harmon Killebrew, 3b	(.194, 0, 2)
Jim Lemon, rf	(.246, 26, 75)
Ed Fitz Gerald, c	(.263, 0, 11)
Ron Samford, ss	(minor leagues, 1958)
Julio Becquer, 1b	(.238, 0, 12)
Faye Throneberry, lf	(.184, 4, 7)
Chuck Stobbs, p	(3–9, 5.04 ERA)

The Senators were not playing this game at full strength, as Albie Pearson, the diminutive (5'5", 140 pounds) outfielder who was Rookie of the Year in 1958, was not available. Their slugger Roy Sievers was a more notable absentee. Sievers led the American League in homers in 1957 and hit .295 with 39 round-trippers in 1958, and there was a precipitous drop-off from Sievers to his replacement, the 28-year-old Cuban, Julio Becquer. The Senators did have two extremely promising young players in 25-year-old outfielder Bobby Allison and 23-year-old third baseman Harmon Killebrew. When Allison, Killebrew, Lemon, Pearson, and Sievers were all available, the Senators' lineup commanded a great deal of respect.

Sox fans showing up for the game got a pleasant surprise when they noticed that the unpaved east parking lot behind right and center field, long a source of choking dust during games, had been oiled over and was no longer a dust bowl. Veeck wanted to pave it but balked at the $90,000 price tag.[12] The pleasantries ended when they got inside the park, however, as 2,087 saw Allison, Killebrew, and Lemon all hit home runs off Sox ace Billy Pierce for an easy, 8–3 Washington victory. With a salary of only $7,500, Killebrew was shaping up as the best bargain in the major leagues; his long blast off the Sox lefty was his eighth in just 22 games. Wynn could not right the ship the following day when the highly-touted 25-year-old Cuban, Camilo Pascual, outpitched him for a 6–4 Senators win in front of the smallest Comiskey Park crowd of the season, 1,710. The bottom of Washington's lineup finished off the Sox, with shortstop Ron Samford and the weak-hitting Faye Throneberry leading their offense. Dick Hyde and Tex Clevenger followed Pascual on the mound and shut the door on the punchless Chicagoans. The Sox had now lost four in row and had scored 14 runs in their last five games.

They had an off-day Thursday, May 7, and a chance to regroup before a big four-game weekend series at Comiskey with the Indians. The Sox's front office, however, grabbed the headlines before the Indians series got under way. Veeck announced to the press a new administrative organization, naming himself president, Chuck Comiskey vice president, Greenberg vice president and treasurer, and Chicago attorney Milton Cohen secretary. Cohen was Veeck's chief legal counsel and was seen as yet another potential thorn in Chuck's side. Veeck also tried to clarify four points to the throng of reporters. First, there would be no more divided operations between himself and Chuck, and he alone would have complete authority on trades and personnel moves. Veeck also indicated that Lopez' job was safe, but by merely mentioning this he made an issue where none previously existed. He noted that all of the front office's attention would be paid to the team on the field, with any consideration for administrative or farm system changes put on indefinite hold. Lastly, Veeck clarified his statement that he was in "full charge" to indicate also that "the executive vice presidency created for Chuck was more of an honorary position to keep the Comiskey name alive in American League baseball than in a position of [Chicago White Sox] authority."[13] It was clear from this point forward that Veeck and Greenberg would be running the franchise.

Obviously this turn of events did not sit well with Charles Comiskey. Columnist Herb Lyon of the *Chicago Tribune* wrote that Chuck would only be satisfied and drop his lawsuits if Greenberg were completely out of the way.[14] Greenberg's departure, however, was not about to happen. Greenberg and Veeck had been together since Veeck bought the Cleveland Indians in 1947, and Greenberg stayed on as the Indians' general manager until 1958, when he was fired. He left amid criticism from the fans and the press, was alleged to have committed the unforgivable sin of working behind the scenes to move the team to the Twin Cities, and was not fully trusted by the players.[15] After his departure, Greenberg sold his interest in the Indians for $350,000 and, at Veeck's invitation, invested in the White Sox. His personal life at this time had gone through great change, and a chance to work with his old colleague and friend in professional baseball was too good an opportunity to pass up.

Greenberg and his wife of 12 years, millionaire department store heiress Caral Gimbel, divorced soon after he left the Indians.[16] After she filed for divorce, Gimbel moved to New York City. The divorce was problematic, and Gimbel and Greenberg got joint custody of the children. Interestingly, the court also ruled that Greenberg's home, not Gimbel's, would be the children's primary residence. To ensure that his children could be near their mother, Greenberg rented a large apartment in Manhattan and commuted between Manhattan and Chicago every week. He flew into Chicago on Monday, lived at the Executive House Hotel on Wacker Drive in Chicago's Loop when he was not at the ballpark, and then flew back to New York City Friday afternoon to spend the weekend with the three children. With his personal life and weekly routine such sources of stress, the last thing he needed was an increasingly contentious relationship with a bitter Chuck Comiskey, but that is exactly what he had.

Greenberg's old team came to town Friday night, May 8, for the biggest series of the young 1959 season. The first-place Indians arrived in Chicago at 15–6, with manager Joe Gordon enjoying the offensive accomplishments of Vic Power, hitting .356, and Rocky Colavito, who had six homers in 21 games and a .325 average. These two met their match when Sox starter Dick Donovan pitched impeccably, but Donovan's teammates at the plate had no success against Cal McLish, and the Indians won, 3–1, sending 19,170 Sox loyalists home disappointed. The South Siders' bats finally woke up on Saturday and Sunday, as they won the Saturday matinee matchup, 9–5, and swept the Sunday doubleheader. In the Saturday game, the small crowd of 6,325 relished the Sox's aggressiveness on the base paths, when Aparicio tried to steal home in the second on Jim Perry's first pitch to Jim Landis. When home plate umpire Joe Paparella called him out on a close play, an infuriated Aparicio kicked dirt all over Paparella's freshly pressed pants and newly shined shoes. Paparella angrily tossed Aparicio from the contest, while the fans loved this uncharacteristic burst of temper from the Venezuelan speedster. Just as encouraging was a quality relief stint by Ray Moore, who had been the Sox's least effective hurler all spring. On Sunday, Bubba Phillips hit his first home run of the season, Landis broke out of his slump with three hits, and Ennis hit his first home run in a Sox uniform as the Sox swept the doubleheader, 5–4 and 5–0. In the second game, Wynn handcuffed the Tribe, throwing a complete-game four-hitter. The elated Chicagoans readied themselves for the longest road trip of the season, a 13-day, 13-game, five-city excursion to Boston, New York, Washington, Baltimore, and Kansas City. Lopez boldly told the press that the goal was to return to Chicago in first place.

High hopes accompanied the team as they flew into Boston on May 11 for a three-game set with the Red Sox. Their road record was 7–2, best in the majors, the pitching was rounding out, and the pop-gun offense was showing some signs of life, with Landis and Phillips warming up their bats and Nellie Fox, who had a 16-game hitting streak, staying hot. The Tuesday night affair turned out to be a 4½-hour, 12-inning marathon with the White Sox prevailing, 4–3. Rudolfo Arias got the win coming out of the bullpen, starter Dick Donovan hit his first home run in two years, and Al Smith's first homer of the season, a two-run shot in the 12th, sealed the extra-inning win. The game was also Ted Williams' first of the season, but the highest-paid player in the game did nothing against Sox hurlers, going hitless without hitting a ball out of the infield.

Thirteen games in 13 days forced Lopez to tinker with the rotation in game two, taking right-hander Bob Shaw out of the bullpen and giving him his first start of the year against Boston's Frank Sullivan. Starting pitching was the Sox's strong suit going into the season, but one of the relievers had to pick up the slack and join Wynn, Pierce, Donovan, Moore and Latman as a spot starter, especially since Moore and Latman had not been as consistent as the Big Three. The 25-year-old Shaw was a logical choice, yielding only three earned runs in 14 relief appearances thus far in 1959 and demonstrating great command and control. The young right-hander from the Bronx confounded Boston's hitters with his fastball and sinker/slider for an easy 4–0 victory. The ex–Tiger yielded only five hits and no walks for the first shutout of his career. After the game, Lopez was ecstatic, declaring, "Shaw will definitely be in my starting rotation now. You might say this gives us six potential starters, but Shaw's now number four." The next day, on the strength of a home run and four RBI by Del Ennis, another homer and three RBI by Earl Torgeson, and a solo shot by Jim Landis, the White Sox pulled off a rare sweep at Fenway Park with an easy 14–6 victory.

While the short trip to New York went quickly, press reports of some significant roster tinkering by the front office made it an anxious journey for several players. Veeck and Greenberg, desperate for more offense, made their third acquisition in two weeks when they purchased the contract of Larry Doby from the Detroit Tigers for his second tour of duty at 35th and Shields. Members of the fourth estate saw this acquisition as a real head-scratcher. Doby was now 35 years old, and his power numbers had been steadily shrinking since 1954. Thus far in 1959 he was hitting .218 with one home run and four RBI, almost identical to the underperforming hitters the White Sox already had. None of this mattered to Veeck, who had one of his heroes back. Doby and Veeck had always been very close, so close that when Veeck signed him for the Indians, the young slugger asked Veeck to be his daughter Christine's godfather.

Veeck took pains to do the right thing when he arranged for Doby to be the first black player in the American League. He paid Effa Manley, owner of the Newark Eagles, $10,000 for Doby's contract. Veeck also promised to give Manley $10,000 more once Doby made the Indians.[17] Veeck's generosity to Doby's old employer was in direct contrast to Branch Rickey's actions when he obtained Jackie Robinson. Doby was an exceptional athlete whose name was mentioned along with Roy Campanella, Monte Irvin, Willie Mays and Robinson as the first black most likely to star in the majors. When he integrated the American League, he also integrated the Cleveland Indians, and the initial reception from his Indians teammates was very chilly. In Doby's major league debut on July 5, 1947, nobody would loan him a first baseman's glove before he took the field. Much credit was given to Veeck, Greenberg, manager Lou Boudreau, and the Indians' coaching staff for orchestrating this historic integration, which was largely overshadowed by Jackie Robinson's arrival in Brooklyn.

In his autobiography, Hank Greenberg discussed Doby's uneasiness filling his historic destiny. Unlike Robinson, Doby at first was not inclined to take lightly the abuse and slights doled out by opponents. Many saw him as too sensitive, his tremendous abilities weighted down by a big chip on his shoulder. In his early seasons, when disputing an umpire's called strike, he would sometimes step out of the batter's box, point to the back of his hand, and say, "You called that on me because I'm colored." Greenberg also claimed that Doby was miffed about the fact that Robinson was getting all of the publicity as the pioneer integrator of baseball, and that any belligerence and defensiveness Doby displayed rubbed both the Cleveland fans and the press the wrong way.

As time went by, however, Doby's immense athletic talent helped him overcome these personal obstacles. Few players in the game had more in their toolbox than the introspective outfielder from Camden, South Carolina. Doby could run, was a peerless fielder, drew walks, and hit for power and average. His performance in baseball through the middle 1950s alone may have assured him his 1998 induction into baseball's Hall of Fame, but for Veeck to pick him up at this stage of his career, after he had just given up young pitching for Ennis and Simpson, did not make a great deal of sense.

Another issue was that the Sox fans' acceptance of Doby, especially in light of Al Smith's troubles, was no guarantee. Doby's first years with the Sox in 1956–1957 did not always go well. David Condon in the *Chicago Tribune* wrote the following in the autumn of 1957: "Lopez [then managing Cleveland], upon trading Doby from the Indian ball club to the White Sox: 'We just traded away 100 strikeouts.' Another quote from an unnamed White Sox in the waning days of the season: 'Don't quote me … but we wouldn't have blown this game if it wasn't for that clown in center field. He'd be some help to us if he wasn't so moody.'"

Condon's article addressed Doby's questionable disposition and lackadaisical play during his first stint with the Sox. The crafty Veeck, however, may have had more personnel chicanery up his sleeve, making some think that his "Doby's a great asset to us" statement was a smokescreen to make him look attractive to other teams. At the same time Doby arrived in Chicago, the Senators trimmed two active players off their roster, and some in the media thought their move set the stage for a blockbuster trade involving their $36,000 a year slugger, Roy Sievers. The plot thickened when it was noted that the Sox were not playing their two young, promising catchers, Battey and Romano; that they had three left-handed–hitting outfielders, Doby, Rivera, and Simpson; and both Moore and Latman had the potential to develop into reliable starters. With the Senators making space on their active roster for some new ballplayers and the Sox being able to dangle names like this in trade discussions, many thought a Sievers-for-several-players blockbuster trade was on the horizon.

Larry Doby's last stop in his Hall of Fame career was 21 games with the White Sox in 1959. He would return to manage the team 19 years later.

If the Doby acquisition created a little paranoia and worry with some of the Sox, it certainly did not affect their play during the short two-game series in Yankee Stadium. They swept the Yankees, thanks to Pierce's shutout pitching on Friday, May 15, and the efforts of Ennis, Lown, and Moore in an extra-inning affair on Saturday, May 16. Pierce's 6–0 whitewash was the first time a lefty had shut out the Yankees in three years, since Herb Score blanked them on August 21, 1956. The win on Saturday boosted their record to an impressive 5–1 in extra-inning affairs.

The exhausted but happy South Siders left for Washington immediately after the Saturday afternoon victory for a Sunday doubleheader against the Senators. Fatigued bats and promising Washington starter Pedro Ramos caused them to waste another good effort by Donovan, losing 4–2, but they bounced back to split the day's action with a 10–7 win in the second game. On Monday night, May 18, a crowd of 3,995 saw them vault into first place with an easy 9–2 victory behind Wynn's dominant pitching. With that win, the Chicago White Sox were atop the American League for the first time since June 29, 1957.

But the South Siders' good fortune did not continue after they made the long trek to Kansas City. The offense went to sleep, and they lost three out of four to the A's, including a 16–0 embarrassment when the Athletics' potent lineup dinged Wynn and Arias for five earned runs apiece and Latman for four, marking the pitching staff's worst day all year. In spite of the disappointing weekend in Missouri, the Sox finished their most difficult road trip to date with nine wins and four losses. While they did not reach Lopez's goal of coming home in first place, they were only one game out, and the hitting seemed to be coming around. Aparicio and Fox continued to get on base; Landis, Lollar and Phillips were beginning to hit; and Simpson and Ennis appeared to be wise additions. They were coming back to Comiskey Park for a 14-game home stand in which they would host first-place Cleveland, Detroit, Kansas City, Baltimore, and Boston.

An unexpectedly huge crowd of 40,018 came out Tuesday night, May 26, to see the matchup against the front-running Indians. Those who came late missed one of the more notable Veeck stunts. Just before the game began, a helicopter landed at second base, creating a small dust storm, and dropped a rope ladder to the ground as it hovered over the field. Four midgets dressed in outer space garb warily descended the ladder. Once they reached the ground, they immediately ran into the Sox's dugout, where one of them took the microphone of the stadium's PA system and announced, "We have come to Earth to carry away the only two men we consider worth joining us, Nellie Fox and Luis Aparicio. However, since they are doing such a fine job here, we've decided to let them stay."[18] One of the "spacemen" was 34-year-old Eddie Gaedel, whom Veeck first hired to pinch-hit in probably the most historic of all his on-field spoofs. Gaedel was first hired by Veeck to help commemorate the 50th anniversary of the St. Louis Browns' chief sponsor, Falstaff Beer. Gaedel, resplendent in the costume of the Browns' mascot, jumped out of a huge birthday cake between the games of a Sunday doubleheader against the Tigers at St. Louis' Sportsman's Park on August 19, 1951. Just when every-one thought the gags were over, Veeck, who had surreptitiously signed Gaedel to a one-day contract, had manager Zack Taylor use him as a pinch-hitter, and one of baseball's immortal moments was born. Many thought Veeck took the idea from a James Thurber short story that appeared in the April 5, 1941, *Saturday Evening Post*, entitled "You Could Look It Up," but Veeck offered a different explanation in his autobiography, *Veeck as in Wreck*. He said that he remembered Hall of Fame manager John McGraw having a clubhouse attendant named Eddie Morrow, a diminutive, gnome-like individual who suffered from kyphosis.[19] Veeck claimed that in his moments of extreme frus-tration, McGraw swore that someday he would be so desperate that he would use Morrow as a pinch-hitter.[20]

During the game itself, Don Ferrarese and Jim Perry pitched like they were from outer space. Sox hitters could do nothing against them, and the South Siders wasted yet another nice effort by Dick Donovan and were shut out, 3–0. They bounced back to split the series with a 5–1 victory on Wednes-day.

After a day off on Thursday, May 28, the Sox hosted a three-game week-end series against the Tigers. The Tigers' poor play at the start of the 1959 season resulted in the first managerial casualty of the year when general man-ager Rick Ferrell axed skipper Bill Norman on Saturday, May 2. On that date, the Tigers were fresh off a 15–3 Friday night loss to the lowly Senators, had a record of 2–15, and had a paltry crowd of 4,771 for a Saturday afternoon affair in arguably the most baseball-crazed city in the American League. Nor-man was released, in spite of the fact that he was 56–49 as the team's leader after he replaced Jack Tighe at the helm just ten months earlier. Ferrell turned to the non-nonsense, 62-year-old Jimmy Dykes, who ran the White Sox with a capable iron hand during the days of Lou and Grace Comiskey. Dykes took over a 2–15 squad and saw them win 16 of their next 23 games, as they entered the weekend series at 18–22.

Detroit's competent play continued at the White Sox's expense Friday night, May 29, when Don Mossi spread five harmless Sox hits for a 4–1 victory. They split a Saturday doubleheader against the Tigers but got creamed on the last day in May, 9–1, by the hard-hitting Athletics. The South Siders fin-ished the month with a 15–13 record, while the outfield's offensive production continued to be the biggest problem. Earl Torgeson led the team with only four homers and 21 RBI. It was clear that newcomers Callison and Cash were not ready. Doby thus far had brought none of the offensive magic that Veeck yearned for, and nobody other than Fox could be relied upon to produce enough at the plate to take some of the pressure off the pitching staff. Veeck and Greenberg would continue to burn the phone lines in the coming weeks.

5

June: Treading Water

Unfortunately, the first publicity the Chicago White Sox received in June 1959 came from reporters covering Cook County Circuit Court and not the sports writers covering the games. Chuck Comiskey decided to go back on his word and appealed the April 30 ruling that denied an injunction to prevent Veeck's CBC Corporation from taking over the team.[1]

Veeck told the press that he was surprised and hurt by this action, since he had changed the table of organization and elevated Chuck to the position of executive vice president. At the time, Chuck said he was satisfied with this plan and that his legal maneuvering had all been aimed at his sister Dorothy for refusing to sell him the team. Veeck also indicated that because of this new development, further efforts to accommodate Chuck in the Sox's organization might never occur. Chuck and his now third group of attorneys had a goal of getting the court to reduce the board of directors to four members, so he and Veeck would have equal power. Veeck's attorneys continued to claim that reducing a corporate board from five to four is against Illinois law. They also pointed out that the Veeck syndicate offered an attractive package to Chuck to settle the dispute with three key components: a two-year contract to serve as executive vice president of the team for $35,000 per annum; a chance to purchase his home—currently owned by the team—at book value; and $5,000 in legal fees. Chuck was holding out for a five-year contract, a chance to purchase the home below book value, $25,000 in legal fees, and a whopping $1 million in escrow to assure payment of all corporate taxes.[2] Judge Thomas Courtney gave each side one week to file their briefs.

Later that night, a frigid crowd at Comiskey Park saw Kansas City win its seventh game in ten contests with a boring 3–1 victory. Sox starter Ray Moore deserved a better fate on a night in which Veeck staged a long, loud fireworks show after the game. Fireworks displays were a trademark of his showmanship, and he was eager to get the ritual started. It would have been much better received by the 8,221 attendees if the Sox had won, particularly since such a victory would have tied them with the Indians for first place.

Baltimore was next up at Comiskey, and on June 2 they sent Hoyt Wilhelm and his famous knuckleball to the mound to face the Sox. Wilhelm, who had not allowed a run in the last 22 innings, was not a likely candidate to help Sox hitters emerge from their offensive malaise, but they got a boost from Mother Nature in the first inning when a huge swarm of gnats descended on the pitcher's mound and engulfed the panicked hurler.[3] Orioles coach Al Vincent came out to help, waving white towels. Sox batboy Johnny Rosisch and umpire Hank Soar sprayed insecticide to no avail. Orioles trainer Eddie Weidner rushed out and sprayed Wilhelm with insecticide, which also proved futile. The Sox grounds crew came out, walking solemnly to the mound while carefully carrying lit newspapers, looking like the villagers storming the castle in an old *Frankenstein* movie. The gnats stayed put, and the crowd was treated to a madcap display of the grounds crew madly shaking and sucking their singed fingers. After 20 minutes, the fireworks expert came out, cleared the field of personnel, lit a smoke bomb on the mound, and fled as fast as he could. The sooty black smoke covered the infield, and the gnats finally flew elsewhere or perished. By this time, Wilhelm was completely out of his rhythm and proceeded to walk Fox and Torgeson and hit Lollar with a pitch. Unfortunately for the Sox, this small offensive eruption proved insufficient, and Baltimore took a 3–2 victory.

Lopez had seen enough and shook up the lineup before the Wednesday game. He put the hot-hitting Bubba Phillips in the third slot of the batting order and dropped Landis to eighth. To get Romano's bat in the lineup, Lopez put Lollar at first and Romano behind the plate. Pierce finally got some run support, holding the Orioles in check while the offense put up nine runs for a 9–6 win. Toward the end of the game, the small crowd roared its approval as the big Chesterfield scoreboard flashed the score of the Senators' victory over the Indians, putting the South Siders in a virtual tie for first place. They moved into first on Thursday, June 4, with a 17-inning, 6–5 victory. Donovan, Latman, Staley, Arias, Lown and Shaw each took a turn on the mound, but Earl Torgeson, who did not enter the game until the seventh inning, went 3-for-6, the third hit a prodigious blast off Baltimore reliever Jerry Walker for the most dramatic victory of the season. After the Sox had wasted opportunities in the eighth, tenth, 12th, and 13th innings to win the game, Torgeson's game-winning round-tripper was met with as much relief as elation.

Clifford Earl Torgeson was a big, raw-boned gentleman of Norwegian descent from Snohomish, Washington. Entering his 13th season in the majors when the 1959 campaign began, the cigar-smoking "Earl of Snohomish" was seen in the locker room as one of the trusted veterans—along with Fox, Lollar, Pierce, and Wynn—who had been successfully tested in many baseball wars.

At 24, he started at first base for the pennant-winning Boston Braves and led all hitters in the 1948 World Series with a .389 average, striking out only once in 20 plate appearances. Everyone expected Torgeson to be the prototypical 6'3", power-hitting first baseman, and indeed, he hit a total of 63 homers his first three years in the majors, but he was that rare athlete who could hit for power but also wear out opposing pitchers. His lifetime on-base percentage was an excellent .385, largely because he had a knack for drawing walks; at the end of his career, Torgeson had 327 more walks (980) than strikeouts (653). For a big man, he also ran exceptionally well and was an excellent base stealer. Torgeson was also a bit of an edgy character and someone you wanted on your side if things got hostile, as he backed down to nobody. Boston's Billy Hitchcock, Pittsburgh's Cliff Chambers, and the Giants' Sal Yvars were some of the more notable sparring partners who regretted their imbroglios with the bespectacled slugger. In June 1957, Torgeson came to the Sox from the Tigers for Dave Philley. With Boone dispatched to Kansas City and Cash proving too green to face major league pitching on a daily basis, Torgeson, with his seven home runs and .292 batting average, was by far the strongest link in the Sox's weak offensive chain.

The four-game weekend series with Boston starting June 5 got off on a bad note when Billy Goodman, one of the few consistent hitters on the squad, was admitted to Mercy Hospital due to chest pains. Considering what a terrible start the Red Sox were experiencing, Goodman might not even be needed. Pinky Higgins' Red Sox were in last place in the American League with a record of 20–26, having been plagued with lackluster pitching and a total lack of clutch hitting. Ted Williams, injured at the beginning of the season, was hitting a very un–Ted-like .205. The Red Sox were 20–27 after the series opener, as the host Chicagoans won a dramatic 5–2 victory, thanks to a gritty pitching effort by Wynn and a clutch pinch double in the eighth inning by newcomer Harry Simpson. Simpson's drive brought Torgeson, Smith and Landis across the plate, and the Friday night crowd of 32,321 suddenly took a

Earl Torgeson, the "Earl of Snohomish," was a no-nonsense veteran with solid offensive credentials in both leagues. Unlike many power hitters of his era, Torgeson walked more than he struck out, had more walks than hits in 1959, and was also a base-stealing threat much of his career.

keen liking to the graceful, well-travelled veteran. The White Sox's bats continued in Saturday's game to the tune of nine hits, but clutch hits were nowhere to be found, resulting in a 4–2 loss. Liking their chances in the Sunday doubleheader with Donovan and Pierce going against Boston starters Ike Delock and Frank Sullivan, the South Siders could only manage a split, winning the first game, 9–4, but dropping the finale, 4–2. Lopez started fan favorite Jim Rivera in both games, and the colorful veteran went 4-for-7 with a home run on the day. After Sunday's twin bill, Rivera was hitting .343; Lopez realized that he could no longer keep him out of the lineup.

In the 1950s, few players captured the imagination of Chicago the way Manuel Joseph "Jungle Jim" Rivera did. Rivera was born in New York's Spanish Harlem and lived in a small apartment with his parents, six brothers, and six sisters. The struggling family stayed together until Rivera's sixth birthday, when his mother died unexpectedly. His father, unable to care for all the children, sent young Rivera to St. Dominic's Orphanage in Blauvelt, New York, trusting his care to Dominican nuns. At 16, Rivera returned to New York City, played baseball, and took up boxing. Rivera quit boxing when a semi-pro team sponsored by a Manhattan bakery asked him to become a regular on their squad. During World War II, he enlisted in the Army Air Corps. He was now a 20-year-old with exceptional athletic ability. Encouraged to take up boxing a second time, Rivera won the Camp Barkley (Texas) light heavyweight title and starred on their baseball team, turning many heads in the process. His accomplishments and success in the military, however, came to an abrupt end two years later. In 1944, the daughter of a high-ranking army officer charged Rivera with attempted rape after making his acquaintance at a dance at Barksdale Field. Due to the harsh, punitive consequences in the Uniform Code of Military Justice at the time, Rivera received a draconian *life sentence* and was sent to a federal penitentiary in Atlanta, Georgia. None of the alleged events had actually occurred, and it took several years for Rivera to clear his name.

His baseball talents proved to be his salvation. Rivera dominated the area's prison baseball league competition, and when his team was playing the Atlanta Crackers in an exhibition game, Earl Mann, the Crackers owner, was in the stands. Mann was impressed by Rivera's talents and worked diligently to get him paroled, and in March 1949 Mann signed Rivera to a contract, sending him to the Crackers' Class D Florida State League squad in Gainesville. Ironically, the team's nickname was the G-Men; the cynics wondered if Rivera was the first "G-Man" in history to have a prison record. Class D pitching proved no puzzle for Rivera; he hit.335, getting himself promoted for the 1950 season to Pensacola, where he hit .333. Rivera played in Puerto Rico over the winter and got a big break when his team played a game against a squad managed by Hall of Famer Rogers Hornsby. Hornsby, impressed with

Rivera's head-first slides, aggressive demeanor, and intelligent approach at the plate, told Rivera that he would be managing the Seattle Rainiers in the Pacific Coast League—the best minor league in the country—and wanted Rivera to come out West with him. Like another legendary Chicago favorite eight years earlier—Andy Pafko—Rivera was named Most Valuable Player in the PCL after he hit .352 with 16 triples, 20 home runs, and 33 stolen bases. The White Sox purchased his contract, but before Rivera played his first game at 35th and Shields, he became a key component in the November 27, 1951, eight-player trade between the Sox and the St. Louis Browns.

Hornsby had just been hired to manage the Browns, and he convinced Veeck, the Browns owner, to get Rivera. The Sox sent Rivera, Joe DeMaestri, Dick Littlefield, Gus Niarhos, and Gordon Goldsberry to the Browns and received Al Widmar, Sherm Lollar, and Tom Upton. However, Rivera's tour of duty in St. Louis did not go as planned. Hornsby was fired in June and Rivera languished on the bench. In July 1952, the Browns traded him back to the White Sox along with catcher Darrell Johnson for J. W. Porter and Ray Coleman.

Rivera became an immediate fan favorite, playing a daring defense in the outfield and stealing bases every chance he had. *Chicago Sun Times* sportswriter Howie Robbins gave him the nickname "Jungle Jim" for his antics while taking a lead off base. Rivera would bend slightly forward at the waist, then dangle his arms—simian-like—prior to sprinting off to the next base. He always used the head-first slide, a rarity in those days, ignoring the risk of injury to give himself more maneuverability at the base to avoid a tag.

In spite of his popularity, Rivera's first season on the South Side ended on a frightful note. He was arrested in the Sox's locker room after the last game of the season and charged with criminal assault by a female acquaintance. The charge resulted from what Rivera claimed was a Good Samaritan act that went badly. After his offer to help a young woman carry her groceries was accepted, she claimed he stayed in her apartment much longer than she intended. She claimed an assault occurred when Rivera took excessive liberties with her that were most unwelcome. Two months later a jury found him not guilty, but Commissioner Ford Frick's office took note of his latest brush with the law and handed out what many thought was a nonsensical punishment. Frick instructed the White Sox that they could not trade Rivera and that the team would be held responsible if he caused any difficulties in the future.

Through it all, one of Rivera's biggest backers was owner Chuck Comiskey, and Rivera repaid Chuck's faith in him repeatedly with his play. In 1953, his first full year with the Sox, he led the American League in triples (16) and finished second in stolen bases (22). Rivera was second in stolen bases in four more seasons (1954 and 1956–1958), and led the league in that category in 1955, when he also led all American League outfielders in assists (22) and double plays (7).

While the fans loved Rivera's hustle and demeanor, the press loved his colorful, frank observations. After receiving an autographed baseball from John F. Kennedy before a game with the Senators, Rivera complained to a reporter, "The guy's got bad handwriting. How can I even prove he signed this? That could be anybody's signature. And he went to Harvard!"[4] When Rivera was introduced to Harry and Bess Truman after hitting a game-winning homer in Kansas City, the ex-president told him that Bess was the real baseball fan in the family. Rivera broke the ice with the former First Lady by saying, "Hiya Bess! Sorry we had to hang one on you!" When asked one off-season by Chuck Comiskey why he always signed his contract without reading it, Rivera replied, "Why read it? Where else can I go if I don't like it here?"

Rivera was back in the Sox's lineup on Tuesday, June 9, at Washington, getting two hits and an RBI, but it was not enough and the Sox lost, 7–4. They were able to bounce back for a 4–1 win the next night and won the series thanks to a stellar effort by Billy Pierce. Pierce threw a complete-game one-hitter against the Senators, winning 3–1, spoiling an almost equally brilliant by effort by Senators starter Camilo Pascual in the process. Light-hitting Washington shortstop Ron Samford's double in the third inning was the lone safety Pierce allowed.

Jim Rivera overcame a hardscrabble up - bringing to become a fixture in the White Sox outfield during the 1950s. Rivera's daring base running, exceptional fielding skills, and clutch hitting established him as a fan favorite as soon as he arrived in Chicago.

By 1959, William Walter Pierce was the White Sox's elder statesman, having become the winningest left-hander in team history. He came to Chicago on November 10, 1948, in probably the best trade the franchise ever made. The Sox got Pierce and $10,000 from Detroit for aging catcher Aaron Robinson, much to the Tigers' regret. Pierce's improvements on the mound proved remarkable. His major league record from 1945 through 1952 was 52–57, and he averaged 4.87 strikeouts per nine innings.

From 1953 to 1958, the little southpaw went 99–64, and his strikeouts per nine innings average rose to 6.23. Pierce explained the huge improvement to sports historian Bob Vanderberg as follows:

> In 1953 I finally came up with a slider, which I'd been working on for a while with [then Sox manager Paul] Richards. It took me some time the to get the grip right—and when I threw a good one to [Yankee nemesis] Hank Bauer and broke his bat, I looked over in the dugout, and Richards was laughing because he realized I finally had a slider. I threw some slow curves, but I didn't have a change up, and I never mastered a good change off the fastball. Those three pitches worked for me, and as long as I was getting by and doing fairly well I just stayed with that combination of pitches.

"Getting by and doing fairly well" is a typical understatement from the premiere White Sox lefty of all time. During his career, he started three All-Star Games (1953, 1955, and 1956) and was on four more All-Star teams from 1957 through 1959 and again in 1961. In 1956 and 1957, he was named *The Sporting News* Pitcher of the Year, and in 1958 he just missed a perfect game against the Senators when pinch-hitter Ed Fitz Gerald doubled for Pierce's fourth one-hitter, the other two being against the Browns and Yankees.

Other teams coveted his services. Frank Lane remembered that before he left the Sox, the Yankees were worried about Whitey Ford's bad arm and were desperate to obtain Pierce in a trade. When Lane told the New Yorkers that he would need a starting infielder, either Jerry Coleman or Hank Bauer, and a seasoned veteran off the bench, the Yankees politely declined. Lane summed up Pierce's importance to the Sox as follows: "If Pierce had been twins, we might've won it all repeatedly when I was there. Pierce, that little guy. You didn't need a relief pitcher when he was pitching. If we're ahead in the seventh by a run, with him out there it's over. He had more courage per ounce than any player I ever saw."[5]

Pierce's adoration by Sox fans was

The great Billy Pierce, premiere starter for the White Sox throughout the 1950s. Pierce, Whitey Ford, Sandy Koufax, and Warren Spahn were the greatest lefties of their era. Pierce had more strikeouts than Ford, pitched 982 more innings than Koufax, had a better World Series ERA than Spahn, and is the only member of this storied foursome to pitch for both AL and NL teams in the World Series. Pierce deserves his place in the Hall of Fame.

based on more than just his on-field success. He was known throughout his career as one of the most unassuming, consistently available, and generous players in the majors. The Billy Pierce Fan Club thought so much of him that they had a shower for his wife when the Pierces were expecting their first child in 1953, and even paid for his mother to come to Chicago for the event.[6] With a salary of $41,000 in 1959, Pierce was among the most highly paid players in the game.[7] It was clear, however, that the White Sox were getting the better end of the bargain.

The Sox moved on to Baltimore and took two out of three from the Orioles to remain in first place by a half-game. By June 15, they were sharing the lead again, as the Indians regained a tie with a win over Boston. June 15 was also the trading deadline, and as the Sox were en route to New York, the rumors started flying. Word leaked out that Veeck and Greenberg had made Senators owner Clark Griffith an offer they thought he could not refuse, $500,000 in cash for the services of Roy Sievers, nearly a fifth of the team's gross operating income. When Griffith refused the deal, they counter-offered $250,000 and five players for Sievers and two additional Senators. "I'm probably the only guy in the world daffy enough to make such an offer and [Griffith] must be the only guy daffy enough to turn it down," Veeck mentioned in the June 16 *Chicago Tribune*. The cash-strapped Griffith would only say that he would not strip his team of their best players for money.[8] Veeck had a long-standing obsession with the 33-year-old Sievers, who hit .306 with 16 homers for Veeck's Browns in 1949 and was named American League Rookie of the Year. Since that time, Sievers had emerged as one of the most consistent power hitters in baseball. He averaged about 32 home runs per year between 1954 and 1958, hitting 159 round-trippers. Given Sievers' historical productivity, he was projected to hit about 20 homers for the remainder of the 1959 season, but by spending a half-million, each round-tripper would cost about $25,000, causing Veeck to back away from the deal.

The pursuit of Sievers gave a clear indication that in spite of the pitching, great defense, and great speed on the base paths, Veeck did not think that the 1959 White Sox had enough power to capture the American League flag. Comments made by Lopez years later bear this out. Lopez mentioned that he often disagreed with Veeck about the composition of the team and their chances of winning without power. Lopez realized that in a park as spacious as Comiskey, having all the sluggers in the world might not guarantee a lineup that would consistently score more runs. Veeck always felt more secure with the long ball.

With the trade not consummated and Norm Cash filling a roster spot by coming off his one-year roster exemption as a military service returnee, the Sox were now one player over the limit. To make room, Greenberg released Del Ennis, obtained just 45 days earlier. As the Sox settled in at Yankee Stadium for a three-game series against the Yankees, three things had the team on edge: five current players were dangled in front of the Senators; management was willing to cavalierly drop $250,000 or $500,000 for one aging player; and a veteran like Ennis, in town for only a month and a half, departed so swiftly.

The Sox dropped three straight in the Bronx, scoring only eight runs in 28 innings, losing 5–1, 7–3, and 5–4 in ten innings. The Thursday extra-inning affair was the hardest to take, as Rivera watched helplessly as a blast by Mantle off Gerry Staley barely made it over the short right field wall for a walk-off home run. After arriving in Boston, the Sox got a chance to catch their breath when the Friday night game was rained out. It was rescheduled for the next day, resulting in an unusual Saturday doubleheader on June 20. Donovan and Wynn had no success against the Boston lineup, as Gene Stephens, Frank Malzone, and Vic Wertz lead the Red Sox to an 8–2 and 9–0 sweep. The next day, Pierce most decisively stepped into the stopper role as he had so many times in the past, throwing a six-hit, complete-game, 3–2 victory. Super-sub Sammy Esposito filled in for Aparicio at short. He and Simpson homered, and Simpson lead the offense with six total bases. One of the hits off Pierce was an eighth-inning single by Ted Williams (raising his average to a paltry .189), treating the fans to another classic match-up between two peerless professionals who had been battling each other for 14 years. Throughout his career, Williams hit .258 with two home runs and 11 RBI against the tough little lefty, but their confrontations cannot be defined that simply. In the 127 times the two faced each other, Pierce was so wary of Williams' ability that he walked him 34 times; his on-base percentage against Pierce was a phenomenal .457.

The Sox hurried home to Chicago on Monday, June 22, for the annual charity game against the Cubs. The North Siders sported a 33–33 record, excellent by the low standards the storied franchise had throughout the 1950s, and good enough for fifth place in the National League. Manager Bob Scheffing had a strong offensive lineup in 1959 with George Altman, Tony Taylor, Alvin Dark, Dale Long, Walt Moryn, Tony Taylor, and back-to-back National League MVP Ernie Banks. The Cubs had bats everyone took seriously, but with mediocre pitching and a lack of team speed, they once again were doomed to the second division. A big crowd of 29,383 witnessed the Cubs win for the seventh time in the last ten contests, 3–2.

Home for a seven-game stretch from Tuesday, June 23, through Sunday, June 28, the Sox took two out of three from the Senators, thanks largely to the efforts of Barry Latman and Early Wynn. Latman pitched brilliantly on Thursday, turning in a complete-game performance for a 4–1 victory. This game had very positive implications for the South Siders. Lopez now had a reliable fifth starter to go along with Wynn, Pierce, Donovan, and Shaw. One of the best developments of the month was that the young Californian could hold the powerful Washington lineup to just one hit over five innings.

Arnold Barry Latman, 23 in 1959, hailed from Los Angeles. He grew up in a prosperous, devoutly Jewish family. His father owned an auctioneering business.[9] Young Barry showed promise as soon as he started playing baseball at age six, but by the time he was ten, his parents had him quit baseball to prepare for his Bar Mitzvah, even though it was three years away. Latman began playing again when he was 13, and before he finished high school the tall, broad-shouldered adolescent threw a perfect game for Fairfax High School, the first high school interscholastic perfect game in Los Angeles in ten years. Before Latman fin-

ished high school, he received generous bonus offers from several major league clubs, but he turned them down to take a baseball scholarship at the University of Southern California. While at USC, he caught the eye of Hall of Famer Ty Cobb, who was so impressed that he started a correspondence with Latman and encouraged him to concentrate on professional baseball.[10] Latman signed a contract with the White Sox in 1955 and pitched at Class B Waterloo in the Three I (Indiana, Illinois, and Iowa) League, where his success earned him a promotion to the Sox's Double A Memphis Chicks squad. After winning 14 games at Memphis, Latman spent 1957 and 1958 at Indianapolis, the Sox's highest Triple A squad, starting 50 games over two years and earning September call-ups to Comiskey Park both years. In September 1958, he got three starts for the White

Twenty-three-year-old Barry Latman's effectiveness as the White Sox's fifth starter in 1959 played a big part in the team's pennant.

Sox, won each one, and posted a 0.76 ERA. At that point, Latman was in the majors for good, with many predicting great things from him. His efforts on June 25 validated their expectations.

The month ended with one of the biggest series of the year, the kind every White Sox fan lived for in the 1950s, four games against the despised New York Yankees. Yankees manager Casey Stengel, playing the role of the aging curmudgeon perfectly, fanned the flames before the series started by stating that the Sox's pennant chances were essentially dead, that "if you keep Aparicio and Fox off the bases they're done." Yet in the two victories against the Senators, Aparicio and Fox went 2-for-8 with only one run scored; the two wins were due to the offense of Simpson (again), Lollar, and Torgeson. The stage was set for a classic match-up between the World Champions and their decade-long pursuers.

The weekend starting Friday, June 25, 1959, became Chicago's biggest baseball event in many years. The Yankees were in town, the Sox pitching staff was the best in the majors, Stengel's curious comments fanned the flames, and the Sox were atop the American League standings while the Yankees unexpectedly languished near the bottom. A crowd of 37,909 came out for Friday night's affair, when the Yanks kept the Sox in check, 8–4. Landis and Phillips scored on pitcher Billy Pierce's triple, but Pierce had had better days on the mound. He gave up six runs and eight hits, knocked out in the sixth inning, with two of the hits being homers by shortstop Gil McDougald and third baseman Hector Lopez. While the Sox managed nine hits, clutch hitting once again eluded them, giving Art Ditmar the win. In spite of the loss, before the game ended the Sox were able to settle a score with the New Yorkers that had been bothering them for years.

Stengel called in his 100-mile-an-hour reliever, Ryne "Specs" Duren, to close out this contest, and once he got to the mound many in the crowd knew the game was over. Duren allowed only one weak single by Landis and struck out eight in three innings of work. When Duren came to the plate with two out in the top of the ninth, Rudy Arias was on the mound for the Sox, mopping up. After glancing into the dugout and receiving a knowing nod from manager Lopez, the flinty Cuban with the intimidating glare sent Duren a purpose pitch with a high-inside fastball, smirking at the bespectacled Yankees fireballer as he warily got up and shook the dust off his uniform. Arias' second offering irked Duren even more, as he spun awkwardly out of the batter's box to avoid getting hit in the ribs. Now flustered and intimidated, Duren stood loosely in the box while Arias wound into his third pitch. This one was just as fast as the first two and hit him squarely on the hip. Now angry and frightened but determined not to let the Sox see that he was in pain, the infuriated Duren jogged to first, jawing at Arias the whole time. The fiery Cuban hurler glared back, conveying through his body language that if Duren wished, he could come to the mound to suffer even more humiliation. Duren did not take the bait but continued his tirade at first, decrying the injustice of it all to first base umpire Charlie Berry, who paid no attention to him.[11] The drama did not affect Duren's ninth-inning performance, as he calmly struck out Aparicio, Fox, and Torgeson to preserve the win.

This outing was the remarkable Duren's 14th consecutive scoreless relief appearance. The last time the 30-year-old, visually challenged flamethrower from Cazenovia, Wisconsin, had yielded a run was nearly two months ago, Al Smith's game-winning hit at Comiskey Park on April 30. Lopez always discouraged his pitchers from intentionally hitting opposing batters, but for years Stengel's moundmen threw freely at the Sox, and he felt it was time to settle the score. Years later, pitching coach Ray Berres explained the history of this beanball event: "Ryne Duren would invariably hit Jim Landis. So we got tired of it that Friday night, and when Duren came up, Lopez told Arias in Spanish to waste the first two pitches way inside and then stick a fastball into Duren's ribs. Arias missed the first one and Duren looked at Lopez. who yells, 'That's right, we mean you can't keep hitting Landis.' Next pitch he hits him. That's the only time I recall Lopez retaliating."[12]

Veeck picked this Saturday afternoon game against the Yankees for one of his zaniest promotions of the year. This was odd, because a Saturday matinee match-up between these two teams never needed any help at the gate. He hired waiters from the Ambassador Hotel's famous Pump Room, sartorially splendid in their formal Elizabethan attire, to serve a variety of very un–White Sox like concessions. The choices included fried caterpillars, eel, seaweed, and barbecued snake, not exactly the type of gastronomic delights the typical South Sider could order in Bridgeport or Canaryville. The 21,162 fans at the game also had a chance to win cuts of iguana, whale meat, and smoked sparrows on skewers. Some have speculated that the smoked sparrows might have had more impact in a game against the Cardinals or Orioles.

While the zany giveaways in the stands were occurring, Bob Shaw and Bob Turley staged a classic pitchers' duel. The heroics of the Sox's young right-hander were overshadowed in the late innings by Harry Simpson. With the Yanks up, 2–1, in the bottom of the eighth, Turley calmly struck out pinch-hitter Norm Cash and induced Aparicio to fly out to Mantle in center. After Fox followed with a walk and Torgeson singled him to third, Turley, clearly tiring at this point, walked Lollar. Over in the Yankees dugout, Stengel, perhaps showing judgment apropos to his advanced years, did not go to the bullpen, and in the Sox dugout, Lopez sent Simpson up to pinch-hit. Simpson was not shy about telling the press that in all of his baseball travels, his New York experience with Stengel was the worst, insisting that the aging Yankees skipper never made him feel welcome but instead kept complaining to him how much he missed Billy Martin, for whom he was traded.

After starring for the Havana Sugar Kings in the International League in 1958, Rudy Arias earned a spot in the White Sox bullpen in 1959 and made 34 appearances with a 2–0 record.

Just as the Sox settled the score with Duren the night before, Simpson could do the same with Stengel. The wispy slugger laced Turley's first pitch for a tape-measure grand slam that hit a railing in the far reaches of the upper deck in right field. The fifth grand slam of Simpson's eight-year career whipped the crowd into a frenzy, and when Arias survived the ninth inning after yielding solo homers to Norm Siebern and Moose Skowron, the Sox had an important 5–4 victory. The next day, the *Chicago Tribune* titled the game's box score with a reference to the Sox's most recent hero's nickname: "Unpack, Man!"[13] This turned out to be one day Stengel wished he had not seen the "Tan Ted Williams" in an opponent's uniform.

A throng of 42,121 enjoyed every minute of the Sunday doubleheader, when everything went right for their heroes. The Sox drubbed the Bronx Bombers twice, 4–2 and 9–2. The Sox were never behind during the nearly six hours of baseball. Donovan got the better of Don Larsen in the first game, and Wynn had no difficult besting Whitey Ford in the second. Bubba Phillips was the offensive star in the first game and homered in the second, and his round-tripper was matched in the finale by Earl Battey, Sherm Lollar, and Al Smith. It was almost as if the White Sox hitters were sending a message not just to the Yankees but also to Veeck, indicating as June drew to a close that they did not need to give away the store for the likes of a Roy Sievers—the current bats on the squad would succeed just fine in big games. The World Champion Yankees left town just one game over .500 at 36–35, five games behind first-place Cleveland, with the Sox in second, just a game behind.

After the game, Greenberg announced that the Sox were sending Johnny Callison to Triple A Indianapolis, and that 22-year-old Jim McAnany would be take his place. Callison expressed disappointment in his inability to hit major league pitching after such a promising debut for the Sox the year before. He left the South Side with a .173 average, 124 points lower than the previous season, and expressed optimism about going back to the minors to regain his batting eye. He also reminded the press that the last time he was in Indianapolis, he led the American Association with 29 homers.[14] Both Veeck and Lopez expressed a desire to have him return to Chicago before the July 31 deadline. The Sox hoped the husky, bespectacled McAnany would bring some of his offensive prowess with him once he got to town. He left Indianapolis hitting .315 with five home runs, seven triples, and 11 doubles to go along with 34 walks. His .395 on-base percentage was the kind of number Lopez could only dream about.

The South Siders ended June on the road, playing the first game of a short two-game set in Cleveland, losing 3–1 and spoiling a nice outing by Pierce. The offense consisted of four harmless singles by Aparicio, Fox, Lollar and Landis, while Cal McLish, emerging as one of the best starters in baseball, raised his record to 9–3. Veeck and Greenberg looked on with envy as Colavito hit his 23rd home run with the season not yet half over.

June was a mediocre month for the 1959 White Sox, as they broke even at 14–14, 39–33 for the season. With the All-Star break six days away, the standings were beginning to mean something:

Cleveland 40–30

Chicago 39–33 2 GB

Baltimore 38–35 3.5 GB

Detroit 38–36 4 GB

New York 37–35 4 GB

Washington 33–39 8 GB

Kansas City 31–39 9 GB

Boston 31–40 9.5 GB

Cleveland continued to get great pitching, had the most powerful lineup in the league, and were very strong defensively up the middle with Woody Held, Billy Martin and Jimmy Piersall. During the first three months of the season, Baltimore's young pitchers proved to be extremely effective, and they had a manager in Paul Richards who knew how best to develop them. Detroit, after starting the year disheveled and disorganized, was 36–23 since changing managers, making Jimmy Dykes look like a genius. The Yankees, although listless and often showing their age, were still the Yankees. Would they eventually realize they had a World Championship to defend and play like it? A scary thought for Sox fans. With all the worthy competition, there was still something about the White Sox that made people take notice, and drawing 470,036 for 33 home games during the coldest three months of the season meant Chicagoans were taking notice indeed. If Latman continued to pitch like he did in June, not even Cleveland could match their starting staff. Offensively they were not driving the ball with any authority, but Aparicio, Fox, Landis, and Rivera were getting on and running bases like no other quartet in the American League. Fox, Lollar, Phillips, Simpson, and Torgeson were providing some big hits at the right time, and while the failures of Callison and Cash had made things difficult, if young McAnany could continue to hit, it would not matter. Al Smith had been a disappointment, but he was about to excel at the plate like he never had before, and helped launch the Sox into the most remarkable three-month stretch in their history.

6

July: We Might Have Something Here

The White Sox's July schedule would determine if they could capture their first American League flag in 40 years. As the month started, they liked where they were, two games behind the Indians, 1½ ahead of the Orioles, and two ahead of the Yankees. If they could end the month in the same position, the Sox would virtually be assured of being in the thick of the pennant race through September. They had 15 home and 13 road games in July, with three of the contests against Cleveland, four against Baltimore, and seven against New York. Play well in July and possibly knock the East Coast teams out of the race; fall short in July and once again it's wait 'til next year at 35th and Shields. The margin for error without a lot of power in the lineup was thin, but every week it seemed the Chicagoans proved they could win games a number of different ways.

They started the month by sneaking past the Indians, scoring six runs on six hits for a 6–5 win. Latman's pitching was mediocre at best, but the opportunistic Pale Hose took advantage of seven walks from the generous Cleveland pitching staff to sneak away from Lake Erie with a big win. They hustled out of Ohio for a night game on Thursday, July 2, in Detroit. The Sox hitters were productive enough to keep things relatively close in spite of starter Bob Shaw's ineffectiveness. The tide turned in the eighth inning, when the pride of Paw Paw, Michigan, Charlie Maxwell, pounded his 18th homer of the year, a three-run blast deep into the left field seats off Rudy Arias. In spite of Al Smith's grand slam off Don Mossi in the ninth, the Tigers prevailed, 9–7. With the win, the streaking Tigers moved into third place, only a game behind the Sox, but the South Siders spoiled any ideas Detroit had about catching them in the standings before they left town. On Friday, in the short-series finale, Al Smith took a Tommy Morgan offering into the seats for a three-run homer in the top of the tenth inning for a 6–5 victory. Smith's success that night could not have come at a better time, since he came to the Motor City sporting a pathetic .223 batting average and was on every Sox fans' short list of major disappointments of the 1959 season.

The mercilessness of the July schedule became apparent right after the win, as the Chicagoans rushed out of Briggs Stadium to fly to Kansas City for a Fourth of July doubleheader. Donovan displayed some jet lag, giving up eight hits and four runs in less than four innings, so Lopez called on Shaw, still fresh after pitching so few innings in his start two nights before. Shaw had his best outing of the season, allowing one lonely single (by A's third baseman Hal Smith) in 5⅓ innings of work. At the plate, the White Sox banged out 17 hits, five of them off Landis' bat and four off McAnany's, while Lollar, Phillips, and Romano homered.

Landis and Shaw were the kind of ballplayers who gave credence to the argument that the Sox did their best to succeed in the present while investing in the future. In 1952, Landis, playing ball at Contra Costa Junior College in Brentwood, California, signed a contract that legendary super scout Bobby Mattick gave him with a $2,500 bonus. The 18-year-old Californian left school and went to Wisconsin Rapids, finishing the year in the Sox's rookie camp under the tutelage of Johnny Mostil. Mostil, a polished American League out-fielder with the Sox in the 1920s, felt Landis was out of place in the infield and worked hard to make him an outfielder. Under Mostil's tutelage, and with his lean, athletic frame, natural quickness, and sure hands, Landis developed into the Sox's second-most promising prospect behind Luis Aparicio. The follow-ing year, he hit .313 at Colorado Springs and was awarded the MVP in the Western League. After two years in the Army, where he got to play some baseball while stationed in Alaska, he hit .429 in his first 13 games at Colorado and earned a promotion to the Southern Association's Memphis Chicks. Facing better pitching, he saw his average dip to a modest .257, but the Sox still pro-moted him to AAA Indianapolis in 1957 and called him up mid-season to play 96 games at 35th and Shields. Splitting the year between Indianapolis and Chicago, Landis had difficulty adjusting to major league pitching. He hit just .212 and struck out once every 4.5 at bat. The handsome Californian opened a lot of eyes, however, with his tremendous ball-hawking ability, strong arm, and quick hands. For all of his offensive woes in 1957, Landis still stole 14 bases, hit three triples, and legged out 11 doubles. He listened patiently while Early Wynn told him that he was swinging at too many bad balls, took to heart Nellie Fox's suggestions about how to use his speed at the plate more effectively, and was all ears when Ron Northey told him to change his batting grip. It all paid off the following season. In 1958, Landis hit .277 with 23 dou-bles, 11 triples (sixth in the American League), 15 home runs, and an AL third-best 19 stolen bases.[1] For his efforts, the Sox rewarded the swarthy speedster handsomely, doubling his salary from $7,000 to $14,000 for the 1959 season.

Jim Landis in his prime was the best defensive outfielder in the American League. Landis was a gifted athlete who had to work at becoming a successful major league hitter. His newfound offensive contributions were a big reason the White Sox captured the 1959 AL pennant.

Bob Shaw went 18–9 to help cement the 1959 AL pennant for the White Sox. He declined a football scholarship at St. Lawrence University to sign with the Detroit Tigers, and the Sox acquired him in 1958. His 11-year career included successful seasons with Milwaukee and San Francisco in the NL.

The 26-year-old Shaw left St. Lawrence College in 1952, giving up his football career, and received a $1,000 bonus to pitch in the Tigers' organization. Shaw spent the next five years making all the minor league whistle stops, playing in Jamestown, Durham, Augusta, Syracuse, Toronto, and Charleston. In 1957, Detroit called him up, but he threw just 9⅔ innings in seven games. Unimpressed, the Tigers' plans for Shaw in 1958 were much the same, and by mid–June he had appeared in only 11 games. When the Tigers decided to send him down to Charleston, Shaw refused to go, determined to pitch in the majors, and threatened to return home to New York City. Upset with his attitude, Detroit sent him with Ike Boone to the White Sox for Bill Fischer and Tito Francona. It proved to be the break that made the right-hander's career. Years later, Shaw summoned up the change as follows: "I won four in a row in relief after joining Chicago. I was with good teachers. Manager Lopez had confidence in me, and then there were Coach Ray Berres and Dick Donovan to advise me. I began throwing my slider the way Donovan threw his. In the winter of '58 in Cuba, I worked on fundamentals at Lopez's suggestion. I began pitching completely overhand instead of sidearm and three-quarter."[2] Berres, at the time the best pitching coach in baseball, thought that when Shaw threw side-arm or three-quarter, he was giving the hitter too much time to see the ball. In spite of having the full faith and confidence of his manager and pitching coach, Shaw was by no means considered untouchable by Greenberg and Veeck. On more than one occasion, he was dangled in front of Cleveland as trade bait for some power hitting. If such a trade had been consummated, or if Shaw were still pitching for the Tigers in 1959, it's unlikely that the White Sox would have ended their 40-year pennant drought.

The Sox lost the second game of the holiday twin bill, 8–3. Third base coach Tony Cuccinello complained that the Athletics failed to instruct their grounds crew to cover the base paths during a hard pre-game rainstorm.[3] In baseball, such claims are usually dismissed as sour grapes, but the 51-year-old Cuccinello was one of the more respected figures in the game, with a long list of notable accomplishments. The colorful little fireplug from Queens was one of only seven players in baseball history to hit over .300 his first and last seasons in the majors. His 15-year career included being on the American League squad for the first All-Star Game at Comiskey Park, and missing the 1945 American League batting title by .0001, when he hit .3084 to Snuffy Stirnweiss's .3085. If Cuccinello had a gripe, people listened.

Smith provided the game-winning hit the next day, as the Sox won the rubber game of the series, 4–3. His home run off longtime Sox nemesis Ned Garver gave Turk Lown the win in relief as the team looked forward to the All-Star break. The White Sox were now 16–4 in one-run games and entered the three-day hiatus with a record of 43–35, firmly entrenched in second place, two games behind Cleveland.

The All-Star break meant a welcome respite from baseball for all the Sox except Aparicio, Fox, Lollar, Pierce, and Wynn. Fox and Aparicio were the leading vote getters for the contest, and Wynn was named the American League's starting pitcher. The National League won, 5–4. Fox went 2-for-5 and Wynn gave up only two hits, a homer by Eddie Mathews and a double by Ernie Banks, in three innings. The Los Angeles Dodgers' Don Drysdale got the start for the Senior Circuit and also pitched well. Few thought that just three months later, these two hurlers would be facing each other on an even bigger national stage.

After the break, South Siders were eager for the season to continue, and 36,742 of them flocked to Comiskey Park on Thursday, July 9, for the start of the important two-game series against the Indians. On that date, Pierce pitched one of his grittiest gems of the year, a complete-game five-hitter for a 4–3 Sox win. In the sixth inning, Bubba Phillips delivered the game-winning hit when he homered off the hard-luck loser, Herb Score. The affable Southerner was providing a workable solution to the White Sox's longstanding third base woes.

John Melvin "Bubba" Phillips was born in West Point, Mississippi, on February 24, 1928. His athletic talent first surfaced on the high school gridiron, when he scored 235 points in nine games. This athletic display led to a football scholarship to Southern Mississippi University, where he played both running back and cornerback and was named a second team Little All American. His record of 25 career interceptions at Southern Miss still stands, and he scored 22 touchdowns in just 32 collegiate games. Phillips reportedly signed a contract with the San Francisco 49ers while they were in the All-America Football Conference, and also led Southern Miss's baseball team in hits in 1948. His baseball skills caught the eye of several major league scouts, and he signed with the Tigers, playing for the Stroudsburg Poconos in the North Atlantic League his first year, and promoted to the Class D Thomasville Tigers for the 1949 season. He continued on a fast track to the majors that was interrupted after his season in Buffalo ended in September 1952 with his induction into the army. The Tigers did not forget him, and Phillips started in left field at Briggs Stadium on Opening Day, 1955. After another lackluster season, Detroit needed to shore up their starting pitching, so they sent him to Chicago for aging veteran Virgil Trucks, who returned to the scene of his greatest accomplishments. Phillips hit a solid .271 for the Sox during his first three seasons on the South Side, pleasing everyone in the organization. "His football training made him a better competitor. He's the kind of kid who accepts coaching, and he's a kid who loves to play," Don Gutteridge attested. John Rigney made his own observations: "Remember that he's a fellow who played football as his major sport and picked up baseball as it came along. On certain plays that a kid who had played baseball all his life would make instinctively, Phillips doesn't know what to do. But he's learning all the time and has a lot of guts. He gives us the strongest arm we've had at third since Bob Kennedy's younger days."[4] In June 1958, Phillips badly injured his foot in a game against Boston and missed six weeks. His replacement, the capable veteran Goodman, hit .299 as a fill-in and complicated the Sox's third base decisions. As a result, the two began splitting third base responsibilities. In spite of his not being an everyday starter, Phillips' clutch hitting was cementing his place as one of the key individuals for the White Sox's pennant hopes.

In the Friday night game July 10, Phillips tripled against the Indians, but unfortunately his blow was half of all the extra-base hits the Sox could muster (the other a triple by Torgeson) as the Tribe restored their two-game lead. A crowd of 41,588 left disappointed as Early Wynn gave up nine hits and five runs in just four-plus innings, while Tito Francona and Rocky Colavito combined for seven hits in an easy 8–4 Cleveland victory. So the Sox could only muster a split against the league leaders, and anxious Sox fans could be forgiven if the series left them questioning the old baseball adage that good pitching stops good hitting.

While disappointed with the results on the field, the Sox's front office was thrilled with the huge turnout. The game was interrupted by a downpour, which knocked out the electricity in the press box and also the lights on the field. To placate the big crowd, Veeck improvised and put the post-game fireworks show on during the rain delay. The Sox's home attendance was now over 548,000 in just 35 games, an increase of 120,000 customers over 1958. Their enthusiasm was tempered the following morning, however, when columnist Herb Lyon wrote that Chuck Comiskey had hosted a dinner for a bevy of baseball executives in town for a mid-season meeting. At a banquet-sized table in the Ambassador East Hotel's Pump Room, Chuck hinted that he had more legal tricks up his sleeve in his endless quest to gain complete control of the franchise.[5]

The next afternoon, Kansas City took Cleveland's place in the visitors' locker room at Comiskey for a short Saturday-Sunday, three-game series. When the Indians left, they took the crowds with them, as only 7,346 paid to see the July 11 matinee. Latman rewarded them for coming out, throwing a sparkling, complete-game four-hitter for an easy 8–3 win. The home stand ended Sunday, July 12, with a doubleheader, as the Sox raised the South Side's pennant hopes to a fever pitch, taking both games, 5–3 and 9–7. This twin bill marked a sort of coming out party for Jim McAnany, the 22-year-old call-up who replaced Johnny Callison. His two-out triple in the second game off Bud Daley in the fifth inning drove in three runs that eventually decided the game. McAnany drove in six runs for the day, and he walked off the diamond at Comiskey late that Sunday afternoon with a blistering .378 batting average.

Stocky, bespectacled James McAnany was the other "rookie from California" who was hidden in the big shadow that Johnny Callison cast. Born September 4, 1936, in Los Angeles, he was signed by Hollis Thurston and Doc Bennett after his sophomore year at USC and given a $4,000 bonus. A bad case of nearsightedness, however, almost cost him his career before it started. McAnany was hit in the head four times in his first season at Waterloo, and each beaning warranted a hospitalization. The White Sox, alarmed by the situation, sent him to their West Coast ophthalmologist, Dr. Herbert Cohn. He surmised that McAnany's corrective lenses were the problem, impairing his peripheral vision and making it impossible for him to track the ball when it came toward him inside. He fashioned a new pair of spectacles with curved lenses that gave McAnany an unimpaired field of vision, and they worked perfectly. In 1957, the young Californian, playing for Davenport in the Three I League, hit .303 with 17 homers. The following year, he won the Hillerich & Bradsby Bat Corporation's Silver Slugger Award when he hit .400 (175 hits in 438 at-bats) at Colorado Springs. This performance was all the more remarkable considering the stressors McAnany experienced before the 1958 season began. He learned of his father's unexpected death while playing in a game at Vero Beach, a loss that cast the young outfielder in the role of family breadwinner, with his mother and three siblings still in California.

The Sox called him up that September, but he went hitless in 13 at-bats. His commitment to the Army Reserve interfered with his preparations for the 1959 season, in spite of the fact that he was now eligible for a discharge as the sole support for his family. This military obligation actually delayed his reappearance at 35th and Shields until June 27, 1959, when the Sox officially ended the brief Johnny Callison era and called him up.[6] McAnany was the seventh starting right fielder manager Al Lopez had penciled into the lineup since Opening Day, and El Senor was now content to have him share the position with the veteran Rivera and start against left-handed pitching. Lopez, not knowing what he had, placed McAnany in the

Jim McAnany's mid-season debut for the White Sox occurred because Johnny Callison did not perform up to expectations. His sensational hitting and fielding in July 1959 convinced manager Al Lopez to platoon him with Jim Rivera in right field for the rest of the season.

eighth slot, with his job simply being to get on base so the pitcher could either sacrifice or be the last out, and Aparicio could lead off the next inning. The wide-eyed rookie with the big forearms and the weight of his family on his shoulders had already proven that he could do much more than that.

The Sox, winners of four of their five games since the All-Star break, travelled to Boston on Monday, July 13. The first-place Indians now felt the White Sox's breath; the Chicagoans' hot start in July left them only a single game behind in the standings. The weak-hitting Sox had suddenly scored 63 runs in their last 11 games. The heroics by Aparicio, Fox, Landis, McAnany, and Phillips overshadowed Al Smith's improved hitting. Smith's average for July was a lusty .362, and he had four hits for 12 total bases in the July 12 double-header against Kansas City. Edward Prell wrote in the *Chicago Tribune* that the usual catcalls Smith heard from the crowd at the start of the Sunday doubleheader were cheers by the end of the day.

In the Tuesday night game at Fenway Park, the Sox took advantage of an apathetic and listless Red Sox team for an easy 7–3 win. Pierce had his way with Boston's lineup throughout the game, and the one inning the Red Sox had success against him actually angered the 20,606 Boston loyalists in the stands. All this occurred in the fifth inning, with the White Sox ahead, 5–2. Sammy White got a hold of one of Pierce's few bad pitches and tripled. Boston manager Billy Jurges failed to pinch-hit for reliever Murray Wall, whom Pierce fanned with ease, and he proceeded to strike out Red Sox leadoff man Don Buddin. When Pierce got the dangerous, hot-hitting (.335 going into the game) Pete Runnels to lift a routine fly to Smith in left field for the final out, the Red Sox fans let loose their years of frustration, booing vociferously and telling Jurges what they thought of him. Two hundred miles down the coast, Whitey Ford beat Herb Score as Cleveland lost, 1–0, to the Yankees, putting the Sox in a virtual tie for first place.

Heavy rains on Wednesday meant a dreaded Thursday doubleheader, which the White Sox split, taking the first game behind Donovan, 4–3, but losing the second, 5–4. Donovan's slider baffled the disinterested Bostonians throughout the game; Buddin and Frankie Malzone were the only Red Sox starters to get hits. Donovan's caution with Ted Williams was another reason for his effectiveness. He walked him twice after Williams reached base his first time up on Jim McAnany's error. The rookie right fielder more than made up for this gaffe, however, at the plate, going 3-for-3 and raising his average to .432. After the game, the Sox rushed to the depot for their train to Manhattan. It was a pleasant journey, since the Yankees swept a doubleheader from the Indians that same afternoon.

The South Siders arrived in New York City buoyed by the knowledge that a travel agency had chartered two airplanes carrying 141 faithful fans from Chicago to Yankee Stadium to cheer them on in their big four-game weekend series with the defending champions. They were among the 42,168 who saw the best pitching duel of the 1959 season when Wynn faced the pride of Big Cabin, Oklahoma, Ralph Terry, in Friday night's opener. Terry entered the game with a 3–6 record and an adipose 4.40 ERA, but on this night he pitched like he was 6–3 and sporting a 0.40 average. The tall, raw-boned right-hander's curve and sinker were almost unhittable. By the top of the ninth, the Chicagoans had managed only two balls out of the infield, a second-inning fly to center by Lollar and Aparicio's short fly to right in the sixth, and no hits. Through those eight innings, Wynn battled Terry tooth-and-nail; the Yanks had managed just one hit off the anchor of the Sox staff, a harmless infield single by Terry, his opposite number.

In the top of the ninth, McAnany, who had had a decisive hand in three of the last five victories, led off with a sizzling line drive right up the middle, a little too close to the tiring Terry for comfort, breaking up the no-hitter and put the lead run on base. Wynn bunted in front of the plate. The frantic Terry fired to second too late to get the fleet McAnany, putting two on with nobody out, bringing leadoff man Aparicio to the plate. Aparicio surprised everyone in the park when he also bunted, pushing McAnany and Wynn to seczond and third with one away. Terry was now in a first-class jam and he knew it; Fox, the toughest out in the American League, strode to the plate, with his .334 average. Terry wanted nothing to do with him and put him on first with a walk. Landis came up and fouled off Terry's first four offerings before rifling a frozen rope between first and second. The Yankees' infield was caught out of position, because Lopez had put on a hit-and-run in most unusual circumstances: game tied, one out, bases loaded, and two strikes on the hitter! Fox broke stride to avoid being hit by the liner, while McAnany, off with the pitch, was almost across the plate before Landis was out of the batter's box, giving the Sox the lead. The flustered New Yorkers were caught off guard a second time when Cuccinello frantically waved Wynn around third base. Wynn, pedestrian gait and all, barely beat Enos Slaughter's throw to Berra: Sox 2, New York 0. The infuriated and demoralized Terry, too stunned to realize fully that he had lost a no-hitter, sat in silence as Wynn faced Siebern, Mantle, and Berra in the bottom of the ninth with little trouble to close out the game. Siebern managed a single but Mantle, who hit only .242 against Wynn during his career, grounded into a double play. Berra, fuming with frustration as he walked out from the batter's box to the plate, popped out to Fox to end the game. For all the frustrations Sox fans suffered through the 1950s at the hands of the Bronx Bombers, Friday, July 17, 1959, erased a multitude of bad memories.

The win was the 50th of the season for the Pale Hose against 37 losses. A Friday night victory in Yankee Stadium was an achievement any time, but this win was special. The Sox broke up a no-hitter. They refused to let a stellar pitching performance by Wynn—now 12–6—go to waste. Their two young outfielders, Landis and McAnany, once again were the catalysts of the offense. They did not buckle under the pressure of facing Mantle and Berra as the tying runs in the bottom of the ninth in New York. These were all high points to savor in a season rapidly filling up with them. Success continued for the Sox in the Saturday afternoon game, when Shaw out-pitched Don Larsen, 2–1, with the margin of victory being McAnany's 14th RBI in less than three weeks. Pitching, daring strategy, and timely hitting were the difference in two straight victories in the Yankees' back yard. With a Sunday doubleheader looming on July 19, could the South Siders dare to fantasize about a sweep and leave town with the Yankees 9½ games out of first by the middle of July?

A pleasant thought, but it was not to be. Latman did not have it in the first game, while Ford and Duren had it bunches, resulting in a 6–2 Yankees victory. The crowd of 53,014 hung around for game two and saw Pierce get uncharacteristically knocked around while Sox hitters had difficulty with Yankees starter Eli Grba. With Duren finishing the second game as well, New York prevailed, 6–4. Duren pitched the last two innings in each contest, and the intimidating All-Star's line for the day was four innings pitched, no hits or runs allowed, five walks, five strikeouts, and three balls hit out of the infield. The short but difficult road trip to the East Coast ended at 4–3, coming to a close with the Sox still tied for first, in many ways a job well done. But they returned to the South Side knowing that the Yanks could have been 9½ out if just a few things had worked out differently on Sunday. The damned Yankees had seemingly crawled out of the coffin before the Sox could put the final stake in their heart.

Nobody mentioned it at the time, but Tuesday evening, July 21, 1959, marked the date in which the Boston Red Sox joined baseball's Age of Enlightenment, more than 12 years after it began. The Red Sox were in the midst of a terrible year and arrived in Chicago mired in last place at 40–51. They started the season under the ambivalent watch of Pinky Higgins, a baseball lifer who was fired after 73 games with a record of 31–42. Coach Rudy York took the helm for one game, with his faithful charges spoiling his managerial debut by losing yet again. Billy Jurges, known to Chicago fans for his time with the Cubs,[7] got the managerial job in early July, and the team responded positively to his leadership for the first few weeks. Boston's record under Jurges was 9–8. With the team going nowhere and playing 1,100 miles away from home, it seemed like a perfect time and a safe place for the Red Sox's version of the "Great Experiment": play a black ballplayer wearing a Red Sox uniform in a major league game. The Red Sox achieved this belated milestone when Jurges sent in 25-year-old Pumpsie Green. The big moment occurred in the top of the eighth inning. Trailing by one run, Vic Wertz pinch-hit for shortstop Don Buddin and powered a single to center field. He noticed some commotion in the visitors' dugout before he took his lead. Time was called, and Jurges summoned the big first baseman to the bench. The lithe, high-waisted Green trotted over to first base, trying hard to look like he had been there before. Green got no further as Pete Runnels lined out, Marty Keough flied out, and Dick Gernert popped out to end the inning. Green's defensive debut occurred in the bottom of the eighth, when Jurges sent him to replace Buddin at shortstop, where he handled no fielding chances in his one inning of work. The historic day ended with the White Sox holding on to their one-game lead thanks to the 2–1 victory.

The Sox swept the two-game set with a 5–4 win on Wednesday, July 22, manufacturing the winning run in the bottom of the ninth with classic "small ball" play. Fox singled, Landis bunted him to second, and Lollar singled him home for the winning run. Since the Yankees had put away the Indians earlier in the day, this 21st one-run victory by the Chicagoans kept them in first place by one game. It was also Green's first major league start. Wynn retired him with two grounders and a pop out, but Green did manage to work Wynn for a walk in the fifth inning.

The first-place Sox hosted the third-place Orioles over the weekend of July 24–26. Baltimore came to 35th and Shields with a four-game losing streak; since Pierce, Wynn, Donovan and Shaw were slated to pitch, a quick improvement did not seem likely. Pierce and Al Smith provided the heroics in the Friday night affair. The only run Pierce allowed was a solo homer in the third inning by left fielder Bob Nieman. Smith got hold of a flat Hoyt Wilhelm knuckler in the bottom of the ninth, sending it 400 feet into the left field stands for a walk-off home run. This contest was the fifth time Smith had driven in the game-winning run in 1959, and the usual mix of boos and apathetic cheers the fans bestowed upon him at the beginning of the game turned into a deafening chorus of praise from the same 29,274 voices.[8]

Saturday's contest turned out to be a tractor pull and a game in which a victory might actually do more harm than good. Paul Richards and Al Lopez used 31 players in the 17-inning, 4½-hour contest in which the Sox prevailed, 3–2. Harry Simpson once again put everyone out of their misery with a sharp single in the bottom of the 17th with one away, driving in Esposito with the winning run. The much-traveled Simpson entered the game hitting only .227, but since so many of his hits come in clutch situations, he was probably the most valuable .227 hitter in the majors.

The real heroes of this marathon, however, were the pitchers. Billy O'Dell, historically a tough foe for the Sox, started and gave up only two runs over 9½ innings. Jerry Walker took his place and gave up only three hits in 4⅔ innings of relief. Billy Loes followed Walker, pitched well, but took the loss when Simpson ended the game with his liner to left. As good as the Orioles' hurlers were, the two Sox pitchers were even better. Shaw pitched brilliantly through 11 innings, yielding two runs, with only one of them earned. Turk Lown took his place in the 12th and delivered his best performance of the season, blanking the Orioles for six innings, while giving up three lonely singles to Chico Carrasquel, Billy Gardner, and Walt Dropo. The White Sox now had a remarkable 13 consecutive wins in one-run affairs; Lown was one of the reasons.

The Sox signed Omar "Turk" Lown on July 23, 1958, after he was waived by the Cincinnati Reds. The Brooklyn native was a highly touted pitching phenom who started his high school baseball career as a catcher and outfielder. One day, when his team was short of hurlers, Lown climbed on the mound for the first time in his life and struck out 17 batters. His brother Bill was

another young Brooklyn baseball luminary; the Dodgers thought so much of Bill that they invited him to a tryout at Ebbets Field. Bill had to work that day, so brother Turk went in his place. Dodgers scout Joey Kleinkauf was so impressed with the 18-year-old fireballer that he offered Turk a contract that same day.[9]

Lown's introduction to professional baseball occurred at Valdosta in the Class D Georgia-Florida League. He toyed with his competitors, striking out 204 in 232 innings with an 18–8 record and 1.94 ERA. Lown spent three years in the army and earned a Purple Heart due to a shrapnel wound in his thigh. His war heroics interrupted his progress on the mound, leading to an extended stay in the minors. In 1950, Cubs gen-

Omar "Turk" Lown was claimed off the waiver wire by the White Sox when the Cincinnati Redlegs gave up on the aging fireballer in 1958. Lown was one of pitching coach Ray Berres' best reclamation projects, going 9–2 as a reliever, saving 15 games, and posting a 2.89 ERA.

eral manager Wid Matthews, who remembered Lown and his coveted fastball when he worked for Branch Rickey in Brooklyn, drafted him out of the Dodgers organization and welcomed him to Wrigley Field. Lown's career with the North Siders could best be described as erratic. He was up and down between Chicago and Los Angeles of the Pacific Coast League until 1955, when he won five games, saved 12, and pitched 114⅓ innings for LA. In May of 1958, the Cubs sent him to Cincinnati for reliever Hersh Freeman, largely because by that time Matthews was long gone and new Cubs general manager John Holland went with youth. Lown spent all of six weeks with the Redlegs before they waived their rights, and he was immediately picked up by the White Sox.

He found the spacious confines of Comiskey Park very much to his liking. He struck out 40 batters in 40⅔ innings, improved his control under the tutelage of Ray Berres, and went 3–3 with eight saves. Lopez paired Lown with his roommate, Gerry Staley, another veteran reliever several teams thought was washed up, and they became the most effective bullpen duo in the American League. Lown's intimidating fastball and Staley's grounder-inducing sinker were figuring in a great many White Sox victories.[10]

The weekend series with Baltimore ended with the Sox splitting the Sunday doubleheader, which cost them the league lead. Wynn threw his second consecutive two-hit complete game against the O's for a 4–1 victory in game one. He got a big assist from Landis, whose spectacular leaping catch at the center field wall robbed catcher Gus Triandos of a three-run homer. In game two, however, 20-year-old Baltimore phenom Milt Pappas padded his record to 11–5, while Latman was no better than mediocre, giving up four earned runs in 5⅓ innings. Pappas confounded the Sox hitters all afternoon, giving up only five hits. With the Indians sweeping their three-game series with the Senators in Cleveland, Pappas' strong effort pushed the Sox into second, a half-game behind the Indians.

While most of the crowd of 35,207 came to Comiskey Park to see the ballgame, a sizable chunk of the women attended because Veeck declared it to be S&H Green Stamps Ladies' Day. Collecting trading stamps was a beloved avocation in many American households in the late 1950s, which made it a perfect Veeckian promotion. Besides getting in free to the doubleheader, every woman received 150 stamps, and the actress Jill Corey, who was starring in the Tent House Theatre's rendition of "Gigi," kicked things off by driving a new Chevrolet station wagon courtesy of Nickey ("with the backward 'K'") Chevrolet around the perimeter of the field. Veeck did not stop there, adding a laundry list of absurd free gifts to unsuspecting women, ranging from 1,000 ice cream bars to 4,000 dill pickles.

Veeck's promotions irked those he referred to as the "stuffed shirts" in the baseball establishment, but most of them were well thought-out marketing devices to draw a bigger audience and enhance everyone's experiences at the game. In a talk at the University of Chicago Business School on May 14, 1959, Veeck presented his theories of baseball marketing.[11] He pointed out that over the years, the White Sox drew fewer females than any other team in the majors. He attributed it to several factors: Comiskey Park's inaccessibility by public transportation, the deteriorating neighborhood surrounding it, and the visually foreboding industrial environment where it was located. While Veeck pointed out that the soon-to-be finished Dan Ryan Expressway and his plans for illuminating a four-square-block area around the park would help matters, he tried hard to attract women spectators before these changes would come to fruition with promotions specifically aimed at the fairer sex.

Veeck also used promotions aimed at women when he owned teams in Cleveland and St. Louis. Aside from the usual Ladies' Day promotions, he and his wife, Mary Frances, had innovative plans to promote the Browns. She would comb through the vital statistics of the St. Louis newspapers and send a team contract to each newborn boy, dated 16 years in advance, along with two tickets for the parents. The parents of infant girls were not slighted. They got two tickets and a poem that Mary Frances herself composed especially for the occasion. Veeck's most important promotions, however, were the fireworks shows. Knowing that concession sales could be the difference between a team earning a profit and experiencing a loss, Veeck thought that if he could slow down the departure of fans after a game, concessions revenues would go up. A great majority of the crowd would stay to see fireworks, and many would buy concessions at the same time. Veeck determined that post-game concession sales increased 40 percent after a loss if there were fireworks, increased 50 percent after a win with no fireworks, and 150 percent after a win that was followed by fireworks.[12] He was well ahead of all other owners in professional sports at developing new revenue streams through marketing research and unorthodox enticements.

The South Siders looked forward to their day off on Monday, July 27, before three important games with the visiting Yankees. If July's goal was to create a two-team race, this upcoming series loomed large. Sweeping the Yankees over the next 72 hours would put the New Yorkers 12 games behind them in the loss column with 45 left to play. The off-day ended on a good note; thanks to Boston's victory over the Indians, the Sox moved back into first place.

The Yankees entered Comiskey Park on Tuesday night having lost four of their last six games. They hoped that 3–7 Ralph Terry could somehow spin the same magic he did a couple Fridays ago when he held the Sox hitless into the ninth inning, only to lose the game. Pierce, always tough against New York, pitched his heart out and was up, 2–1, in the bottom of the eighth. After Fox singled, Smith came through once again in the clutch, homering deep into the left field grandstand for two critical insurance runs. New York was able to score in the ninth after a rare error by Aparicio, but 43,829 fans went home happy with a big 4–3 Sox victory. McAnany, who was struggling with his first batting slump, snapped out of it after Terry hit him with what looked like a purpose pitch, whizzing a sharp single right by the surprised hurler later in the game.

A heavy cloudburst sent a huge crowd of 43,599 home after six innings on Wednesday night with the score knotted up at four apiece. The Sox knocked Whitey Ford out in the second inning but did little against his successor, Duke Maas. Bob Shaw did not have his best stuff but managed to preserve the tie. The night was not a total loss, however, since the huge throng roared its approval when the big Chesterfield scoreboard recorded another Red Sox victory over the Indians.

Thursday's match-up was a red-letter day for the young Yankees starter, 25-year-old Chicago native, Eli Grba. The pride of Bowen High School who signed with the Red Sox after a great career in the tough Chicago Public League, Grba lived the dream of every South Side ball player by getting to pitch in Comiskey Park. While he pitched well, giving up only two earned runs over seven innings, he could not match Wynn's efforts, which were the main reason for the Sox's 3–1 victory. Wynn was now 14–6, throwing yet another complete game and receiving a critical insurance run in the eighth inning off the bat of the now irreplaceable Al Smith, who singled in Aparicio while facing Ryne Duren. The game turned out to be the final nail in New York's coffin. They fell 10½ games behind the league-leading Sox and 11 behind in the loss column. The month ended with an easy 7–1 victory Friday night, July 31, when Barry Latman silenced the Washington Senators' big bats while Torgeson, Landis, and McAnany each got two hits off Pedro Ramos.

The White Sox ended July with a record of 20–7, their best one-month record in nine years, back when Paul Richards' young Go-Go Sox team went 20–5 in May 1950. With the Indians going 20–12 in July, the South Siders found themselves in first place at the end of the month by one game. More importantly, the American League pennant race for 1959 was now a two-team competition. The Orioles fell during the month, going 13–17, and the always-feared Yanks fared no better at 12–16. Their poor July performances left them both teams at least ten games behind. The upstart Kansas City Athletics, vaulting into third place after a 19–11 July, were not taken seriously. They could hit and were much improved since the season started, but did not have a deep enough roster to play at an extended .600 clip. Sox fans loved looking at the standings with two months to go:

Chicago 59–40
Cleveland 59–42 1 GB

Kansas City 50–50 9.5 GB
Baltimore 51–52 10 GB
New York 49–51 10.5 GB
Detroit 50–54 11.5 GB
Boston 44–57 16 GB
Washington 43–59 17 GB

7

August: The South Side Rises Again

With the Chicago White Sox's pennant express steaming ahead in July, on Saturday, August 1, Veeck got caught up in the excitement before the game against the Senators. Having played 16 games in 16 days, Lopez gave the weary starting staff a break by penciling in Ray Moore to start the middle game of the three-game series. Shaw and Latman's effectiveness had limited Moore's opportunities; he had not started a game in seven weeks. All the Sox wanted from the veteran right-hander was to eat as many innings as he possibly could. Veeck, however, had much grander plans for the game. Knowing that Moore was an avid outdoorsman, Veeck bought a hunting dog named Young Blue and brought it into the dugout, promising to give it to Moore if he won the game. Few in the crowd knew there was a hound in the Sox's dugout, let alone that he was being used as a behavioral incentive for one of the players. Moore left after retiring the side in the eighth, looking to be a hard-luck loser—and out one fine hunting dog—with the White Sox trailing, 1–0. But in the bottom of the ninth, submariner Dick Hyde came in to relieve Camilo Pascual and was victimized by center fielder Bobby Allison's error as the Sox salvaged a 2–1 victory. Even though Gerry Staley got the win, Veeck gave Moore the dog for his strong showing.

Ray "Farmer" Moore, the best pitcher to ever call Meadows, Maryland, his hometown, was a character right out of *Outdoor Life* Magazine. The 33-year-old right-hander loved hunting, fishing, all things outdoors, and country music. During the off-season, Moore worked his tobacco farm and pursued his woods and waters hobbies. When he turned 19, he enlisted in the Army and was sent to the Philippines at the end of World War II. His baseball talent caught the eye of a fellow soldier, Rex Bowen, who was a scout for the Dodgers. By 1947, Moore was pitching in the Dodgers organization, and he debuted for the Dodgers on August 1, 1952. The pitching-rich Brooklynites did not really have a place for the rangy right-hander, so from 1952 through 1954 he was yo-yoing between Brooklyn, Ft. Worth, and St. Paul.

In October 1954, the Dodgers traded him to the Orioles for infielder Chico Garcia. The Orioles' organization was a perfect fit for Moore. He went from a team with one of the most established pitching staffs in the majors to an upstart organization looking for hurlers and managed by one of the game's all-time great pitching tutors, Paul Richards. Moore had good seasons in 1955, 1956, and 1957, recording 33 wins and 30 losses with 302 strikeouts in 564 innings. The White Sox got him in a controversial multi-player trade with Baltimore that took place in December 1957. The Sox sent starter Jack Harshman, Larry Doby, minor league pitching prospect Russ Heman, and future major leaguer Jim Marshall to the Orioles for Moore, Tito Francona, and Billy Goodman.[1]

Some Sox fans were suspicious of the trade, not seeing past the departure of Harshman, overlooking ex–American League batting champion Goodman, and unaware of Francona's great potential. Once the 1958 season got underway, however, Moore did his best to placate the trade's critics. He pitched 136⅔ innings in 32 games, starting 20 of them, and finished 9–7. In spite of his occasionally spotty performances in 1959, the job he turned in to earn another hunting dog on this Saturday afternoon demonstrated his value as a back-of-the-rotation starter. The Sox swept the series the next day by taking both ends of a Sunday doubleheader, 3–2 and 9–2, with Shaw upping his record to 10–3 while Sox hitters had their way with a promising Senators rookie whose fame would come later–Jim Kaat.

A tough, two-week, four-city road trip awaited the Pale Hose, but the euphoria from the weekend sweep put everyone in a good mood. Chuck Comiskey was so elated he announced that he would call off all legal fighting with Veeck over team ownership until after the season was over.[2] Despite being in first place by three games, the team had some anxieties. Donovan was still on the shelf with a sore arm, and Wynn suffered a freak injury when the team picture was taken. He bruised his heel when a bench he was standing on collapsed, giving everyone a scare.

Another unneeded distraction was the 1959 season's second All-Star Game on August 3 in Los Angeles. Nobody was sold on the idea of a second All-Star Game, and sports columnists from across the country wrote scathing pieces criticizing it. Baseball executives were not pleased either. Indians general manager Frank Lane complained bitterly about All-Star manager Casey Stengel using an exhausted Cal McLish, the mainstay of Cleveland's starting rotation (along with Baltimore's O'Dell, Wilhelm, and Jerry Walker) instead of his own Ryne Duren. Orioles manager Paul Richards complained that "[using my pitchers] messed up my rotation for at least four days, and I have a big series with the White Sox coming up." Stengel's frank response: "I don't care what they say. These pitchers were all warmed up and if they didn't feel good they didn't have to play. They all wanted to pitch."[3] Two of the White Sox figured prominently in the contest. Early Wynn agreed to pitch two innings as a means to test his sore heel, and Nellie Fox singled in the go-ahead run in a 5–3 American League victory.

With Donovan out, the Sox called up 24-year-old Ken McBride to start the series opener in Baltimore on Tuesday, August 4. The Sox had purchased the young hurler's contract from the Red Sox just three days earlier, a move seen by many as surprising, since Boston was going nowhere in 1959 and a promising young pitcher with a sinking fastball could be a perfect fit in a hitter's park like Fenway. McBride pitched well and did not tire until the eighth inning, when Lopez replaced him with Turk Lown, who could not protect the 2–0 he inherited. Billy Klaus nicked Lown for a game-winning single in the eighth: Orioles 3, Sox 2.

On the following day, the White Sox played a dreaded mid-week doubleheader. Latman made it more palatable with a complete-game, three-hit shutout in the opener, but Baltimore hit Wynn hard and handed the Sox a 7–1 defeat in game two. More frustrating than Wynn's poor outing was the offense's complete inability to handle the offerings of Orioles starter Arnie Portocarrero.

The series finale the following evening turned out to be one of the strangest games of the year. The Thursday, August 6, night game was even longer than the previous two marathons these teams had earlier in the year. On June 4, the Chicagoans trimmed Baltimore, 6–5, in 17 innings, thanks to Earl Torgeson's walk-off home run. On July 25, great relief work by Lown and a game-winning single by Simpson in the 17th put the Orioles away. The August 6, O'Dell-Pierce match-up went 18 innings and after four hours ended in a 1–1 tie. With the Sox up, 1–0, in the bottom of the eighth, outfielder Willie Tasby singled in Bobby Boyd to tie the score. Hoyt Wilhelm came out of the Baltimore bullpen to pitch an amazing ten innings of relief, giving up only two hits to the exhausted Sox hitters. Wilhelm's terrific effort was only one out short of the equivalent of a no-hitter. He pitched 8⅔ innings without yielding a safety before Goodman nicked him for a single in the bottom of the 17th. Pierce, however, outdid everyone in this game, pitching an incredible 16 innings before Turk Lown finished the last two frames. After Billy Klaus singled in the bottom of the 15th, Smith saved the tie for the Sox with a brilliant throw to Lollar, who nailed the sliding Wilhelm as he tried to score the winning run. When Lown coaxed Walt Dropo to hit a weak grounder to Lollar at first for the final out in the 18th, Baltimore's curfew law, which stated that no inning during weekdays could start after 11:55 p.m., took effect. Baltimore took the series, 2–1–1, and the Indians were suddenly 1½ games behind the first-place Chicagoans. The Sox had an off-day the following Monday,

August 10, causing many to question why Lopez would leave Pierce in so long. In two months, that decision would come back to haunt him.[4]

When the team arrived in Washington, Lopez announced that he would be resting Lollar, due to a strained knee ligament, which had the starting catcher mired in a 5-for-34 hitting slump. The Sox made up for their poor showing in Baltimore by sweeping the hapless Senators, 4–1, 4–3, and 9–0, largely thanks to the excellent pitching of Shaw, Staley, and Wynn, and the hitting of Billy Goodman. The reliable veteran went 5-for-8 with three two-out RBI. The Sox looked forward to a trip to Detroit, three games ahead of the second-place Indians.

The rangy William Dale Goodman was born March 22, 1926, in Concord, North Carolina. The pride of Winecoff High School was ambidextrous and excelled as both a pitcher and catcher. Equally skilled at basketball and football, he concentrated on baseball only after signing a contract with the Concord Weavers in the Carolina Victory League, abandoning his left-handed activities and catching the eye of Atlanta Crackers scout Claude Dietrich. While signing a 17-year-old to a Double A contract might seem like a risk, the Crackers gave Goodman $1,200 to sign, and in 1944 he toiled under the watchful eye of ex–Cubs outfielder and future Hall of Famer KiKi Cuyler. Goodman did not miss a beat after a stint in the Navy during World War II, hitting .389 for the Crackers in 1946. The Red Sox took note and bought his contract from Atlanta for $75,000, a huge sum for a player in those days, and sent him to Louisville. His major league debut was April 19, 1947, against the Philadelphia Athletics, and he appeared in 12 games for the Red Sox before being sent down to Louisville. Goodman's extra time there paid off; he hit .340 with 52 walks and only 27 strikeouts. The Red Sox called him back September, and he was in the big leagues to stay.[5]

A natural hitter with a keen batting eye, Goodman won the American League batting title in 1950, hitting .354 and finishing second in the Most Valuable Player balloting. He was a mainstay in the Boston offense until traded to Baltimore in June 1957 for pitcher Mike Fornieles. The all-purpose athlete played six different positions for Paul Richards' Orioles while hitting .308. Goodman's stay in Baltimore, however, was rather brief; six months after arriving, he went to the Sox as a key component of the seven-player trade in December 1957. For the Sox in 1958, Goodman hit .299 with a .355 on-base percentage, striking out only 21 times in 425 at-bats. His contributions and veteran presence were proving invaluable to the Sox in 1959 as they pursued their first pennant in 40 years.

As if to celebrate the Sox's emergence as the best team in baseball during the 1959 season, *Sports Illustrated* featured Aparicio and Fox on the cover of its Monday, August 10, edition.[6] The South Siders arrived in Detroit and took two out of three, with Fox, Goodman, Lollar, and Torgeson heading the offense, which scored 20 runs in their two victories. Lollar's sore knee appeared to be completely healed; in the last two games, he went 6-for-9 with two home runs and five RBI.

The most overlooked individual during the most successful decade in Sox history was their first-string catcher, John Sherman Lollar. Lollar was a quiet leader who, despite being one of the most productive and respected players in the league, always toiled in the shadows of the era's most illustrious catcher, Yogi Berra. Lollar's decision-making skills and leadership roles came early. His father died unexpectedly in 1934 when he was eight years old, forcing his mother to sell the family grocery store in Fayetteville, Arkansas. She became a nurse in a VA home to support Lollar, his two sisters, and his brother. Young Sherm got a job as the batboy for the Fayetteville Bears in the Class D Arkansas-Missouri League. Since his high school eliminated baseball during the Depression, all of Lollar's playing during his adolescence occurred on club teams or sandlots. He finished high school at the age of 16 and enrolled at Pittsburg (Kansas) State Teacher's College in 1940. Lollar's baseball playing during college years was in the amateur Ban Johnson League. His big break occurred when he took a job at the Baxter Springs Lead Mine and played on their highly regarded semi-pro team.[7] The Baxter Springs Miners a few years later would feature a young outfielder from Commerce, Oklahoma, who could outrun everyone on the team and hit a ball 450 feet: Mickey Mantle.

As World War II loomed on the horizon, the Baxter Mines, in spite of its inherent dangers, was a good place to work: steady pay, a good baseball team, and best of all an exemption from the draft since mining lead was considered critical to the war effort.[8] The Miners had a pitcher named Stan West who played baseball in the Double A International League for Baltimore (then a minor league city) during the summer. West recommended Lollar to the Baltimore club, and they signed him to a contract in 1943. Lollar's hitting turned some heads in 1944 when he had 15 homers and 72 RBI in 126 games, an effort that was a prelude to one of his best years in pro ball. In 1945, Lollar won the International League's MVP award, hitting .364 with 34 home runs and 111 RBI while committing just 13 errors in 139 games. The Indians bought his contract and invited him to spring training in 1945, but manager Lou Boudreau was sold on another young catcher, Jim Hegan, who had spent 1943–1945 in the military. Boudreau preferred Hegan because he was bigger, four years older, and more of a holler guy than Lollar, but told Lollar he would still be on the Indians in 1946 as a back-up. Lollar wanted none of it, asked Boudreau to send him back to the minors so he could play consistently, and resigned himself to his fate when Boudreau refused. Appearing in 28 games for Cleveland in 1946, Lollar had a poor first year in the majors, hitting .241 with one home run and nine RBI. He was traded with infielder Ray Mack to the Yankees for outfielder Hal Peck and two pitchers, Gene Bearden and Al Gettel. Once in New York, Lollar learned that the Yanks had four other skilled catchers on their roster: Gus Niarhos, Charlie Silvera, Aaron Robinson, and future Hall of Famer Yogi Berra. Part of the Yankees' answer to this numbers problem behind the plate was to ship Lollar to the Triple A Newark Bears in the International League. The Yankees called him up for 11 games in 1947 and also kept him on their World Series roster. Although he went 3-for-4 with a single and two doubles during the Series, the Yankees settled on Berra and Niarhos as their primary catchers in 1948, and Lollar, injured for part of the season with a cut on his throwing hand, played in only 22 games.

Finally in December 1948 he left New York, traded to the lowly St. Louis Browns. The Yankees finally realized that Lollar had too much trade value to languish on the bench. He went to St. Louis along with pitchers Red Embree, Dick Starr, and a desperately needed $100,000 for pitcher Fred Sanford and catcher Ray Partee. Lollar, now 24, finally got the break he needed to become a starter, and he proved up to the challenge by hitting .261 with eight homers in 1949 and blossoming into an All-Star in 1950, when he hit .280 with 13 home runs, 64 RBI, 64 walks, and only 25 strikeouts while starting 125 games. His arrival on Chicago's South Side occurred after the eight-player swap between the Browns and the White Sox in November 1951.

The trade meant many things to Lollar. Playing for a team with an established fan base meant a pay raise, and his first White Sox contract for the 1952 season was for $12,000. He was also pleased to join a much better team; the Browns were 52–102 in 1951, while the young, improving Go-Go White Sox were 81–73. Moving to a team with 29 more wins and staying in the starting lineup was the kind of trade players dreamed about. Most importantly, it meant being under the daily tutelage of Sox manager Paul Richards, a great catcher in his time who was considered to be one of the best mentors in the game.

Richards noted a lack of assertiveness in Lollar and often discussed it with him. "Paul told me to show a little more animation. He wanted me to be a little more agile in receiving, and to show more zip in returning the ball to the pitcher," Lollar said in an article by Red Gleason in the *Saturday Evening Post* in 1957. "He recommended that I run to and from the catcher's box between innings, instead of just strolling out there, and had me catch with my left knee on the ground, which moved me up, closer to the plate, and also down, closer to the ground."[9] Richards' tips worked, and coupled with Lollar's consistent hitting success, the Sox were set at the most important position on the field for years to come. He made seven All-Star teams (1950, 1954–1956, 1958–1960) and won the Gold Glove Award three times (1957–1959). While throughout the 1950s he never quite matched Berra's offensive production, many felt the great Yankees backstop could not approach Lollar's skill at handling pitchers. The Sox's pitching staff was proving this to be the case on a daily basis with him behind the plate in 1959.

Lollar continued to contribute when the Sox arrived in Kansas City on Friday, August 14. Besides helping Shaw pitch a complete-game, five-hit victory, he hit two home runs and drove in four runs for an easy 5–1 victory. The team got bad news the following day, however. Billy Pierce's yeoman 16-inning effort nine days earlier in Baltimore left him with a badly strained right hip, and he lasted only 1⅓ innings in a 2–1 loss to the Athletics. A rare base running gaffe by Jim Rivera gave Kansas City the win. Rivera, pinch-running for Lollar on third base with the game tied, missed a suicide squeeze sign from the bench, and when Jim McAnany laid down a perfect bunt, Rivera was out by 30 feet, squandering an opportunity to tie the game.

Much to Jungle Jim's chagrin, his gaffe had a much wider audience than just the 14,497 fans in Municipal Stadium. In response to the pennant fever that was sweeping Chicago, WGN-TV took the rare step of broadcasting the road game back to Chicago. The costly set-up involved a television truck with four cameras beaming the signal back to its Chicago broadcasting towers through a telephone hook-up. Although the technology available at the time made such an arrangement quite costly, the broadcast proved well worth the trouble and expense. In the Chicago area, the game drew a bigger audience that WBBM's *Gunsmoke*, WNBQ's *Cimarron City*, and WBKB's *Story of the Century*. To prove what a draw the 1959 Sox were with younger viewers, the most popular 10:00 p.m. television show in Chicago, *Shock Theatre* (that night showing *The Return of Frankenstein* with Bela Lugosi and Nina Foch) did not have one-tenth the market share that the Sox did.[10]

Dick Donovan came back for his first appearance in 26 days for the Sunday, August 16 finale, but he proved nowhere near ready as the A's took an easy 7–2 victory, whittling the Sox's lead in the American League to three games. Yet in spite of two disappointing losses to Kansas City, the Sox ended a tough road trip 7–5–1 and had scored at least four runs in six of them, a rare feat for this team on the road. Another encouraging sign was that in the games in which there was little offense, the pitching usually came through.

The South Siders returned to Chicago and got good news on their off-day Monday, August 17, when Dr. Joseph Coyle at Mercy Hospital diagnosed Pierce's injury as a strained lumbar muscle and ligament, severe enough to cause an evulsion, with the ligament injury loosening a small piece of bone from his hip, but the condition was not debilitating enough to prevent him from missing more than two starts. Kicking off the 11-game home stand with a 6–4 win over the Orioles, Wynn, McBride, and Staley pitched just well enough to hold the Orioles at bay. The size of the crowd showed that Chicago was catching a case of pennant fever; 34,547 came out for a Tuesday night game against a non-contender. The following day, the Sox once again had trouble hitting Billy O'Dell and lost, 3–1. They also dropped the Ladies' Day Thursday game, 7–6, in a sloppily played contest made worse by the ineffectiveness of Latman, Moore, and the middle of the lineup, which went 0-for-5 with runners in scoring position. Before the finale, Veeck presented skipper Al Lopez with a huge two-layer cake for his 51st birthday, but with the Sox's poor play and Cleveland winning to move just 2½ games behind, the Sox's skipper was in no mood to celebrate.

The celebrations, however, did not end on Thursday. Veeck and Comiskey decreed Friday night, August 21, to be "Nellie Fox Night." It was commonplace for teams in the 1940s and 1950s to have a "day" or "night" for a star player, and these fetes were usually highlighted by a rather garish showering of gifts on the individual. On this date, David Condon wrote in the *Chicago Tribune:* "Fox is assured of recognition as an immortal because, game in and game out since 1950, he has delivered more than Nature intended him to deliver. Nellie Fox has made himself a great ballplayer. Fox has a better batting eye than anyone in baseball, according to Rogers Hornsby … and Fox is the little lion with the heart of an elephant."[12]

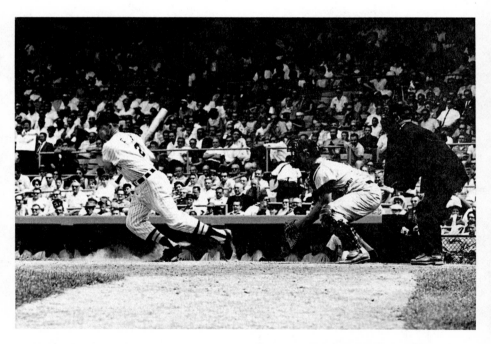

The legendary Nellie Fox, with his trademark bottle bat and bulging tobacco cheek, was one of the toughest outs in the history of the game. The Hall of Famer's diminutive size betrayed a fierce competitiveness and intense determination few players in the history of the game ever matched.

The gifts ranged from the useful (a $7,500 Cadillac sedan, a $2,200 Vauxhall station wagon and $70 worth of cigars) to the absurd ($250 worth of S&H Green stamps). His teammates chipped in and gave him an automatic shotgun. None other than Sox Fan #1, Mayor Richard J. Daley, opened the ceremony with a statement of adulation and praise. Once the game started, Chuck Stobbs, the Senators' flinty starting pitcher, had something for Fox as well. It was a first pitch fastball that he rudely planted right on Fox's diminutive derriere, causing the crowd of 37,986 to roar its disapproval. For what little he did at the plate on his special night (no hits in three at-bats after being hit), the diminutive second baseman may have been better off swinging his new shotgun at the pitches, but he was picked up nicely by Phillips and McAnany, who combined for five hits as the Sox won another one-run game, 5–4. Latman and Russ Kemmerer matched up in a classic pitching duel the following Saturday, with Latman shutting out the powerful Senators, 1–0. They won it in typical White Sox fashion. Lollar, the slowest man on the team, singled, stole second, and scooted to third when the rattled Kemmerer's next offering was a wild pitch. Lollar jogged home with the only run of the game on Phillips' timely single. With the Senators on their way out of town, the Sox girded themselves for a visit from the Bronx Bombers.

The biggest sporting event in Chicago in the 1950s was a doubleheader between the Sox and the Yankees, and the largest crowd of the season to date, 44,520, came to Comiskey Park August 23 for a Sunday twin-bill against the third-place New Yorkers. Game one featured Wynn against Art Ditmar, and Elston Howard broke it open with his 20th homer of the season in the fifth inning. Lopez stayed with Wynn through seven innings, and Gerry Staley pitched the eighth. The Sox three-run deficit became seven runs after eight innings, as Staley gave up four runs in one of his poorer outings of the year. Young Ken McBride mopped up in the ninth, allowing no runs: final score Yankees 7, Sox 1. The Sox managed four total bases off Ditmar, a double by Fox and singles by Battey and Cash. Adding to the disappointment and tension, the big Chesterfield scoreboard in center field flashed Cleveland's 1–0 win over the Red Sox before the conclusion of the game.

Shaw took the mound in game two and saved the day. He scattered six hits in a complete-game shutout, 5–0. Lollar's 19th homer of the year off Ralph Terry got things going in the right direction for the South Siders. Shaw's record was now a surprising 13–4, and he picked a great time to excel, as Cleveland swept the Red Sox in a doubleheader. A make-up game with the Yankees on Monday ended the series, and Lopez went deep into the rotation, giving Moore another start. Moore handcuffed the Yankees for six innings, and the Sox won, 4–2, as Cash and Landis combined for five hits. The team realized what an important game this was to win. They gained a half-game on the idle Indians, moving two games ahead in the standings. Even more importantly, the loss left the Yankees 13½ games behind with only 30 left to play. Sox loyalists took this as a good omen, since the last time a Sox team was 13½ games ahead of the Yankees was August 24, 1919, when they won their last pennant. Moore's effective pitching was another shovel of clay on top of New York's already closed pennant coffin.

Stengel could not leave Chicago without taking a swipe at the White Sox organization. He whined about the preparation of Comiskey Park's infield, saying that the grounds crew "packs the base paths hard but keeps [the] back part soft. They had it fixed so their runners could run and they also had it fixed so that ground balls we hit would slow down enough for them to grab 'em near the grass and throw us out."[13] An unnamed Yankees starter also took a swipe at Sox fans, saying, "Look what happens after a double header [at Comiskey Park]. They have a police lieutenant with a big night stick accompany Casey Stengel across the field so none of those lunatics don't get at him."[14] The reality was that Stengel had known Acting Police Captain John L. Sullivan of the nearby Deering Steet Station for years, and was thankful for the courtesies the Chicago Police extended him whenever the Yankees were in town.

Before the Sox ended the month with a four-game series in Cleveland—that now looked to be the biggest series of the decade—the woebegone, seventh-place Red Sox came to Chicago. The novelty of playing for new manager Billy Jurges had worn off, and Boston came in with a record of 57–68. While Jackie Jensen, Frank Malzone, and Pete Runnels were having good seasons at the plate, Ted Williams' demise continued. Hitting just .235, he was often platooned with Gene Stephens. If the Red Sox had a bright spot at this point, it was the play of their pioneering black second baseman, Pumpsie Green, who had debuted against the White Sox in July. Under Jurges' tutelage, Green fit in at second base very capably and came to Chicago hitting .308. The Sox took two out of three from the Bostonians, winning Tuesday, August 25, 5–4, on the strength of Goodman's clutch, two-out double in the bottom of the ninth. After dropping the second game by one run, they earned their seventh victory of the 11-game home stand when Latman dominated the apathetic Bostonians, 4–1.

The only loss in the series occurred on "Al Smith Night," one of the more novel promotions in Veeck's repertoire. Sox fans had never warmed up to Smith for a variety of reasons, and by 1959 they rode him so ruthlessly that he forbade his family from coming to home games. Veeck announced that anyone with the name Smith, Smythe, Smithe, Schmidt, or any close derivative would be allowed in the park for free and directed to sit behind their namesake in the left field stands. They also received buttons declaring "I'm a Smith & We're All for Al." To raise the luckless outfielder's spirits, Veeck told him that the $2,500 pay cut he took at the start of the season would be given back to him and made a promise of more bonuses in the future. Unfortunately Smith did not distinguish himself on his special night. He went 1-for-4 with a strikeout and a miscue in the field that led to Boston's winning run.

Smith's failure to produce while in the limelight was completely overshadowed by Veeck's biggest personnel move to date. During the series against Boston, he finally landed what he had been coveting all season—a power hitter. The Pittsburgh Pirates put Ted Kluszewski on waivers, and Veeck immediately claimed him, sending minor leaguer Bobby Sagers and the clutch-hitting Harry Simpson to the Pirates. Veeck was ecstatic. He felt that the presence of a veteran power bat like Kluszewski's would immediately result in more runs from the middle of the lineup, and that opposing hurlers had no choice but give Landis, Lollar and Phillips better pitches to hit. Not everyone, however, embraced the Big Klu-for-Simpson deal with open arms.

Al Smith came to the White Sox with Early Wynn in the controversial trade that sent local hero Minnie Minoso to Cleveland. Smith's torrid pace at the plate in July was a big factor in the team winning the 1959 AL pennant.

The 35-year-old Simpson left Chicago hitting only .187 in 84 games, but it was undoubtedly the most productive .187 in the team's history. Simpson had five game-winning hits in only 75 at-bats, including a season-changing grand slam against the Yankees. He was a smart, effective base runner on a team that relied on speed, and also a very capable outfielder. No one could possibly criticize Kluszewski's credentials, but he had never been in a pennant race, and now—with only five weeks left in the season—would be facing pitchers he had never seen. The 34-year-old Kluszewski, however, was exactly what Veeck had been lusting for. Suddenly the sting Veeck felt from not being able to pay a half-million for Roy Sievers two months earlier did not hurt so much.

Theodore Bernard Kluszewski was born September 10, 1924, in Argo, Illinois, an industrial town southwest of Chicago, where his father was a factory worker. By the late 1930s, Kluszewski was an athletic legend on Chicago's South Side, gaining fame for his football abilities and scoring 30 points in a high school basketball game. Kluszewski was modest about his accomplishments and used to joke that he was the "runt" of the family litter, with siblings even bigger than he was. Since Ted was 6'2", 235 pounds, with 18" biceps, the press never knew if he was kidding, but never had the nerve to ask. Kluszewski got a scholarship to Indiana University to play football and led the Hoosiers to their only undefeated Big Ten season in 1945, starting at fullback and often playing both ways in a 9–0–1 season. His catch in the end zone against Purdue sealed a Big Ten title for the Hoosiers. Kluszewski also played baseball at Indiana, where in 1945 the Cincinnati Reds held their spring training.[14] The Reds took note of the big, multi-sport letterman and invited him to work out with them. Liking what they saw, they immediately offered him a princely $15,000 signing bonus at a time when the average major league salary was $5,000. In his first year in organized ball, the young slugger hit .352, winning the batting title in the Sally (South Atlantic) League, playing for Columbia. Promoted to the Memphis Chicks in the tougher Southern Association in 1947, Kluszewski toyed with Double A pitching, hitting .377, and the Reds called him up for nine games in September. His first full season followed, and in 113 games he hit .274 with 13 home runs. The Reds knew they had their first baseman for the next decade.[15]

Kluszewski quickly became one of the most feared hitters in the majors, hitting 136 homers and driving in 362 runs from 1953 to 1955. He hit over 40 homers each of those seasons, joining the rarefied company of Babe Ruth, Jimmie Foxx, and his contemporary Eddie Mathews as the only players in history to do so. From 1952 through 1956, he had more home runs (187) than strikeouts (168), an uncanny accomplishment for a power hitter.[16] A back injury limited his home run total to 35 in 1956, and the Reds dealt him to Pittsburgh for Dee Fondy in December 1957. He never found his stroke in Pittsburgh, hitting only four homers in 100 games in 1958 while being platooned with young Dick "Dr. Strangeglove" Stuart.[17] So the big question regarding the acquisition of this local legend was which Big Klu did the White Sox get—the one who once was of the most productive power hitters in history, or the one who had 12 homers over the past two and a half seasons.

Kluszewski unsuccessfully pinch-hit in the first two games against Boston, which the Sox split, but started at first base in the rubber game and went 2-for-4, helping Latman to an easy 5–1 victory. After that win, the team immediately left for Cleveland, ahead of their weekend hosts by only 1½ games. Momentum was clearly with the Indians. Throughout the season, Cleveland's starting pitching had been almost as good as the Sox, but their bullpen was more erratic. They did not have the team speed the Sox possessed, but with Francona, Held, Minoso, and Piersall, they were not exactly clogging the base paths, and were also a very capable defensive team. The Indians' clear advantage over the Sox was at the plate. After 127 games, they had 146 home runs, nearly double the Sox total of 77. Colavito had 38 and Held had 24 of those, while Francona was hitting .375. With Minoso and Power hovering around their usual .300 clip, the White Sox pitching staff would be sorely tested.

The Sox looked to take any edge they could in this critical series. The *Chicago Tribune* reported that Emil Bossard, the Indians' head groundskeeper, boasted that the Chicagoans would not steal a base all weekend. A columnist asked him how he could possibly soak down the base paths in Municipal Stadium any further; his cryptic reply: "That's my secret."[18] When the first pitch was thrown by Mudcat Grant to open the series Friday night, few realized that the South Siders' 40 years of frustration and futility would vanish in less than 48 hours. The Sox did the impossible, fulfilling the wish everyone had but did not dare mention; they swept the Indians, 7–3, 2–0, 6–3, and 9–4. In front of a crowd of 70,398, Lollar hit his 20th home run to break a 3–3 tie, allowing Shaw to register the critical first game as a win, 7–3. The baseball gods were smiling on the Sox during Lollar's long blast to center. The ball actually hit Minnie Minoso's glove and bounced over the fence.

McBride was scheduled to start the Saturday afternoon affair but reported to the locker room with tonsillitis. Lopez conferred

Big Ted Kluszewski. Kluszewski was a sensational three-sport athlete at south Chicago's Argo-Summit High School and went on to gridiron greatness at Indiana University. He is one of the few sluggers in history to hit 40 home runs three straight seasons, and the only one to strike out less often than homering while doing so.

with pitching coach Ray Berres and reluctantly sent Donovan, erratic and injured most of the year, to the mound, hoping for the best. The big right-hander rose to the occasion with his best showing of 1959, a complete-game, five-hit masterpiece. With the Sox now up by 3½ games, the Indians' hope of drawing 75,000+ for the doubleheader on Sunday was dashed. Nevertheless, 66,586 came out and sadly witnessed Wynn quietly outpitch McLish, 6–3, and those who stayed around for game two saw the Sox swing some rare heavy lumber in an easy 9–4 win for Latman.

The weekend could not have gone more perfectly for the Chicagoans. The Indians had the lead only once the entire weekend, after the bottom of the fifth in the first game of the doubleheader. The Indians, now 5½ games out of first with 24 left to play, would have to go 18–6, with the Sox playing at a mediocre .500 clip, to have even a puncher's chance of catching up. If there was any consolation for the Indians, it came from the fact that baseball was alive and well on Lake Erie in a great, proud city that just one year before listened to sad rumors about losing their beloved team to Minnesota. Over the three days, the Indians drew 165,091, an incredible weekend gate for any era. Their attendance was vastly improved over 1958, with this weekend accounting for almost 12 percent of their total draw for the season.

After going 20–7 in July, the South Siders played .700 ball for the second consecutive month, posting a 21–9 for August. Just as the last time the Yankees were 13½ out and the Sox won the pennant, the last time they played over .700 ball in two successive months was August and September 1917, a month before they won their last World Series. The only American League standings that mattered in Chicago:

Chicago 80–49 .620
Cleveland 75–55 .577 5½ GB

Without admitting it, Sox loyalists at this point were also interested at peeking at the pecking order in the Senior Circuit, daydreaming about whom their heroes might get to play in October:

San Francisco 73–57 .562
Los Angeles 71–59 .546 2 GB
Milwaukee 70–60 .538 3 GB

8

September: Forty Years, but Worth the Wait

When Al Lopez turned the calendar in his office to September, he noticed that the season would be over in a mere 27 days. The White Sox had 25 games left and the Indians had 24. Aside from being 5½ games behind, Cleveland also had one less game to play. The White Sox's record was 80 wins, 49 defeats, and two ties. If the teams ended the season tied for first, the Indians could only hope the league would have the Sox finish those two non-decisions. Chicago had 13 home games and 12 road games; Cleveland had only eight home games and 16 road games. This was not as big an advantage for the Chicagoans as it seemed, since Cleveland's road record was an excellent 37–24. Both teams were scheduled to play all seven of their American League foes. The Sox were happy they would play each other only four times, with three of the contests at Comiskey Park. Entering September, their lead was more than the number of games left against the Indians, a big advantage for the South Siders.

Although worn out on their travel day of Monday, August 31, the Sox were thrilled to see a crowd of about 10,000 greet them at Midway Airport when they arrived after their triumphant weekend in Cleveland. On Tuesday night, September 1, a crowd of 27,218 left Comiskey Park wondering if a 5½-game bulge would be enough, after seeing the White Sox do their hitless wonder imitation and lose, 4–0, to the Tigers. Shaw pitched well but got no offensive support, while the Tigers' Jim Bunning only allowed a single by Aparicio and two by Kluszeski. However, as if to prove Tuesday night was an aberration, the White Sox took both ends of the doubleheader on Wednesday, September 2, whipping the Tigers, 7–2 and 11–4. Donovan was brilliant in the first game, and in the fifth inning of game two, the Sox scored 11 runs when two were out. With Kansas City falling meekly at Cleveland, 6–3, the White Sox were back to a 5½-game lead and had all day Thursday, September

3, to rest up for the weekend. Coming up was one of the biggest series of the year: a Labor Day weekend at 35th and Shields against the Indians.

Frank Lane, the Indians' general manager, blew into town full of his usual bluster and enjoying every opportunity he had to provide his unique fodder for the press. In practically the same breath, he said that if they did finish first, "the White Sox will be the worst team ever to win a pennant,"[1] but in a less bitter vein pointed out that Luis Aparicio and Willie Mays were the only two individuals in the Major Leagues worth $1,000,000 on the trading market. The veteran baseball executive then got serious about the pennant race. He said that over the season, Nellie Fox was the most valuable of all the Sox, but that as the season progressed Jim Landis proved to be equally irreplaceable. He also admitted to some ambivalent feelings regarding the White Sox's success, since he, Chuck Comiskey and John Rigney were the architects of this amazing team, while his current creation was still nipping at the Sox's heels in the race. Lane's last comment to the media was that the Indians needed a weekend sweep if they were to have any chance of overtaking the Chicagoans by the end of September.[2]

While the Indians and Sox got ready for their big series, baseball executives from around the country gathered four miles north of Comiskey Park in downtown Chicago's Conrad Hilton Hotel to plan for the upcoming World Series. Executives from the White Sox, Indians, Yankees, Orioles, and Tigers were present, along with representatives from four National League teams, the Giants, Dodgers, Braves, and Pirates. The San Francisco Giants contingent announced that if the Giants, National League leaders at the time, won the pennant, the World Series games would be held in the new Candlestick Park instead of Seals Stadium. Commissioner Ford Frick slated Wednesday, September 30, as the opening date for the 1959 World Series. If Milwaukee and Chicago were the contestants, the Series would be scheduled in seven consecutive days, due to their close proximity. If either Los Angeles or San Francisco was the National League entry, open dates for travel would be scheduled when the teams moved from one city to another. Frick also added that sometime in early September, teams would be instructed to print tickets, with the costs covered by the league office.[3]

Most people expected the huge weekend series to be the curtain call for the challengers from Ohio. A surprise returnee for the Indians was second baseman Billy Martin, back in the lineup earlier than expected after being hospitalized for multiple facial fractures from his beaning at the hands of Tex Clevenger. Martin was not expected to see much action and would wear a football helmet with a face mask when he batted. As the series began, the White Sox's magic number was now only 18, with 22 games left to play.

Jim Landis, Sherm Lollar, Al Smith and Early Wynn were responsible for the Sox win in the critical first game Friday night in front of 45,510 boisterous Sox fans. Wynn held his old team in check for eight innings, yielding only one run while the Sox held a precarious 2–1 lead. With two out in the eighth, Minnie Minoso doubled to right center and Tito Francona followed with a single to left. Al Smith charged the ball, grabbed it on a high bounce, and fired a missile to Sherm Lollar. Lollar dove at Minoso, and home plate umpire Frank Umont called him out, sending Minoso into a rage. Jimmy Piersall, who had been bench jockeying Umont from the Cleveland dugout throughout the game, also came out to argue. Umont immediately threw Piersall out of the game. The huge crowd got more excitement and satisfaction than they expected for one night, but the good feelings did not last long; the White Sox's 6½-game lead diminished to 4½ games less than 48 hours later. Cal McLish and Mudcat Grant both won one-run decisions on Saturday and Sunday, 6–5 and 2–1. Over 106,000 fans saw the series, the largest draw for a three-game set in Comiskey Park's history. Many of them noted the performance of the guy that "got away," ex–Sox Tito Francona. His three RBI were the difference in Saturday's matchup, and he went 6-for-8 in the last two games.

Lane gloated about the weekend results. He also flippantly made fun of the trade the White Sox made with the Pittsburgh Pirates, proclaiming that "I'd much rather pitch to Kluszewski than Simpson any day."[4] Indians coach Jo-Jo White jumped in and teased the Chicagoans through the media, saying, "don't print those damn World Series tickets too soon."[5] A more reserved Joe Gordon, the Indians' manager, told the press that he hoped to be only 2½ games out by the next night, since they had a doubleheader in Cleveland against Detroit and the White Sox would entertain Kansas City in a twin bill at the same time.[6]

In Monday's contests, Gordon did not get his wish, and Sox fans settled for the status quo, as the Indians took two from the Tigers and the Sox swept their twin bill from the Athletics. Billy Pierce put some anxieties to rest with his best outing since the marathon game in Baltimore in game one, and center fielder Jim Landis contributed in both contests with three singles, two doubles, and a triple. Landis' hitting had become exceptional in the last two weeks, and one reason was the new thumper who followed him in the lineup and batted fourth, Ted Kluszewski. American League pitchers, unfamiliar with Kluszewski's weaknesses but intimidated by his power and reputation, were giving Landis much better pitches to hit. Coach Don Gutteridge commented on the young center fielder: "Day after day he catches balls and makes them look easy. We hit the same things against other teams and they fall in for hits. But he's such a quiet guy, and goes about his business without making a disturbance, that nobody pays attention. You talk about your most valuable players—he's it!"[7] Manager Al Lopez echoed Gutteridge's sentiments, exclaiming, "He can go farther than any other center fielder in the league. If the ball stays in the air he'll catch up with it. He takes the extra base by himself, too, on plays where the coach can't help you."[8]

Lopez himself received some well-deserved accolades from none other than Leo Durocher, the NBC "Game of the Week" broadcaster, when he said about the Sox skipper,

> He's not going to lose. Not this guy, Al Lopez. This is a different team than the [1951] Dodgers. The Sox are tough right down the middle—catcher, pitcher, infield, and outfield. They have good defense, pitching, and speed. You can win with two things you need, and the Sox have three. If they had the fourth—power hitting—this would be strictly no contest. They'd be 20 games in front. And Lopez is one of the great managers of all time. He's never finished worse than second.[9]

The nine-game home stand ended Tuesday night, September 8, as the biggest crowd since June 11, 1957, saw a 3–2, ten-inning victory over the Athletics, giving the White Sox a three-game sweep. Wynn pitched the entire game for his 19th victory, putting the South Siders five games ahead of the idle Indians. The total ticket count of 46,598 included 28,238 paying customers and 18,360 Ladies' Night guests. The huge crowd boosted the Sox's season attendance to 1,340,439, breaking the previous record of 1,328,234 in 1951.

While Commissioner Frick earlier in the day gave the White Sox, Indians, Braves, Dodgers, and Giants permission to start printing World Series tickets at their Leagues' expense, the White Sox issued a statement saying that they would delay doing so. The front office gave three reasons: they had not picked out a design, did not yet know what to charge, and had not yet established an equitable distribution plan.[10]

Nine games in eight days on the road followed, with stops at Washington, Baltimore, Boston, and New York. During this same stretch, Cleveland traveled east as well, with ten games over the same eight days, against the same rivals. The Sox had to like their chances of surviving this trip still in command of the American League. If they had their worst road trip of the season and went 2–7, Cleveland would still have to go 8–2 to tie them for first.

Major League rosters expanded from 25 to 40 on September 1, and the Sox had six new faces in the dugout on Thursday, September 10. Outfielders Johnny Callison and Joe Hicks, first baseman Ron Jackson, catcher Cam Carreon, infielder J. C. Martin, and pitcher Gary Peters would finish out the season but be ineligible for the World Series. Lopez did make a post-season roster move by declaring that Ken McBride, whose effective appearances in August were cut short when he was sidelined by tonsillitis on August 23, was well enough to return and contribute. Lopez reconsidered McBride when he learned that September 1 call-up Joe Stanka, whom he intended to put on the World Series roster, had a nagging groin injury. The Sox also revealed that Chuck Comiskey's tumultuous year had now affected his health. Between the legal in-fighting and the tense pennant race, he suffered a severe ulcer attack the last weekend in August, cancelling his plans to accompany the squad on this road trip.

On Wednesday, September 9, the Indians wasted no time going to work, taking both ends of a doubleheader against the Orioles, 3–2 and 4–1, behind stellar pitching by Jack Harshman and Jim Perry. Luckily, Shaw came through just as effectively for the Sox against the Senators, earning his 15th win with a complete-game, 5–1 victory. A typical Sox rally in the top of the seventh inning sealed the win when Kluszewski walked, Goodman reached on an error, Smith, Rivera, and Shaw singled, and Aparicio lofted a sacrifice fly, giving the Sox four runs on three total bases. But their lead was whittled down to 4½ games. It remained there at nightfall on Thursday, September 10, after Hoyt Wilhelm and the Orioles rebounded to beat the Tribe, 6–1, and Camilo Pascual dominated the White Sox, 8–2. After the game, the Sox announced their World Series roster, and one name conspicuous by its absence was Callison's. Jim McAnany, whose extraordinary hitting in July and timely contributions in August betrayed his status as a rookie call-up from Indianapolis, was placed on the roster at Callison's expense. Other than McAnany, Cash, McBride and Romano were the only other newcomers included in the post-season plans.

On Thursday, September 11, the biggest event of the year occurred for seven members of the White Sox before they even got to Griffith Stadium. Representative John Kluczynski, a 63-year-old Democrat who represented Illinois' Fifth Congressional District, gave a luncheon in the Nation's Capital to honor the Sox. Coach Don Gutteridge and seven players were present, along with Vice President Richard M. Nixon. Never one to miss a photo opportunity, Nixon posed with Rep. Kluczynski, Turk Lown, Bob Shaw, and Billy Pierce for a photograph that the *Associated Press* disseminated throughout the country. A common folk legend about this event is that the vice president, known for mixing up names, appeared because he thought the Democratic congressman from Illinois was related to a famous White Sox first baseman, perhaps thinking that all Polish names were alike. He did offer a brief speech before the festivities adjourned: "Let's set the record straight," he said, in his best Nixonian bluster. "When you're playing Washington, I'm for Washington. While being for Washington is like being for the underdog, when I go to see them, they win. They've won the last five times I've seen them. I was invited to go tonight, but I've been thinking it over. After meeting all you nice fellows and listening to your plans for spending your World Series money, I can't bring myself to do it. I'm going to stay home tonight."

As it turned out, by staying home with Pat, Checkers, Tricia and Julie that evening, Nixon did not do the White Sox any favors after all. Pascual fanned ten batters, Donovan could not get through the fourth inning, and three Senators hit home runs for an 8–2 rout. Over the 1959 season, Pascual, who had been perfecting his slow curve and change-up to go along with an already good fastball, had developed into one of the best starters in the American League. One of the Senators' round-trippers was Harmon Killebrew's 40th, tying him with Rocky Colativo and Ernie Banks for the most in the majors. The game also featured the debuts of J. C. Martin, who pinch-hit for Turk Lown in the eighth inning, and Gary Peters. Peters flashed a little of his future brilliance by striking out baseball's Mr. Paradox, Billy Consolo. With the loss, the Sox reduced the magic number to 11, since Baltimore, the South Siders' next opponent, drubbed the Indians, 6–1.

Friday, September 11, turned out to be one of the most disappointing and damaging nights of the season. Looking like the team that every true Sox fan worried about in June, they were shut out for 25 innings and lost both ends of a doubleheader, 3–0 and 1–0, the second game taking 16 innings. With the Indians losing in Washington, the Sox lost a big chance to distance themselves further from the Tribe. Worse, the extra seven innings of the second game had the effect of making the day's events almost a tripleheader, with more wear and tear on position players and pitchers alike.

Pierce threw eight innings of very good baseball in the first game but took the loss because his teammates hit .111 (3-for-27) against Jack Fisher. In the 16-inning affair, they hit .118 (6-for-51) against Jerry Walker, who pitched all 16 innings. In game two, Latman had perhaps his best outing of the year, a 9⅓-inning effort in which he gave up only five hits, which went completely to waste. Jerry Staley logged the last 6⅓ innings and was the hard-luck loser.

After the game, an exhausted Nellie Fox let his hair down with the press, declaring that "we have to get through the Baltimore series to win the pennant; the Orioles and Athletics have been giving us the most trouble, not Cleveland."[11] Fox praised the Orioles' manager, Paul Richards, by saying Richards "did more for me than anyone in baseball. He changed me to using a heavy bat and I bunted .313 with it," he joked. One reason Fox felt the Sox had limited success against the Orioles was because several players, including himself, played for Richards when he managed the Sox and they "try too hard to beat him." Fox pointed out that he was not concerned about the team's chances and credited Aparicio, Landis, and manager Al Lopez for keeping the team in first place, explaining to the press, "Aparicio has made me a better player, [and] Landis is the best defensive outfielder in the league. Our defense is set up real good with Pierce and Donovan back in shape. Lopez has to get a lot of credit for holding together a club that was supposed to finish far down in the standings."[12]

Early Wynn won his 20th game of the season the next day, a complete-game seven-hitter, as the dormant White Sox bats awoke for ten hits and an easy 6–1 victory. Adding to the excitement in the victory was Jim Landis' theft of home in the eighth inning. Even though the Indians shut down the

"Little Looie" Aparicio, the Magician of Maricaibo, shown stealing second, beating Pumpsie Green's tag. His ballet-like gracefulness redefined the shortstop position, and his uncanny knack at stealing bases made him one of the best table-setters of all time. Aparicio was the first Venezuelan voted into baseball's Hall of Fame.

Senators 7–2, on Gary Bell's three-hitter, the magic number was now in single digits at nine. Cleveland had 13 games remaining, eight away—three in New York, two in Boston and three in Kansas City—and five at home. At home, they had one game against the Sox and four against Kansas City to end the season. The Sox had 11 games left, three at home and eight on the road. The home dates were with Detroit. Two road contests in both Boston and New York, one game in Cleveland, and three in Detroit would close out the season. Cleveland's slim pennant hopes hinged on Sunday, September 13, when they would be in Yankee Stadium for a doubleheader.

At the same time, Bill Veeck disclosed the team's plans for World Series tickets while speaking at an Executive Club meeting at the Sherman Hotel. Veeck announced that instead of selling the tickets in the customary four-game package, the tickets would be sold one game at a time. Season ticket holders and what he referred to as "old time White Sox fans" would get first crack. "We've been combing the stands recently in search of old timers who regularly attended Sox games. These loyal fans will be given first crack at tickets just as if they were season ticket holders," Veeck explained. He pointed out that the ticket office conducted a study of where the heaviest ticket orders originated throughout the season, and that this study determined the allocation of World Series tickets by area.[13]

Sixty percent of all World Series tickets would be sold in Chicago, with two-thirds of them allocated for the South Side. A group vaguely described as "out of towners" would get 20 percent, and the remaining amount (12.4 percent) would be evenly divided between the south, west, and northern suburbs. As the ticket requests arrived at the Comiskey Park office, they were divided into bins according to the return address. Veeck's vow to be impartial was such that he set up a committee of ten prominent Chicago area executives, socialites, and prominent White Sox fans to make the actual ticket selections. The membership of the selection group was varied. It included Ben Amsterdam, a retired CTA streetcar conductor who had been a White Sox fan since 1908; Joseph Hardy, president of the Ryerson Steel Corporation; and John I. Kirkpatrick, the vice chancellor of the University of Chicago.[14]

The Chicago newspapers also carried a large advertisement in their main sections on how non-season ticket holders could order the tickets. Each application was good for only one game, and no order could be made for more than two tickets. The front office explained that these policies were set so "as many White Sox fans as possible can see the World Series." Prices were $14.40 per set of two reserved grandstand seats and $20.60 per set of two box seats. To stave off any disappointments and misunderstandings that might occur, the front office ended the advertisement with the following:

> IMPORTANT NOTE! If we receive more orders than we have tickets available … orders will be drawn by lot—NOT on a first-come-first-served basis. No orders will be processed before the deadline and every properly executed order will have an equal chance to be filled.[15]

The front office took pains to be sensitive to the fact that more than most other teams, the Sox were a team of the common man. Sox brass were also trying to be sensitive to the great significance a World Series on the South Side of Chicago, after a 40-year absence, really was.

During the 1950s, the number of Sundays in September that the South Side faithful would be cheering for the Yankees were few and far between, but September 13, 1959, was one of them. The Yankees pulled through in a most appreciated way, knocking off the Indians in a doubleheader, 2–1 and 1–0, while Bob Shaw bettered his record to 16–6 by beating the Boston Red Sox, 3–1, with some stellar relief help from Billy Pierce (called in to put down the left-handed duo of Gary Geiger and Pete Runnels) and Turk Lown. Billy Goodman, whose finest years in professional baseball occurred in Fenway Park, made sure the 26,720 fans in attendance did not forget him by getting his biggest hit of the season, his first home run in two years, with two out and Jim Landis on base in the fourth inning. Sunday, September 13, was also State of Maine Day at Fenway Park, as the Red Sox honored Massachusetts' neighbor to the north. Part of the commemoration on this pre–PETA date was a bear cub awarded to the first player on either team who hit a home run. That honor, of course, went to the improbable Goodman, and after the game Al Lopez, coach Johnny Cooney, and Goodman were photographed feeding a bottle of milk to the three-foot-tall bruin in the dugout. In the locker room after the game, Goodman was relieved that the White Sox had made arrangements with the Boston Zoo to take his gift. The Sox, however, were even more relieved when they read about the Yankees' exploits that same afternoon.

The first game in the Indians' most disappointing Sunday in many years ended when Mickey Mantle hit a walk-off home run with Tony Kubek on first base in the 11th inning, victimizing a brilliant but tiring Jack Harshman and wiping out a 1–0 Cleveland lead. Cleveland managed nine hits off Bob Turley but left 12 men on base in their most critical game of the season. It was fitting that Mantle hit the game-winning home run but rather unusual that it would occur under these circumstances, since the Yankees' future Hall of Famer batted only .133 off Harshman during his entire career. The second contest was even more disappointing for the still game but emotionally crushed Indians, a 1–0 defeat. Duke Maas beat Jim Perry when Hank Bauer drove in Yogi Berra with a weakly hit ground ball. Whatever respect any Chicagoans felt toward the Indians' valiant efforts paled in comparison to the excitement over the Sox's magic number being trimmed to six games. Donovan could not lower it the next night when the Red Sox roughed him up, 9–3, while the Indians salvaged their final game in the Bronx. After the game, the Sox travelled south to visit the Yankees while the glum Indians moved on to Boston.

After swapping opponents, the two contenders ended up with different results; Boston shut out the Indians, 1–0, and Billy Pierce beat the Yankees, allowing three hits in seven innings. When Pierce's back weakened, Shaw handled the last two innings and saved the win. Sherm Lollar hit a game-tying single in the eighth, and Rivera's sacrifice fly scored Earl Torgeson with the lead run. Mickey Mantle reached both Pierce and Shaw for home runs. Batting right-handed, the incomparable slugger hit his 30th round-tripper of the year off Pierce in the first inning. In the ninth, while batting left-handed with Shaw on the mound, he hit his 31st. In spite of Mantle's performance, no outfielder on either team factored as much in the victory as the Sox's Rivera. His dipped-glove catch of Hector Lopez's frozen rope in right field started a game-ending double play, which saved the game. The popular veteran always seemed to save his best performances for biggest contests. The next day, the Sox lost and Cleveland won. Yankees manager Casey Stengel, having had a week's worth of contests against the two remaining contenders for the American League crown, was asked what he thought of the teams. "I know which team I'd rather be on," he said diplomatically. Not mentioning any team by name, he nodded toward the visitors' dugout, just recently vacated by the Chicagoans, and added, "That group, over there, that is a great team."

Both Chicago and Cleveland enjoyed a rare late-season day off on Thursday, September 17. The White Sox were on their way back home for the season's final three games at Comiskey Park, while the Indians trudged on to Kansas City. The magic number was down to three, and Chicago's lead expanded to 5½ games. While optimistic Sox fans were hoping that the Sox could clinch by Sunday, it would take a sweep of the Detroit series to clinch the flag at home, and they expected little help from the eighth-place Athletics, Cleveland's next opponent. The A's had been mailing it in since the end of August. As they prepared to entertain the Indians on Friday, September 18, Kansas City was 4–12 in September.

Throughout Chicago, the entire city was caught up in the delirium of a Chicago World Series, for the first time in 14 years, becoming a likelihood instead of a pipe dream. South Sider Clarence Lyle changed the flags on his Oklahoma Petroleum Company service station to white athletic sox, each one being size 11, in honor of his favorite shortstop. He also played with the company slogan, "Put a Tiger in Your Tank!" by posting a sign that said "Not a Tiger but an Aparicio—GO GO GO!" Not to be outdone, the aldermen in the Chicago City Council passed a resolution changing the name of 35th Street from Wentworth Avenue west to Halsted Street to "White Sox Pennant Pathway" from September 16 until the Sox clinched the pennant. The decree ended with the following: "Be it further resolved, that bells ring, whistles blow, bands play, and general joy be unconfined when the coveted pennant has been won by the heroes of 35th Street, the Chicago White Sox."[16]

Apparently not knowing when a good thing should end, 37th Ward Alderman Paul T. Corcoran got carried away with all the excitement and proposed an amendment to the resolution renaming Addison Street "7th Place." This thinly veiled jab at the consistently also-ran Cubs was wisely rejected by the rest of the City Council.[17]

WGN Television announced that if the White Sox won the pennant, Chicagoans would have two television networks to choose from to watch the Series. As the local carrier for White Sox games during the season, they would also broadcast the Fall Classic, and do so in color. The other outlet was WNBQ, the Chicago outlet for NBC Television, which had the contract to televise the World Series nationally.

The White Sox also disclosed their plans for Comiskey Park's first World Series in 40 years. There would be no on-street parking allowed anywhere near 35th and Shields. Wentworth Avenue between 32nd and 39th streets, previously demolished as part of the Dan Ryan Expressway project which was under construction at that time, would be available for parking, and the Sox organization exhorted the owners of the property along that stretch to keep the parking rates at one dollar per vehicle. The team contracted for the services of additional Andy Frain ushers and added 500 vendors, 25 women's rest room matrons, 25 ballpark courtesy patrollers, 15 tradesmen, 15 grounds crew members, and 20 full-time cleanup men. The Sox indicated that they also spent $23,000 for three new washrooms and for renovations in all existing ones. In spite of the loss of revenue, the small section of 750 bleacher seats the team roped off at the beginning of the season would remain closed. Since virtually everybody coming to the game would have a ticket in hand prior to their arrival, the front office expected the pre-game crowd outside the park to be orderly and manageable. The only tickets available for sale at the park would be the 1,248 bleacher seats, and the ticket sales department knew individuals would be cueing up many hours before game time—probably lining up the night before—to purchase them. Consequently, they would be sold out long before the contest would begin.

While they had been out of practice for post-season duty since 1945, the Chicago Police Department was also well prepared for the Fall Classic. Aside from a special detail from the Deering Street Station outside the park, 100 uniformed policemen and 25 plainclothesmen would be patrolling inside the park. John L. Sullivan, the acting captain of the Deering Street Station (and Casey Stengel's personal bodyguard), had been planning for the Series with White Sox staff almost every day since early September.

Meanwhile, word leaked out that Frank Lane, never one to summarily reject a rash or foolish move, had convinced Leo Durocher to quit his $65,000 baseball broadcasting contract with NBC Television to take over as manager of the Indians. A source close to Durocher indicated that Lane had approached Durocher six weeks earlier to replace Joe Gordon and try to work some "Durocher magic" to get the Tribe into the World Series. Lane apparently did this while telling the press all through the summer that Gordon had his full support and was the best man to lead the team. Once Gordon got word of this story, he entered into a bitter exchange with Lane, who privately said that there were "four or five men" he preferred over Gordon and added, "if I can get one of them, I will." Gordon, taking the high road, issued a statement from Kansas City, simply saying, "As far as I know right now, I'm still the manager. I feel I have done the best job I possibly could do under the circumstances."[18]

Pennant anticipation intensified Friday night, September 18, when Bob Shaw shut out the Tigers on five singles, 1–0, thanks to Sherm Lollar's 21st home run of the season in front of 37,352 fans. Even though Cleveland, as expected, had an easy time dispatching the Athletics, 11–2, the magic number was now at two, and the Sox were at home for the next two days. While the city waited in anticipation, however, the Hollywood script everyone secretly hoped for never came. The still-fighting Indians scored a total of 26 runs against an apathetic Kansas City pitching staff, and won 13–7 on Saturday and 4–3 Sunday. The Tigers, meanwhile, were not about to roll over and witness a pennant clinching from the visitors' dugout at Comiskey Park. They beat the Sox by a score of 5–4 in both remaining games.

So the magic number of two looked great on Friday night, September 18, but that "two" had lost some of its luster by Sunday afternoon, September 20. Nobody would mention it, but everybody seemed to have a little flicker of anxiety about this last week of the season. Both teams had off-days on Monday, Wednesday, and Thursday. The White Sox traveled to Cleveland for a single night game on Tuesday, September 22. They were scheduled to finish the season with a weekend series in Detroit, three games starting Friday, September 25, and concluding Sunday, September 27. Cleveland's last weekend of the season would be at home, four games against the hapless Athletics, a team they just swept the weekend before on the road. If the Sox lost Tuesday night, the Indians would be just 2½ games out of first and would have four games left to play against perhaps the weakest team in the majors. Sox fans did the best they could to put such a scenario out of their minds.

Manager Al Lopez let his hair down a little bit before the big single game in Cleveland and admitted to the press that he was having trouble sleeping because of the tension in the pennant race. In comparing the 1959 race to his experiences taking Cleveland to the top in 1954, Lopez added that this race was tougher, explaining that "[In 1954] we had a 5½ game lead and played the Yankees in a double header and beat them. So we were 7½ ahead with only ten to go."[19]

On August 20, the *Chicago Tribune* had a feature called "*Will They, or…*" in which the reader who submitted the best letter of 150 words or less regarding the White Sox's pennant chances would have it printed. Rocco S. Cimmarusti of 519 North Laramie, one of the many Sox fans in Chicago's Austin neighborhood, sent a well-reasoned missive, explaining:

> I am pulling for the White Sox to win the flag, because Chicago fans deserve it. I really believe they will win, and I'm basing my hopes that Pierce will come back strong and Donovan will awaken to the fact he can pitch. If he does, Cleveland will not beat us out. It's not going to be easy but in the end the Sox'll win out. Don't be surprised if it goes to the last game. I look for Cleveland to crack in the stretch. The boys around second, Fox and Aparicio, are great plus Landis in center. Look for these scrappers to pull the Sox together until they clinch it.[20]

For the big Tuesday night contest in Cleveland, Mr. Cimmarusti had to settle for Bubba Phillips in center instead of Jim Landis, but the rest of Al Lopez's lineup was undoubtedly to his liking. All the regular starters except for Landis and Lollar were in their places. With Phillips in center, Goodman started at third base, and Johnny Romano replaced Lollar, who had injured his hand during the Sunday loss to Detroit. Wynn climbed the pitching mound at the huge stadium in front of a crowd of 54,293. While the attendance total was by far the biggest for a non-weekend game in the Major Leagues that year, the Indians' front office felt that the number would have been more than 70,000 if the Tribe were closer than 3½ games with only four games left to play. Chicagoans were able to see the game on WGN Television with Jack Brickhouse and Vince Lloyd doing the play-by-play. Broadcasting road games, and especially road night games, was a complicated and expensive undertaking in 1959, and the game's availability to the Chicago television audience further emphasized the significance of occasion. Wynn's mound opponent was Jim Perry, the 23-year-old who one year ago was pitching in the Eastern League. The lanky pride of Williamston, North Carolina, was invited to the Indians' spring training camp because they needed batting practice pitchers. He did not take himself too seriously, and once he arrived in camp made a point of telling every scout they should pay more attention to his more talented younger brother, future Hall of Famer Gaylord Perry. The Indians' front office never dreamt that Jim Perry would have 12 wins and a 2.65 ERA by late September.

The first encouraging moment for the South Side faithful occurred in the bottom of the first inning with two out, when Wynn fooled the .363-hitting Tito Francona with a curve ball for a strikeout looking. The Sox, as they did in the first, went down meekly in their half of the second, unable to solve any of Perry's offerings. In the bottom of the second, Wynn, at his prickliest and competitive best, felt Minnie Minoso was too close to the plate and hit him with a pitch. Catcher Russ Nixon followed with a solid single, easily sending the fleet Minoso to third. Rocky Colavito, the man with 40 home runs, strode to the plate with two on and nobody out and hit a fly ball to left fielder Al Smith, not deep enough to scare anybody, but maybe deep enough to score Minoso. The Cuban Comet tagged up after the catch, only to be cut down on Al Smith's great throw to Romano. Suddenly there were two out, and the slow-footed Nixon was at second. This was a much better scenario, except for the fact that Woody Held, the American League's premier power-hitting shortstop with 29 homers, came up next. Wynn handled the dangerous Held masterfully, inducing him to pop up to Kluszewski at first base for the third out.

Momentum swung the other direction after Held's weak pop-up. In the top of the third, after Jim Rivera flied out to center, Bubba Phillips singled up the middle. He stayed there as Wynn got underneath a Jim Perry fastball and popped out to Held at shortstop. Leadoff man Luis Aparicio came up with two out and laced a double past Colavito, against the 320-foot marker on the right field wall. Colavito, who along with Roberto Clemente, Carl Furillo and Andy Pafko had one of the strongest throwing arms in the game, fired to second instead of home, allowing Phillips to score: 1–0, White Sox. Perry next walked Fox, afraid to give him anything good to hit with Aparicio on second. Billy Goodman, third in the lineup, followed. Like he did so often in his career, Goodman came through convincingly in the clutch, doubling down the line past Colavito in right, scoring Aparicio and allowing Fox to scamper to third. Kluszewski followed. Perry, who had never faced him before but was well aware of Big Klu's reputation, intentionally walked the sleeveless slugger. The move paid off for the Tribe. The inning ended with Fox on third and Kluszewski at first when Johnny Romano grounded out to shortstop: 2–0, White Sox. The score stayed that way until the fifth inning.

In the Indians' half of the fifth, Wynn got too cautious with Woody Held and walked him. Indians manager Joe Gordon pulled the weak-hitting third baseman, George Strickland, sending veteran Chuck Tanner up to pinch-hit. Just as quickly, Tanner returned to the bench when Wynn struck him out and Held remained at first. Gordy Coleman pinch-hit for Perry and beat out a roller to Aparicio at shortstop. The irascible Jimmy Piersall came up next and singled to center, sending Held across the plate and Coleman to third. Up next, the dangerous Vic Power represented the lead run. The cagey Wynn induced the All-Star to hit a two-hopper to Aparicio at short, who flipped it to Fox, who in turn threw a strike to Kluszewski. Piersall was forced at second and Power was out by several steps at first: Sox 2, Cleveland 1, on the strength of the Chicagoans' clutch defensive play.

Much as it had the second inning, the double play seemed to energize the White Sox's offense in the top of the sixth. Mudcat Grant, who beat the White Sox for the first time in his career a few weeks before, came in to pitch for Perry. It was evident right away that Grant was having trouble keeping the ball down. Johnny Romano came up first and hit a deep blast to the 410-foot sign in center which Jimmy Piersall brought to earth for the first out. Al Smith followed and got hold of another high offering from Grant, which landed in the left field seats for his 16th homer of the year. As a rattled Grant dolefully watched Smith round the bases, Rivera shook Smith's hand as he crossed the plate before getting set in the batter's box himself. Grant delivered a fastball, once again not where he wanted to, and Rivera unloaded on it, hitting another home run deep into the left field seats. The White Sox had managed back-to-back homers—a rarity in the Go-Go White Sox era—in the most important game of the year. The score now stood at 4–1, White Sox, as Bubba Phillips kept the hit parade going with a single over third base. Grant finally got it together against Wynn and Aparicio, inducing ground balls to short from both of them, to end an inning that would provide the final nail in the Cleveland coffin.

In the bottom half of the sixth, Francona singled, stayed at first when Minoso flied out, but got all the way to third on Russ Nixon's single. Francona scored, cutting the Sox lead to two runs, on Rocky Colavito's sacrifice fly to center. Lopez quickly summoned Shaw from the bullpen and put Lollar behind the plate. Shaw got Held to ground out, ending the sixth. In the Indians' half of the seventh, Lopez pulled out all the defensive stops he could. Phillips came in from center field to play third as ball hawk Jim Landis entered the game in center. Shaw got the pinch-hitting Elmer Valo to ground out to Phillips at third. Gordon next sent pitcher Jack Harshman up to pinch-hit. This move was not as odd as it seemed; Harshman had good power and had hit six homers in only 82 at bats in 1958. The move did not work, as Harshman grounded out weakly to Kluszewski at first. With two out, Piersall and Power both singled, but Shaw, whose sinker was working well, induced the dangerous Tito Francona to ground out to Nellie Fox. Harshman pitched two effective innings of relief, not yielding anything and inducing Joe Gordon's critics to wonder what might have been if Gordon had called on Harshman instead of Mudcat Grant back in the sixth inning. After Harshman set down Shaw, Aparicio, and Fox in the top of the ninth, the entire city of Chicago sat on the edge of their chairs.

The Indians, worthy opponents throughout the season, gave no quarter. Shaw had now been in the game long enough for the Indians to familiarize themselves with his offerings, and after Woody Held popped out to Fox at second, Jim Baxes lined a single off Shaw's glove, and the fleet Ray Webster came in to run for him. After Harshman singled and speedster Carroll Hardy ran for him, leadoff man Piersall came up, One of the best contact hitters of his era, the pesky center fielder hit a vicious liner that handcuffed Nellie Fox for another single. Piersall now had three hits in the biggest game of the season, and luckily for the White Sox, Webster could only get to third base, as Fox was able to keep the ball in front of him. The Indians had the bases loaded with the always dangerous Vic Power due up. Lopez sprang from the dugout and made his move, decisively striding to the mound, dismissing Shaw while the veteran closer Gerry Staley strode to the mound.

For added insurance, Lopez had both right-hander Turk Lown and lefty ace Billy Pierce throwing at game speed in the White Sox bullpen. The noise level in the massive horseshoe on Lake Erie was deafening. Staley wound and fired a slider, spinning toward the plate low and outside. Power got good wood on the ball, lacing it back up the middle on two hops, but Aparicio swiftly cut it off, took two steps to force Piersall at second, and fired a strike to Ted Kluszewski, completing the Sox's third double play of the game and clinching the South Side's first pennant in 40 years.

The White Sox infielders mobbed Staley, followed by a parade from the dugout led by Al Lopez. Earl Torgeson was the first one from the field into the locker room, where Early Wynn and Billy Goodman, removed from the game earlier, had been nervously waiting. Goodman leaped on Torgeson's back, while catcher Early Battey, smiling from ear to ear, made his entrance. "Whoooeeee! What a heart attack!" Battey cried out. Coaches Don Gutteridge and Ray Berres embraced each other. When Berres spotted Staley, he embraced him and told the heroic reliever "after 22 years I finally made it!" Al Smith and Jim Rivera, producers of the critical back-to-back home runs off tough Mudcat Grant, were frequent subjects for photographers, pouring beer on each other's heads. "The gold dust twins!" Rivera declared to the admiring press.

Things were just as crazy in Chicago, albeit for a variety of reasons. The American Research Bureau said that WGN Television's broadcast of the game had an incredible rating of 56.6 between the hours of 9:30 and 10:00 p.m., which meant that 89 percent of all the television sets in the Chicago area were tuned to the tense proceedings in Cleveland, almost twice as big as the previous record of 32.1 on June 24, 1958.[21]

Gerry Staley, a much-traveled sinker baller who starred in relief for the 1959 White Sox. During that season, the four-time American League All Star struck out twice as many hitters as he walked, going 8–5, saving 15 games, and posting a sparkling 2.24 ERA.

Soon after the game was over, however, a great many of the viewers had the scare of their lifetimes. Chicago's fire commissioner and acting director of the Civil Defense Corps, diehard Sox fan Robert J. Quinn, took it upon himself to turn on the Chicago area's 110 air raid sirens to commemorate the pennant. Needless to say it was a poor idea.

Quinn was Mayor Richard J. Daley's childhood friend from the gritty Back of the Yards neighborhood. He rose from the lower ranks of the Chicago fire department to assistant fire commissioner just four days after Daley took office in 1956; soon after, with no explanation to the press, Daley named him commissioner.[22] When the Sox clinched, Quinn was nine months into the worst year of his life. He was under fire, defending his decisions and the actions of the Chicago Fire Department during the city's worst disaster since World War II, the horrific Our Lady of Angels fire in which 92 children and three nuns lost their lives on a brutally cold afternoon in early December 1958. Quinn was already under media scrutiny for what was perceived as the Fire Department's slow response to the fire and the fact that their ladders were initially too short to reach the school's second-floor windows. Pictures of the fire, with scores of choking, panicked school children pressed so tightly windows that firemen could not break them open, was indelibly etched in the memory of many Chicagoans. Now, just nine months after that tragedy, Quinn's ill-conceived nuclear air raid alerts cast another negative spotlight on his office.

The blaring of the air raid sirens caused near-bedlam throughout many parts of the area. The Bell Telephone Company said that its switchboards were flooded with a volume of calls as large as they had received 14 years earlier when President Franklin Roosevelt died. Hospital supervisors called to see if they should evacuate patients. One woman called from her basement, where she huddled with her three children. Another man called after locking himself in a closet with a bottle of beer. Still another caller checked on the proceedings from a pay phone, saying that he was en route to Wisconsin to avoid the atomic bombing of Chicago. A survey by the *Chicago Tribune* indicated that half the callers that evening to the newspaper thought the city was under Soviet attack, and half felt the sirens were because of the White Sox. On a follow-up question, 90 percent said they were extremely angry and threatened reprisals at the polls in the next election. Mayor Richard M. Daley, Bridgeport resident and lifelong Sox fan, minimized the reporters' questions about the air raid noise and brazenly suggested that the Chicago City Council had authorized the sounding of the sirens. The reporters were not quick enough to call him on that statement, but another important individual was.[23]

That person was Robert M. Woodward, the director of Illinois Civil Defense, who, two days later, called the alert completely unauthorized and said there would be a federal investigation.[24] He filed a formal protest with the North American Air Defense Command (NORAD) in Colorado Springs, the federal office in charge of national civil defense. Woodward sympathized with the dismayed and frightened public, saying that for years civil defense officials had been attempting to educate them that an air raid alarm other than one at 10:30 a.m. on Tuesdays would indeed be a true crisis and emergency. A red-faced Quinn was forced to promise in writing never again to use the sirens for anything other than their warning purposes.

While the celebratory air raid sirens are looked upon with amusement now, the decades have erased the memories of the sheer terror and confusion the wailing blasts created. The anger and fear the Chicagoland citizenry felt were well expressed in various letters to the newspapers:

CHICAGO—What is the difference between teen-age hoodlums turning in false fire alarms and firemen turning in false air raid sirens? IRATE CITIZEN

CHICAGO—Anyone so stupid as to sound the air raid siren simply to celebrate a baseball victory should immediately be removed from office. MRS. J.V.

CHICAGO—In the light of the stupid and capricious lack of judgment displayed by our top city officials in sounding the air raid sirens to celebrate a baseball victory, isn't it time for the city council to put the control of these sirens into more mature and responsible hands? LESLIE L. LEWIS

Even a jubilant White Sox follower was upset by the proceedings:

CHICAGO—A few minutes ago the air raid siren erased everything from our minds except Russia and a screaming baby. They wouldn't attack now," I said. "Khrushchev is here." "On the contrary," said a neighbor from his back porch. "It would be a good chance for them to get rid of him. We are proud of our White Sox, but in the future let's save the sirens for disaster." MRS. WILLIAM W. ADORJAN

A sarcastic, but undoubtedly jealous, North Sider chimed in:

CHICAGO—The sounding of the sirens for the White Sox victory was a good thing for Chicago. Civil defense has for years tried to educate us as to what to do when the sirens blow. Obviously many Sox fans don't know. Now maybe they do; they should turn to Conelrad on their radios. A CUB FAN

But perhaps to disprove A CUB FAN's point, not everyone did the wrong thing:

CHICAGO-Fire Commissioner Quinn has the audacity to talk about how people are supposed to stand by for orders from Conelrad when the alarm siren blows. We tuned in on Conelrad and heard nothing but music, but we went to the basement anyway. J.W.S.[25]

Bedlam ensued at Chicago's Midway Airport soon after the pennant was won. With the air raid sirens wailing in celebration, a jubilant crowd of 25,000 awaited the American League champions, whose chartered United Air Lines plane did not land until 2:30 a.m. Some Sox fans had trouble filling the time.[26] A small group was arrested for breaking into the American Air Lines hangar and looting cargo, while at 1:30 a.m., downtown in the Loop, a small band of six rowdies was arrested for destroying the State Street Council's exhibit at the corner of State and Madison.

Luis Aparicio was the first individual off the plane; he spied the crowd and whipped them into a frenzy, yelling "Go Go Sox!" Mayor Daley strode to the ramp and greeted the team, along with Bill Veeck, as the players quickly departed in 12 taxicabs which were waiting on the tarmac. Their swift departure gave the huge crowd only a brief glimpse of its heroes, but that would be rectified on Thursday, September 24, with a Loop parade to honor the champions.

Veeck's wife, Mary Frances, was waiting at the airport with Mayor Daley and his wife, Eleanor. When the plane landed, the crowd rushed forward as everyone pushed closer for a glimpse of the players. In the ensuing crush, Veeck's wife lost one of her shoes, which was miraculously found in the crowd by Mrs. Daley.[27] Veeck, his wife, and Hank Greenberg partied all night at The Singapore on Rush Street and at Fritzel's at 201 North State.[28]

The city quickly planned Thursday's midday victory cortege to go south on State Street from Wacker to Adams, west on Adams to LaSalle Street, and north on LaSalle through the heart of the financial district, where most of the ticker tape confetti showered down. Mayor Daley, Chuck Comiskey, and Bill Veeck led the parade, followed by a large truck, six bands and a fleet of about 15 convertibles, each one carrying two members of the team. Pulling up the rear was a funeral car carrying the remains of a dead Indian. The official party for the team was scheduled for that night at the Conrad Hilton Hotel. Conrad Hilton himself attended the bash, sponsored by Comiskey, Veeck, Greenberg, and Al Lopez. Aside from everyone associated with the team, an estimated 500 other revelers came to the festivities, which ended when many in the entourage went down to the hotel's Boulevard Room nightclub to continue the party.[29]

Meanwhile, while the White Sox portrayed Cleveland as a dead Indian, articles in the press after the Tuesday night game portrayed their front office more like a tribe of bitter, cynical Indians. David Condon in the *Chicago Tribune* wrote of his experiences in the Cleveland press box with general manager Frank Lane during the tense contest. Condon wrote that as Lane strode up the ramp to his perch, he was spied by an angry Indians fan, who spewed: "Hey, big mouth, go on home…. Are yuh countin' the crowd? It'll be easy to count 'em next year—There won't be none … and you get a nickel a head for each of us."

As the game started and progressed, it became clear that Lane had as much contempt for his team as this heckler had for him. Lane candidly trashed a coach, six players, and the manager for all to hear: "That guy at third [coach Jo-Jo White] he doesn't think at all.

Colavito can't drive in a run except when he drives himself in on a homer. We're two runs behind. Damn, we'd have been out of that jam if Colavito hadn't been asleep on that hit. He takes his time picking up the ball and then throws [to the wrong base]." When manager Joe Gordon sent Chuck Tanner up to pinch-hit and a reporter mentioned that Tanner hit a home run in his first Major League at bat, Lane sarcastically said, "And he hasn't hit one since." Later on, with Vic Power batting, Lane predicted: "This'll be a double play. All Power does is hit into double plays. Power couldn't hit a homer if the fence was behind second base." When Mudcat Grant gave up back-to-back homers to Al Smith and Jim Rivera, Lane's disgust became palpable: "There ought to be a fine against pitching fastballs to Rivera or Smith. They couldn't hit curve balls with a bull fiddle—but we give 'em fast balls." When pitcher Jack Harshman came up, Lane let him have it also, but saved a little of his irritation for his much-maligned manager, Joe Gordon, saying: "Harshman couldn't hit me. He's batting .161. Gordon's the only one who thinks Harshman's a hitter. Gordon quit, didn't he?" His disappointment ended with ridicule of the Indians' hard-working catcher, Russ Nixon, for hitting into a double play.[30]

After the game, to add insult to injury for a team that just lost the pennant, Lane stormed into the locker room and fired the long-suffering Gordon, replacing him with pitching coach Mel Harder. Gordon deserved a better fate, but kept his dignity and wits about him in spite of Lane's cruel, insensitive act. When asked where he would be during the team's final series of the year, he quipped, "Up in the press box with Lane, second guessing the new manager." Lane embarrassed himself even further the next day, rehiring Gordon 24 hours later, giving him a two-year contract to run the team![31]

Before the World Series started, the White Sox had the small matter of finishing the season with a three-game series against the Tigers, with third base coach Tony Cuccinello managing the team. Al Lopez was staying in Chicago, scouting the Los Angeles Dodgers when they played the Cubs at Wrigley Field Friday afternoon, September 25, then going north to Milwaukee to check on the Braves, who were hosting the cellar-dwelling Philadelphia Phillies that evening.

Sherm Lollar did not make the trip to Detroit, either. The team had a great deal of concern about his hand injury, and he checked into Mercy Hospital to give the deep bruise on his fifth metacarpal bone a greater chance of healing. Lollar was expected to be discharged before Monday, September 28, so he could participate in all workouts before the World Series opener.

Sox fans saw a different team in the 1959 season's meaningless final series at Briggs Stadium. On Friday, Cuccinello put Billy Goodman at second base, young call-up J. C. Martin at third, and gave both Joe Hicks and Norm Cash some time at first base. Cash's mental lapse at first cost the White Sox the ball game. The Sox were up, 5–3, going into the bottom of the ninth when Gerry Staley lost his effectiveness and the Tigers prevailed in the meaningless contest after Cash argued a call at first, allowing the go-ahead run to score. The Saturday affair, in front of a tiny crowd of 3,386, was a 10–5 victory, thanks to Johnny Callison, whose grand slam in the eighth inning off Ray Narleski put the game out of reach. Regrettably, it would be his last hit in a Chicago White Sox uniform. On Sunday September 27, the last day of the season, Shaw upped his record to 18–6 with the aid of a rare triple play.

Perhaps it was fitting that the final weekend of the White Sox's first pennant-winning season in 40 years would be a game against the colorful manager who presided over 13 seasons of that long drought, Jimmie Dykes. He reminisced with the press that when he ran the team, ruefully pointing out, "I didn't have it so good. Was I ever close to winning a pennant there? In 1937 we finished third but nowhere near the top. We didn't worry about pennants in those days. The depression—remember? The biggest worry was about the weather, especially on Sundays. If it was good it meant we'd have a few more hundred than otherwise. Harry Grabiner would ask about the weather report each day before anything else. Putting in lights in 1939 saved the White Sox. Too bad Lou Comiskey never lived to see the sight."[32] Dykes, perhaps so as not to take any luster off the Sox's pennant achievement, modestly forgot that he also guided bare-bones White Sox rosters to a third-place finish also in 1941. When he managed the war-torn squad of 1943 to fourth place, he was referred to as the "Miracle Manager."

George Kell was another illustrious ex–White Sox firmly entrenched in the Motor City with a glowing opinion of his old team. He called Jim Landis the key to the White Sox's pennant drive, Nellie Fox the league's most valuable player, and said that Sherman Lollar, for years one of the best catchers in the majors, was having the best year of his career. When asked about White Sox pitching, the first name he mentioned was Dick Donovan, saying that Donovan's rough competitive qualities will serve him well in the World Series. He added that Pierce, no longer able to overpower batters with a fastball like he used to, now had a slider and slow curve to maintain his effectiveness. As far as Early Wynn was concerned, Kell just referred to him as the stopper and "the inspiration." While both Dykes and Kell had nothing but praise for their old ball club, neither of them went out on a limb predicting anything for the World Series.[33]

While White Sox fans eagerly awaited the October of their lifetimes, a few of them took notice that the last day for the 1959 baseball season was also the Opening Day of the National Football League season, and the beloved Chicago Cardinals had their premiere season opener at the renovated Soldier Field. Walter Wolfner was busy contacting the Chicago press earlier in the week to ramp up attendance. Wolfner could not stop talking about how promising the Cardinals would be, saying "Fans won't recognize our defensive team ... the Cards have a defensive backfield, superior to any in the club's history, superior to the defensive backfield of 1947, when we won the league championship. Remember the Cards are the last team to win a real professional sports championship in Chicago." Wolfner extolled the virtues of the Cardinals' new stadium, Soldier Field:

> Fans won't recognize the place.... Soldiers' [sic] Field gives the Cardinals unlimited parking at 25 cents per head, and this may be one reason our season ticket sales are running far ahead of 1958. We play only four home games this season [*note:* two home games were scheduled to be played in Minneapolis] and this may be why season ticket sales are running far ahead of 1958 ... our top season ticket, four $5 seats, sells for $18. We also have a special package deal where a season ticket for one adult, in a certain section, costs only $10, and he can bring in two youngsters, under 14 free. Even for the Bears game![34]

Those 21,892 Cards fans who showed up at Soldier Field September 27 may not have agreed with Wolfner's proclamations about the defense, but they certainly got their money's worth of football. The Big Red amassed an incredible 569 yards of offense and smothered the Washington Redskins, 49–21. The contest was the breakout game for two young Southerners who would leave an indelible mark on the franchise, Bobby Joe Conrad and John David Crow. For those truly diehard Cardinals fans, the icing on the cake was the fact that the Green Bay Packers beat the despised Bears, 9–6. Heady times for the South Side, indeed; a Bears loss, a rare Cardinals romp—and in four days the White Sox would host the opening of the World Series!

The Rest of the American League at the End of the 1959 Season

CLEVELAND INDIANS

The Cleveland Indians, worthy opponents of the White Sox throughout, finished with a record of 89–65, five games behind the pennant-winners. The Indians were in first place for 87 of the 165 days in the 1959 season, their high point being a 3½-game lead on Tuesday, May 5. They relinquished their first-place standing for the last time on July 28, when the White Sox took over as American League leaders for the rest of the year. The hard-hitting Indians finished first in the American League in home runs (167), team batting average (.263), and slugging percentage (.408). Their powerful lineup was led by outfielders Rocky Colavito (.257, 42 home runs, and 111 runs batted in), Minnie Minoso (.302, 21 HR, and 92 RBI), and shortstop Woody Held (.251, 29, 71). Colavito's home run total, tied by Harmon Killebrew, was the highest in the American League; in the National League, only Milwaukee's Eddie Mathews (46) and Chicago's Ernie Banks (45) had more. Colavito's 111 RBIs were only one behind the American League leader, Boston's Jackie Jensen, and was seventh-highest in the majors. Cleveland's excellent pitching was anchored by Cal McLish (19–8) and Gary Bell (16–11), and helped immeasurably by Mudcat Grant and surprise newcomer Jim Perry. If Herb Score (9–11 4.71 ERA) had been more effective, the 1959 American League pennant race may very well have had a different outcome. The Indians had a winning record every month of the season and played better on the road (46–31) than they did at home (43–34). They had a winning record against every team in the American League except New York, against whom they finished 11–11, and Chicago, to whom they lost 15 out of 22 games.

NEW YORK YANKEES

The World Champion New York Yankees never really got started during the 1959 season, finishing with a record of 79–75, a distant 15 games behind the White Sox. The Yankees were through entertaining any pennant thoughts as early as September 1, when they were two games under .500 at 64–66, and incredibly did not spend one day in first place in the entire 1959 season. Their poor record of 12–16 in July sealed their destiny, and they had losing records against every quality team in the American League except Cleveland. If the Yankees had not fattened up on Kansas City (17–5) and Washington (15–7), they would have finished under .500 for the first time since 1925.

DETROIT TIGERS

The Detroit Tigers finished a poor fourth, with a losing record of 76–78, 18 games out of first place. They started the year with a miserable record of 2–13 in April, sliding to 2–17 when manager Bill Norman was fired. Veteran skipper Jimmie Dykes took the helm and finished his part of the year with a winning record of 74–63. If the Tigers had played the entire year like they did under Dykes, they would have challenged the Indians for second place. With Dykes managing the team, Detroit had the best record in the league for the months of May and June combined, 36–23. Like most teams, they fared very well against Kansas City (15–7) and also easily handled New York (14–8), but they broke even with Boston and were under .500 against every other squad. The 1959 Tigers were a slow team, stealing only 34 bases, and had a high 4.20 team ERA. Their lack of execution in close games killed them as they went 17–27 in games decided by one run. In spite of these insufficiencies, some Tigers had great seasons in 1959. Three starting pitchers come to mind: Don Mossi, 17–9; Frank Lary, 17–10; and Jim Bunning, 17–13. Right fielder Harvey Kuenn won the American League batting title, hitting .353. Center fielder Al Kaline hit .327, second-best in the American League, with 27 homers and 94 RBI, while left fielder Charlie Maxwell had a career year with 31 home runs and 95 RBI.

BOSTON RED SOX

The Boston Red Sox, like Detroit, benefited from a mid-season managerial change, but they still were never in the pennant race. Manager Pinky Higgins was dismissed after 73 games with a record of 31–42, and Rudy York lost the only game he managed as an interim. The Red Sox, however, responded to new skipper Billy Jurges, who led them to a 44–36 record, on the strength of a 31–22 record in August and September. To his credit, Jurges developed the first black player on the Red Sox, Pumpsie Green, into a legitimate major league second baseman, while the team ended the year in fifth place, 19 games behind the White Sox, with a record of 75–79. Boston's offense was buoyed by Jackie Jensen, whose 112 runs batted in led the American League, and the great hitting of Pete Runnels, whose .413 on-base percentage was the second-best in the junior circuit. Sadly, the great Ted Williams could not contribute as expected. The aging immortal hit only .254 with ten home runs and 43 RBI, hampered by injuries all season. Boston's pitching left a lot to be desired. They gave up 589 walks and had a lackluster 4.17 team ERA.

Baltimore Orioles

The Baltimore Orioles turned a lot of heads during the first half of 1959, going 41–38, but could not sustain their success during the second half, when they went 33–42. They finished sixth, 74–80, 20 games behind the White Sox. Manager Paul Richards continued to improve the Orioles' pitching, as the starting trio of Hoyt Wilhelm (15–11 with a league leading 2.19 ERA), 20-year-old Milt Pappas (15–9, 3.27) and All-Star Billy O'Dell (10–12, 2.93) anchored a staff with the second-lowest team ERA (3.56) in the league. Baltimore's lack of a consistent fourth starter and weak hitting doomed them to the second division. They were last in the majors in runs scored (551), and their team batting average (.238) was second-worst in all of baseball. The Orioles' inability to generate base runners hurt them throughout the season; Gus Triandos hit 25 home runs but had only 73 runs batted in, and left fielder Bob Nieman had 21 homers but only 60 RBI.

Kansas City Athletics

The Kansas City Athletics once again finished seventh, 22 wins under .500 at 66–88, 28 games behind the White Sox. Their season would have been a complete disaster if they had not gone 19–11 during July, when they pulled off the American League's longest winning streak of the season, 11 games between July 19 and July 30. The Athletics were 14–8 against Baltimore and 11–11 against Boston, but did not do well against any other opponents, and the Yankees beat them 17 times in 22 games. Bob Cerv, Roger Maris, and Dick Williams combined to hit 52 home runs, but their pitching was poor. After starter Bud Daley (16–13, 3.16), the hurlers were woefully insufficient, posting the worst team earned run average in the Major Leagues at 4.35.

Washington Senators

The Washington Senators' power hitting was their only strength. Cellar dwellers for the sixth time in the last 13 seasons, the Senators were a full month's worth of games behind the league-leading White Sox with a record of 63–91, finishing 31 games behind. In spite of hitting 163 home runs, only four less than the Cleveland Indians, the Senators had the lowest team batting average in the majors. Their inability to get men on base in front of third baseman Harmon Killebrew (42 home runs, tied for the league lead), left fielder Jim Lemon (33, third in the AL), center fielder Bob Allison (30), and Roy Sievers (21) resulted in the third-smallest run production in the majors. Washington scored only 619 runs in 1959, worse than every team in baseball except the Philadelphia Phillies and Baltimore Orioles. While the Senators were a competitive 37–41 during the first half of the season, they went winless from July 19 through August 5, losing 18 straight. This three-week period doomed the second half of their season, when they won only 26 games and lost 50. Camilo Pascual developed into one of the best starters in baseball (17–10, 2.64 ERA, second best in the majors), but the Senators' thin bullpen caused them to go a dismal 11–26 in one-run games. Washington went 12–10 against both Boston and Detroit, 6–16 against Chicago and Cleveland, and lost 15 out of 22 to New York.

9

October: Bridgeport in the Spotlight

With the Chicago White Sox making baseball meaningful on Chicago's South Side for the first time in 40 years, the grand old Baseball Palace of the World at 35th and Shields suddenly had more autumn activity than most Bridgeport residents could remember. The usual routine at Comiskey Park when the longer shadows of October came calling would be a five-hour visit for practices from their erstwhile tenants, the Chicago Cardinals, four or five days a week, followed by the attentions of maybe 15–20,000 fans on no more than six Sundays when the Big Red, always hoping for a bigger crowd than what would arrive, would play their home games. Now the Cards were gone, having moved 24 blocks north and eight blocks east to Soldier Field. The usual cacophony outside the park was the same, with the rushing streamliners of the Pennsylvania Railroad and other eastbound and southbound lines speeding by on the huge eight-track artery just west of the ball park that terminated four miles north at Chicago's Union Station. Two blocks east, equally busy veins of rail carried the pride of the Canadian National, New York Central, and Rock Island Lines in and out of LaSalle Street Station with a more muted but similarly insistent roar. To have even more activity inside the park, as hundreds of people readied the somber arched baseball cathedral for the Fall Classic, was a novelty indeed.

The grounds crew tore out all the grass circling the infield and replaced it with 1,500 square yards of fresh sod. One day prior to the start of the World Series, the load of telephone calls to the Comiskey Park switchboard became so heavy that the fuses blew, leaving the entire organization with no telephone service on the eve of the Fall Classic. The U.S. Postal Service delivered ticket orders from as far away as Sweden and France.[1] The Sox's front office, with their painstaking plans to distribute tickets fairly, were embarrassed when the first name drawn out of the lottery to receive the precious passes declared

himself to be an avowed Cubs fan. As expected, the ticket issue posed real
risks for Sox fans. The excitement of seeing their heroes on the big stage far
overshadowed their good judgment when it came to getting a chance to see
a game. Counterfeit tickets were everywhere, and despite color-coding the
tickets (Game One ducats were pink; Game Two, apple green; Game Six,
lemon; and Game Seven, burnt orange), hundreds of people were duped with
poorly printed blue-and-white imitations. In spite of the efforts of Chicago
Police Captains Joseph Graney and Thomas Sullivan, scalpers were still asking
as much as $125 for an infield box seat.[2] Chuck Comiskey commented at
length about the ticket situation:

> I really believe that we could sell every seat in Comiskey 25 times. At least a hundred
> people have asked me for from 100 to 150 sets of tickets, and I mailed back $4,000 worth
> of checks to personal friends last Friday, plus another 200 checks with the amount left
> blank. One man I know, who has a box of eight all year and gives seats to his customers,
> is of course, eligible for another box of eight for the Series. He told me he was thinking
> of leaving his regular box empty … and sitting in the extra box. Then when suppliers
> of his came in they would look at the empty box and say: "Well, he didn't give them to
> anybody else, either." I don't suppose he'll do it, but he's thinking about it.[3]

The World Series always meant big money for baseball, but it meant
even bigger money to the host cities. The Chicago Association of Commerce
said an additional $10 to $12 million would fall into Chicago's coffers if the
Series lasted six games.

A few individuals working the Series had also worked at the Sox's last
one; M. G. "Frenchy" Sharp was one of them.[4] The 62-year-old beer vendor
from 41st and Kedzie would be selling Budweiser to the fans 40 years after
he had hawked Chevrolet beer in the 1919 "Black Sox" series. By coincidence,
the two elderly gentlemen working the Western Union Telegram lines in the
press box both worked as telegraph operators for the same company covering
the Series four decades earlier. The *Houston Chronicle* hired Dickie Kerr, a
White Sox starter who beat Cincinnati twice in the 1919 World Series while
steering clear of the betting scandal, to cover the World Series for them. It
would not be a World Series without Casey Stengel present, and *Life* magazine
paid him $5,000 to cover the games in both cities. For the Chicago games,
Stengel settled into the LaSalle Hotel, the dignified old hostelry in the heart
of Chicago's financial district that was still recovering from the party Veeck
threw for the gathering media the previous Monday, three days before the
World Series opener. Stengel settled in and thoroughly enjoyed himself, holding court for anyone who would listen and imparting what passed as his
unique brand of wisdom. The *Chicago Daily News* commissioned Nelson
Algren to write his impressions of the games played in Chicago. Three of his
World Series reviews, "Nelson Algren Writes Impressions of the Series," "Algren
Writes of Roses and Hits," and "Nelson Algren's Reflections: Hep-Ghosts of

the Rain," were revised and printed 14 years later in his work *The Last Carousel*.[5]

Before the Series started, media coverage became a source of controversy. Jack Brickhouse from the White Sox booth and Vince Scully from the Dodgers shared the television responsibilities. The games would be televised simultaneously by local outlet WGN and national outlet NBC, with NBC's Chicago affiliate, WNBQ, handling the feed. The radio rights belonged to NBC, so Chicago's storied WCFL, "the Voice of Labor," would not broadcast the games, as they had all season. The national radio broadcasts for the Fall Classic usually had the two teams' home announcers split time covering the Series, but this would not be the case in 1959. Thomas Gallery, NBC Sports Director, had a long-standing grudge against the legendary voice of the Sox, Bob Elson.[6] Elson was a giant in Chicago radio since before the Depression. He worked the original All-Star Game at Comiskey Park in 1933. His nationwide coverage of significant sporting events was so beloved by President Franklin Roosevelt that Roosevelt personally arranged for Elson's leave from the Great Lakes Naval Training Center in 1943 so that he would hear Elson's voice broadcasting the 1943 World Series.[7] While at Great Lakes, Elson earned an endearing nickname that stayed with him until his passing—"The Old Commander." By 1959, some considered the aging Elson's formal, mellow delivery as too somnambulant and uninspiring for baseball, but he was an integral part of White Sox culture. Instead of Elson, Mr. Gallery and his ill-advised NBC cohorts chose Mel Allen, the voice of the Yankees, and Philadelphia's Byrum Saam (he of "Have a Phillies cigar!!" fame) to cover the excitement of the moment, which helped fans get over it. Before his passing, Elson said that this snub was the biggest disappointment of his award-winning career.[9]

By the late 1950s, Chicago was the convention capital of the country, and the National Recreation Congress held a convention in Chicago during the first week of October. Dr. Leonardo B. Garcia, a psychiatrist with the Mental Health Institute, addressed the group on the eve of the World Series. Dr. Garcia felt the occasion was a perfect time to discuss the psychoanalytical aspects of World Series mania:

> We are glad to reassure Sox fans that the euphoria of the moment does not mark them as bereft of all sense. It is a temporary condition, although we trust the Sox will strive to make it permanent—at least through the chill season ahead when the hot stove league is given to rehearsing past glories. The condition of the fans is no worse than temporary insanity. The hometown gallery tends to identify itself and its team with the cause of right and justice, and that its sometimes morbid manifestations of hostility toward the umpire arise from the feeling that he may be interfering with a satisfactory denouement.[10]

Most Sox fans did not know what to do with Dr. Garcia's insights.

Chuck Comiskey offered a more personal note about the Series' significance. He mentioned being happiest for the fans who stayed with the team through all the lean years. He noted that his grandfather had put over a million dollars in the team after the Black Sox scandal, a huge personal blow from which he never recovered. He was very pleased that he achieved something himself, and the meaningful satisfaction of knowing he succeeded while competing against more experienced men. When asked if he considered the 1959 Sox to be *his* team, Chuck could not have been more direct, emphatically pointing out that

> I own 46 percent of the stock. No other single stockholder owns as much. I brought in almost all the boys who are playing out there. I led with my chin in trading off Carrasquel so we could bring up Aparicio. I first had my eye on Nellie Fox when I was running our Waterloo affiliate and he was with Lincoln. I was here when we got Pierce, I took lots of criticism for the deal that sent Hatfield and Minoso, and got us Wynn and Smith. There are youngsters out there whom I signed for our farm clubs. There's Staley, the only player we ever received from the Yankees, and then there's our great catcher, Lollar. I got him from Veeck when he was with the Browns.[11]

It was obvious by his response that Comiskey had been waiting to answer this question. Many thought it was now time for Chuck to start receiving the credit he deserved, not only for the team's remarkable decade, but also for the 1959 World Series appearance. In an effort to continue putting the emphasis on the Sox's founding family and away from the Veeck group, he went on to say, "My mother kept the team together. She was a fine executive and a fine fan. Lane was a capable, hard-working executive. John Onslow made room for Fox, and Rigney and I worked together. We thought alike, through all the years we stuck to the principle that the farm system would eventually build a great White Sox team."[12] His comments about his unwanted partner, Veeck, however, were much more cryptic. While he did offer a slim acknowledgment of Veeck's contribution, it had nothing to do with baseball, evasively explaining:

> He has had some great promotions. I can't say that all them were great, but I don't think he will, either. Once the season started we concentrated on baseball. We have difficulties, of course, but there are many ways to solve them—to the advantage of all concerned. I don't intend to get out of the White Sox. I'm confident all of us will find a happy formula. I saw Dorothy the other day and kidded her about selling out a year too soon.[13]

Comiskey and Veeck did make one wise decision together just prior to the start of the World Series when they signed manager Lopez to a $55,000, one-year contract for 1960, a big raise from the $40,000 he was getting for 1959. This put him significantly above the highest-paid players on the team, Fox, Lollar, Pierce, and Wynn, who were all in the $40-$45,000 range. A grateful Lopez indicated that he had every intention of bringing back his coaches, Berres, Cuccinello, Gutteridge, and Cooney, to continue serving as his lieutenants. The Sox skipper was not the only one rewarded for his efforts. *United Press International* mentioned that Maracaibo, Venezuela, would present their favorite son, Aparicio, with the keys to the city upon his arrival home after the Series.[14]

During the buildup to the Fall Classic, Chicagoans spent more time reveling in the Sox's good fortune than they did worrying about whom they would be playing. When they did pay attention to the race in the Senior Circuit, however, they noticed that it was the tightest pennant chase since 1951, when the Giants knocked off the Dodgers on Bobby Thomson's "Shot Heard 'Round the World." The same two teams, now settled in San Francisco and Los Angeles, were engaged in a tense struggle with the Milwaukee Braves. The Giants were perhaps the most dangerous of the three from the Sox's perspective, and they had a three-game lead as late as Wednesday, September 9. They finished the month by winning only five of their last 16 games and watched helplessly while both Milwaukee and Los Angeles overtook them, ending the season tied for first. The Cubs, of all teams, were more responsible than anyone for the National League race ending all knotted up. They beat the Giants in a crucial game on Tuesday, September 22, when big George Altman hit a walk-off homer off Sad Sam Jones to seal a 5–4 victory at Wrigley Field. The next day, the pressing and tense San Franciscans lost again on a Cubs walk-off homer, this one in the bottom of the tenth inning with two out by pinch-hitter Cal Neeman. The Giants' Eddie Fisher was one pitch away from preserving the tie when he served the gopher ball to Neeman, a reserve catcher with a .168 batting average. Crestfallen and completely dispirited, the Giants moved on to end the season in St. Louis, where they quietly mailed it in, losing two out of three and finishing the season in third place, three games but a million heartbreaks behind Los Angeles and Milwaukee.

During the last weekend of the season Milwaukee entertained the lowly Phillies while the Cubs hosted Los Angeles at Wrigley Field. By midnight Friday, September 25, the Dodgers moved one game ahead of the Braves when they beat the Cubs, 5–4, in a matinee affair and the Phillies surprised the Braves, 6–3, that night. Lopez scouted both of these games, taking notes on both potential World Series opponents by driving from Chicago to Milwaukee after the Cubs game. Less than 18 hours later, both teams were tied again for first. Warren Spahn beat Robin Roberts, 3–2, in a classic pitching duel between two future Hall of Famers that lasted less than two hours. The Cubs, enjoying the spoiler role they had perfected by knocking out San Francisco just a few days before, toyed with Los Angeles and coasted to an easy 12–2 victory. On Sunday, with both contenders playing their final game of the season, Milwaukee's Bob Buhl dominated the Phils, 5–2, to assure that the Braves' season would continue a little longer, the victory assuring them a tie for first place. However, any hopes the Braves had that the Cubs would help them out on Sunday were dashed early when the Dodgers jumped to a 2–0, second-inning lead off Cubs starter Bob Anderson, and the Cubs' lineup accomplished very little against Roger Craig. A lopsided 7–1 victory by the visitors meant that a three-game playoff for the National League pennant would start in Milwaukee on Monday, September 28.

Through a press release, the Braves learned that they had support from an organization usually apathetic about baseball—the Chicago Transit Authority.[15] It issued a statement declaring that the company was pulling for the Braves, since an "Interurban Series" could raise some badly needed revenue. Their North Side elevated line shared track and connected with the North Shore Line, an interurban light-rail electric railway that connected Chicago's Loop with downtown Milwaukee. These two lines could provide two-hour, door-to-door transportation between Comiskey Park and Milwaukee County Stadium if the Braves met the White Sox in the World Series.

The scheduling for the three-game National League playoff was a disaster for both teams. Intent on having the World Series start in Chicago on Thursday, October 1, Commissioner Frick's office scheduled the playoff opener with no time off after the regular season finale on Sunday, September 27; the first game was the next day in Milwaukee. The Braves were already home, and the Dodgers only had to travel 90 miles from Chicago to get there. Immediately after that game, both teams had to fly to Los Angeles for Game Two on Tuesday, September 29, and stay there for a third game the following day, if necessary. The winner of the third game on Wednesday, September 30, would immediately fly back to the Midwest to start the World Series on Thursday, October 1, in Chicago. Obviously, the Sox were pulling for a three-game playoff. There would be a huge advantage in playing a team that would have to endure two Midwest-to-Los Angeles flights in a span of less than 48 hours while they themselves enjoyed three days off.

Since the pitching staffs of both Los Angeles and Milwaukee were worn out and they both wanted to open the Series in Chicago with quality starters, managers Walt Alston and Fred Haney sent two back-of-the-rotation lefties to the mound to start the playoffs. Danny McDevitt, who finished the 1959 season at 10–8, got the start for the Dodgers, facing the Braves' Carlton Willey, 5–8. Alston pulled a nervous McDevitt when the Braves nicked him for two runs in the second inning, replacing him with young Larry Sherry. Willey was more effective, lasting into the sixth, when catcher John Roseboro's solo homer put the Dodgers up by a run. Sherry, at the start of the best week of his life, baffled the Braves with his devastating slider for 7⅔ innings, allowing no runs and only four hits, and the Dodgers took the first game, 3–2.

Both teams flew to Los Angeles immediately after the game. The pitching match-up for Tuesday in the Coliseum was more suited to playoff baseball, with Lew Burdette facing Don Drysdale. When Drysdale gave up Eddie Mathews' 46th home run of the season in the fifth inning for a 4–2 Milwaukee lead, Alston took him out of the game. Burdette looked strong until the bottom of the seventh, when the Dodgers pulled off one of the more controversial plays in post-season history. After Norm Larker singled, Roseboro hit a grounder up the middle that looked like a sure double play. Braves shortstop Johnny Logan covered second and threw cleanly to Joe Torre at first, but Larker, ignoring second base, ran directly at Logan like a special teams player on a kickoff. Logan was at least four feet away from the base when Larker lowered his shoulder and pancaked the defenseless Logan in the chest, knocking him six feet behind second base. After Logan left the game on a stretcher, Felix Mantilla switched from second base to shortstop. Two innings later, Mantilla's throwing error cost the Braves the game and the pennant.

So the Dodgers won their fourth pennant in ten years and the first ever for a West Coast team, going from seventh place in 1958 to first in 1959. Larker's controversial base running and the fact that there was no consequence for such an intentionally reckless play gave some Sox fans pause, since the Sox's slick-fielding double play combination was a big reason they got to the World Series. Optimists pointed out that Aparicio and Fox were both much more elusive and nimble around the base than Logan, and that the Sox's great pitching would probably keep Larker off the bases anyway.

With the World Series contestants finally set, the *Chicago Tribune*'s Thursday, September 24 edition gave a complete scouting report, written anonymously by "a veteran American League manager," in an article entitled "Scout Rates Sox Tough Series Foe." The article had some very frank assessments not usually made public:

Aparicio—Likes to hit pitches out and away. Keep the ball down on him and occasionally tight.

Fox—One of the finest bunters in the AL, ideal #2 man in lineup, with Aparicio on gives Sox an early scoring threat.

Landis—Superlative defender, fine arm. Fast ball hitter who has trouble with low curves, which he chases.

Kluszewski—Slow curves and changeups on the inside are his weaknesses, likes to hit fastballs. Good glove man despite size, great hands.

Lollar—Key to the team's success. Take-charge guy in a quiet way. Strictly fastball hitter, keep it low.

Phillips—Will give a high fastball a ride, keep everything down and away, he'll go after the curve. Solid on defense and has strong throwing arm.

Smith—Likes fastballs; break him a curve down and away. Adequate on defense, doesn't need much range because Landis is next to him.

Rivera—Can't hit fastballs anymore so pump it past him. Vulnerable to changeups, keep the ball tight. Great outfielder who can still run; good arm. Aggressive player who is always trying.

Goodman—Magician with the bat, can hit to all fields, spray hitter who could be the surprise of the Series. Can have trouble when you crowd him inside; pitch him outside and he'll punch it to left field. Every once in a while he'll jerk one to right. No gazelle in the field but handles his position well.

Torgeson—Low-ball hitter who seldom goes for a bad ball, making him one of the best "waiters" in the game at the plate. Keep the ball away and curve him. Good base runner despite age.

Cash—Likes the fastball; pull hitter; keep pitches outside.

Esposito—Another high ball hitter but will chase the curve; one of the top utility players in the league.

When it came to White Sox pitchers, there were even fewer negatives:

Wynn—Top Sox pitcher. Throws most everything—fastball, screwball, curve, knuckler—with good control. Rough competitor and smart. Gets a big advantage with a slow windup, giving a sudden snap as he comes through his delivery, making it difficult for the batter to time the ball. Has mastered the art of mixing speeds.

Shaw—Most improved young pitcher in the league. Good sinking fastball, fair curveball and consistently in the strike zone.

Pierce—One of the best lefties in baseball. Good fast ball, curve, and control. Helps self at the plate, never lets up.

Donovan—Knows how to pitch; has good weapons in sinker, slider, and curve, which he keeps down and away from hitters. Like Pierce and Wynn, will help himself occasionally at the plate.

Staley—Gives a lot of motion and has pinpoint control with his sinker low and away. Good screwball; real artist who knows how to pitch and is not afraid.

Lown—Control not as sharp as Staley's, but can fire the ball and usually keeps it low.

The job that Lopez and Berres did with the pitching staff did not go unnoticed. Four Sox hurlers—Lown, Shaw, Staley, and Wynn—had a combined record of 57–23, and each one was an indifferent castoff from another team. The Cubs had Lown for seven years, when his record was 30–34. Shaw's dismissal from the Tigers got very little attention, and nothing was said when the Sox picked him up. Staley lost his effectiveness when he went from the Cardinals to the Reds, and when the Reds tired of him and dispatched him to New York, the Yankees used him in only three games. Stengel saw him as a washed-up 35-year-old, primarily relying on a worn-out knuckleball, yet under Berres' tutelage, when he came to Chicago in 1956, he went 8–3. The Indians gave up on Wynn, only to be haunted by his peerless performances that kept them out of the 1959 World Series. In the 1950s, no manager handled pitchers better than Lopez, and Berres had emerged as baseball's best pitching coach.

The *Tribune* also ran reports on the Dodgers on Thursday, September 27, authored by "an unnamed expert of the baseball wars," entitled "Sox Study Scout's Report on Dodgers":

Hodges—Slowed down with leg injury, but still a good defender. Pull hitter, tremendous power on the inside corner, won't swing at breaking stuff on the outside corner.

Neal—Best defensive second baseman in the league. Good runner, rare combination of speed and power. Can hit breaking pitches so move ball around to get him out.

Wills—Streak hitter on a hot streak; high ball hitter, pitch everything low. Fast and sharp defensively.

Gilliam—(switch hitter) Exceptional eye at plate; hits high pitches best; good bunter and base runner.

Snider—Good power to all fields, no holes in his strike zone. Lefties now give him trouble, change speeds for best results. Wild swinger who will strike out.

Demeter—Best arm in their outfield. Good power, can hit inside pitches, but will chase bad balls and can be handled with assorted pitches.

Moon—Good high ball hitter, power to all fields, good bunter who is fast. Keep the ball down.

Roseboro—Fastest catcher in the league. Has power on inside half of the plate, and can hit breaking balls. Keep pitches inside and mix deliveries.

Larker—Best bunter on team, good fast ball hitter. Good power to left but breaking balls get him out.

Fairly—Young, inexperienced, but dangerous. Good sense of strike zone and good speed. Pitch him tight fast balls.

Zimmer—Wild swinger who is powerful for his size. Fierce competitor who battles all the way.

Furillo—Still good throwing arm, has slowed some. Best player in the clutch. Breaking balls won't get him out; pitch him down and away.

Repulski—Pinch hitter who can be retired on good curves and pitches away. Still has power and can turn on inside offerings.

The Dodgers led the majors in fewest errors, led the NL in stolen bases (84), and were third in runs scored. The Sox had yet to face an opponent with the Dodgers' team speed. Their pitching staff fell into two groups; those who already had great success in the majors and those who were on the verge of doing so:

Drysdale—Fastest righty on staff, good curve and slider. Strikeout pitcher whose control can be erratic. Temperamental at times and can beat himself. Good fielder and hitter.

Podres—Best pitcher on the club in big games, much World Series experience. Throws everything but a knuckler, best at changing speeds. Hits and fields well.

Koufax—A lefty Drysdale, but even faster, with a good curve and change. Strikeout threat. Has known to tire, erratic some days, and fields poorly.

Craig—Fine control, good curve and slider, fair fastball. Pitches to spots; coming into own after mediocre past.

Klippstein—Good stuff and fine control; hampered by recent back ailment. Effective in short relief; cool and experienced.

Sherry—Gaining confidence with good stuff. Control only fair, but rarely hit hard; great slider. Can hit; one of the game's best hitting pitchers.

Los Angeles' pitching staff had the most strikeouts in baseball, a remarkable total of 1,077 batters (almost seven per nine innings), over 200 more than the next team on the list, San Francisco. While excelling at amassing strikeouts, the same Dodgers staff issued more walks than any other team in the National League and ranked third-best in team ERA.

The White Sox led the majors in fewest opponents' runs (588), most offensive stolen bases (113), and lowest team ERA. While Sox pitchers had 316 fewer strikeouts than the Dodgers, but they walked 89 fewer batters. Most individuals assumed the Chicagoans were the superior fielding team, but if so the margin was thin. While the Sox's great double play combination ended up on an August 1959 cover of *Sports Illustrated,* the Dodgers executed 154 double plays to the Sox's 141.[16]

It was evident to all that both teams matched up very closely. The Dodgers had a decided edge in power hitting, but otherwise the teams were similar offensively. Four games in cavernous Comiskey Park might negate the Dodgers' home run advantage, and the Dodgers' hitters had also not faced pitching as good as Chicago's all season. Alston had managed in two other World Series, winning in 1955 and losing in 1956; Lopez had managed in one, losing to the Giants in 1954. One variable that favored the Sox was the fact that the Dodgers could be emotionally and physically spent. Every game in their schedule for the last month was a critical contest, their pitching staff was consequently running on fumes, and they had only one day to prepare for the Series opener, which was starting 2,000 miles away from home. On the other hand, Sox hitters often had trouble against power pitchers, which the Dodgers had in spades, and they had never played in the maddening Los Angeles Coliseum before. That football stadium disguised as a baseball field was known to give visiting teams fits, with its odd fencing, terrible sightlines, and hacked-up turf.

For what it was worth, the great Ty Cobb predicted a White Sox victory. "Chicago will win the Series. They will revolutionize baseball," said the greatest player of the deadball era, obviously identifying with a team that relied on defense, pitching, and speed, the three foundations of the game in his day. Tigers manager Jimmie Dykes, no stranger to 35th and Shields, predicted the Sox to win in six, "because they're a greatly underrated outfit. If they can keep the ball in the park they should win." Perhaps the most important endorsement of all came from the small clique to whom the public paid the most attention, the New York odds makers. They made the Sox 6–5 favorites to win the first game and placed the same odds on them winning the World Series.[17]

10

October: Let the Games Begin

The first Sox fan to get his name in the paper on the eve of the first World Series in 40 years was 54-year-old Anthony Beale, from the 500 block of Drake Avenue, Libertyville, Illinois. Five minutes after Beale was lucky enough to buy his tickets to Game One, he made one of the bigger mistakes of his life by selling them to Sam Incardona and Joseph Dragel, two plain-clothes Chicago policemen working the fraud detail around Comiskey Park. They were part of Deputy Police Commissioner Kyran Phelan's 500-man special World Series task force, and Beale earned the distinction of being the first person arrested during the 1959 Series for ticket scalping. Phelan's special force made 17 arrests the morning of October 1, the most remarkable one being the apprehension of Chicagoan Maurice Freeman, a 56-year-old automobile salesman living in the 5000 block of Marine Drive in Chicago. Freeman had 14 grandstand seats that he was attempting to sell for $25 to $50 apiece. The fine for each of the 17 ticket-scalping miscreants was $25, but the Chicago Police added their own mean little wrinkle to the punishment. To further ruin the Game One experience for the "Unfortunate 17," Chicago's finest thumbed their nose at due process and detained them in a lockup with no chance for bail until the game was over. Another gentleman from Napoleon, Ohio, complained to the police about buying a bleacher ticket from a stranger for $5, only to find out at the gate that he had purchased a rain check, not a ticket.[1] For all some fans knew about *caveat emptor*, it might as well be the name of a White Sox farmhand with an Italian heritage.

Bill Veeck himself had fun settling a score with a long-time adversary over the issue of tickets. Lou Perini, one of the original "Three Little Steam Shovels" (the nickname given a trio of East Coast developers who owned the Braves), sent his office boy, Don Davidson, to see Veeck for some additional tickets for his Milwaukee contingent. Veeck, remembering the cold shoulder he always seemed to get from Perini when he owned the Browns, refused to comply. Each major league team could purchase 100 tickets to the Series through the league office, but it was customary for the two pennant-winning clubs to grant them more if they wished. Taking a swipe at someone he considered one of baseball's "stuffed shirts," Veeck told a group of reporters, "Nobody gave me anything when I was out of baseball, particularly Perini. In fact, he took my 12 seats away from me last year. I had a promise of 12 from the Braves in August, '58 … then at the World Series, I was told I had none. Not one or two, but none. Mr. Perini wants 12 for himself. Okay. Now this is the day of reckoning. I am doing what Perini wishes he could do. I'm taking care of my fans first."[2] The press was happy to get another story about Veeck once more pulling a member of the baseball establishment's chain. For the first game of the Series, Veeck sat in the press box with Hank Greenberg, while his wife and their oldest son, Mike, sat on the aisle steps of the third base side of the upper deck. Comiskey and his guests sat in the owner's box along the third base line. No decorative bunting or other patriotic artifacts hung inside the old park. The White Sox issued a statement saying that the club was "proud of its interior and wanted the fans to see it just as it was for league play. We confined all our decorations to the outside of the park." Veeck also instructed the Andy Frain ushers to pass out roses to the first 20,000 women to walk through the gates. Two South Side immortals, Red Faber and Ray Schalk, the heroes of the 1917 World Series, threw out the first pitch.

Game One

As the crowd of 48,013 settled into their seats, the Dodgers looked and played like the travel-weary team they were. Roger Craig was no puzzle whatsoever for the White Sox lineup, while Early Wynn was in complete control throughout the game. The Sox got two runs in the first inning, seven runs in the third, and two more in the fourth. Ted Kluszewski hit a pair of two-run homers, one off Craig and the other, an absolute moon shot, off Chuck Churn. The big first baseman drove in five runs and led the Sox's hit parade, going 3-for-4. Analysts of the game could have predicted Big Klu's big day; it was the fifth homer he hit off Craig in just 24 at-bats during his career. Jim Landis and Al Smith also had two hits, but perhaps the most encouraging statistic was the fact that the Sox were 4-for-8 with runners in scoring position. In the ecstasy of the moment, nobody noticed that the South Siders got just one hit in the last five innings against Clem Labine, Sandy Koufax, and Johnny Klippstein. Charlie Neal and Gil Hodges each had two hits off Wynn, who found another level of intensity when he needed to, keeping Los Angeles hitless with men in scoring position. Staley closed the last two innings for the victors with his usual effectiveness, but by that time the Dodgers had lost interest.

Afterwards in the jubilant White Sox clubhouse, a broadly smiling Kluszewski described the best game of his career to the press. "I wasn't sure the
first one was going to leave the park, but I knew that the hanging curve ball
from Churn would be long gone, if it ever landed." He continued, "I never
lost my power over the last two seasons, but platooning with Dick Stuart in
Pittsburgh bothered my timing and consistency."[3] Skipper Lopez cautioned
that the way the Series could go, the Sox could just as easily be on the losing
end of an 11–0 whitewash as the Dodgers were on this date.

It was a good day for everyone at Comiskey Park. In a year when the
minimum wage in the country was a dollar an hour, Nicholas J. LaPapa, President of Vendors Local 236, reported that the lowest-earning vendors on this
glorious Thursday afternoon earned $75 in commissions and another $15 in
tips, five times their usual take for an afternoon game.[4]

Game Two

The corner of 35th and Shields resembled Times Square on Friday, October 22, 1959, as the Sox found themselves favored by the odds makers, 6–5,
in Game Two and 9–5 to take it all. Mayor Richard J. Daley settled with a
small entourage in his box seats to watch Bob Shaw face the seasoned World
Series veteran, Johnny Podres. Observers noticed Daley engaged in lively dis-
cussions with one of his younger guests, none other than the Junior Senator
from Massachusetts, John F. Kennedy. Before the game, the American flag
became stuck halfway up the flagpole, with the color guard inanimately standing at attention below. Many fans thought this was another one of Veeck's
pranks until a trim, athletic, 29-year-old woman named Roni Wear deftly
shimmied 60 feet up the flagpole and freed the jammed pulley so that Old
Glory could continue its ascent. Wear, one of the few female steeplejacks in
the country, made a favorable impression on the big crowd.[5] A much more
famous celebrity made a poor impression: Nat King Cole. The Chicago native
completely botched the National Anthem, hitting wrong notes and covering
up a memory lapse of the final lyric by ad-libbing: "…O'er land and o'er sea,
and the home of the brave."[6] Could these pregame miscues be portents of
things to come?

The Sox jumped on Johnny Podres for two runs in the first inning, and
the Dodgers started the game playing just as erratically as they had in Game
One. Podres found his groove, and both he and Shaw had things well in hand
until the fifth inning, when Charlie Neal homered to make it a one-run game.
Neal's blast just reached the front row of the left field bleachers. Sox fan
Melvin Piehl reached for the ball and spilled his beer in the process, giving
left fielder Al Smith an unexpected beer shower which became the most

famous photo of the entire Series.[7] Shaw fell apart in the seventh after he had easily retired Roseboro and Wills. Chuck Essegian, the ex–USC fullback, pinch-hit for Podres and hit a long home run to tie things up. A rattled Shaw then walked leadoff man Junior Gilliam. Lopez made a mistake at this juncture, leaving Shaw in the game, even though the veteran Turk Lown was ready in the bullpen. Charlie Neal came up and hit his second homer of the contest, driving in Gilliam in front of him. The shell-shocked Shaw went to the dugout and Lown finished the inning, one batter too late: Dodgers 4, White Sox 2.

Larry Sherry retired the Sox in order in the seventh inning. With the White Sox down to their last six outs, Kluszewski and Lollar singled to start the eighth. Lopez sent Torgeson in to pinch-run for Kluszewski, but left Lollar, the slowest man on the team, at first. Even with Esposito ready to pinch-run, and Battey and Romano ready to catch, Lopez chose to leave Lollar on the base paths. Smith came up and hit a booming drive to left field. Torgeson scored easily on the drive, but Lollar, thinking the ball could be caught by left fielder Wally Moon, hesitated around second. Once he saw Moon had no chance to catch the long fly, Lollar ran as hard as he could toward third. Third base coach Tony Cuccinello, knowing it was late in the game, that Lollar was the tying run, and that three Dodgers would have to handle the ball flawlessly to get him out, waved Lollar home. The only problem was that Lollar's slow top gear was no match for the Dodgers' fielding acumen. Moon threw a strike to Wills, who wheeled and made a perfect throw to Roseboro, who caught it cleanly when Lollar was still 14 feet from the plate. Lollar was so "out" that he slowed to a trot and resignedly walked into the tag. Cuccinello had committed the cardinal sin of making the first out of the inning at home plate, with two proven hitters—Goodman and Rivera—next in the batting order. Sherry retired both of them to end the eighth, and his devastating slider dispatched Cash, Aparicio, and Fox on three easy ground balls in the ninth to end the game: Dodgers 4, White Sox 3. Few in the departing crowd of 47,368 could get over what they saw. The World Series was all knotted up and on its way to the West Coast.

After the game it was apparent that, in spite of Lopez's decision to let Lollar run for himself, Cuccinello would be the first individual to receive the rapt attention of the media. "I sent him all the way," Cuccinello told a huge throng of reporters. "He's running on the 3–2 pitch. I figure the way the ball's hit he's got to score. I was watching the ball, not Lollar, and didn't know he slowed up at second. When he went by me, then I could tell [that he would be out]. If I'd figured the relay was going to be done that way, I wouldn't have sent him in."[8] Lollar and Torgeson both agreed that the ball could have been caught. Lollar offered no excuses but explained what he was thinking: "I thought there was a chance it could be caught, so I stopped dead at second. Otherwise if he does catch it, I have no chance to get back to first."[9]

Bob Shaw addressed reporters as he exited the White Sox's locker room, saying, "I made three bad pitches in a row. I lost my timing a little. It's not a matter of getting tired; you start bending over instead of getting your arm up as you should. It was 3 and 1 to Essegian. I should have made him hit the ball I wanted him to hit. But then I had to throw a strike, instead of pitching for a spot. Neal's first home run was a high slider and the second a poorly located fastball." Curiously, Shaw added that the Sox scouting report on Neal was wrong.[10]

Over in the Dodgers' locker room, a relieved group of victors were eager to get back to Los Angeles and had lots of criticism for the White Sox organization. The Dodgers were rather ungracious toward their rivals. Reserve catcher Joe Pignatano was one of the first to vent:

> We're gonna beat 'em in five just so we don't have to come back here. They gave our wives lousy tickets and the whole club is teed off about it. They got our wives stuck way out in the right field corner where they have to crane their necks to see around the girders.[11]

Veteran pitcher Clem Labine chimed in, saying, "the White Sox wives will sit under the clock in the Coliseum, including Bill Veeck." The most stinging comments, however, came from Podres. He told the press that he was not all that impressed with the White Sox, dismissively pointing out, "I think over-all San Francisco and Milwaukee are better clubs. They have more power. Defensively, though, the White Sox are the best I've seen. But when a guy hits a couple of homers like Neal did, what good is all your defense?"[12]

Chicagoans had to make do with a televised World Series for the next three games; none of them thought the Fall Classic would not return to the South Side the following Thursday. This was the feeling even though the Dodgers were in a position to end it with a sweep in their quirky home field, where most of the White Sox had never played. Those who had their televisions on Friday night after the Dodgers victory might have seen the premiere on CBS Television of an odd new show called *The Twilight Zone*. The first episode was entitled "Where Is Everybody?" With over 275,000 tickets sold in advance for the next three World Series games on the West Coast, the White Sox would not be asking the same question.

Game Three

The Sox spent $50,000 to charter an airliner for the round trip between Chicago and Los Angeles. With the Series occurring on the West Coast for the first time, Major League Baseball chartered seven planes to transport both teams, their officials, family members, league officials, and the media. American, Continental, and Trans World Airlines all had commercial flights between the two cities, and all reported being booked solid. American also mentioned that their Chicago to San Francisco route was almost filled as well, mostly with individuals who also booked a second flight between San Francisco and Los Angeles.[13] The journey was a novelty to the South Side pennant winners, since no American League team at that time was west of Kansas City.

The Sox set up shop at the Biltmore Hotel, and on Saturday, October 3, they had a two-hour practice in the Coliseum.[14] Their first impression was that they were playing baseball on a football field—which they were. The infield was flat, not crowned, making the mound appear higher than it really was. There was mostly dirt in the large area behind the plate and the field, and the turf was in rough shape. Fair territory had large patches of dead brown grass, and the ancient stadium had hosted a football game the night before, when 11th-ranked USC defeated 14th-ranked Ohio State, 17–0. The facility was so beholden to football that the Dodgers had to reimburse USC for the cost of 2,000 tickets, the number of seats lost for the Ohio State game because of the construction of the temporary press box for the World Series.[15]

Sox players stared incredulously at the "Chinese Wall" in left field. Exactly 251 feet down the left field line was a huge cyclone fence, 42 feet high and 142 feet wide, extending into a deep part of left-center, 390 feet from the plate. While fielding balls off the high fence during practice, left fielder Al Smith noted that unlike the Green Monster in Boston, balls did not bounce off, they just fell to the turf. During batting practice, Aparicio and Goodman hit routine fly balls high off the screen in left field. Young Jim McAnany was the only Sox to hit one over it, while Rivera cleared the cyclone fence in right field wall with a 340-foot shot. Donovan, Sunday's starting pitcher, sarcastically suggested that Aparicio play both shortstop and left field, with the three outfielders covering left-center to right field. Sightlines were another problem in this baseball venue built for football. The field was surrounded by a very low fence with a huge expanse of bleachers above it. When it was filled with individuals dressed in light colors for hot weather, the background for catching a baseball was terrible.[16]

All the teams that played there complained about losing sight of the ball during day games in the sea of white shirts. Al Lopez took some consolation in the fact that four of his starters and two other players had played there previously. Ex–National Leaguers Kluszewski and Lown were the only ones who had played regular season games in the Coliseum. Kluszewski played in eight games, going just 5-for-24 with one RBI, and Lown pitched one perfect inning in the Coliseum with the Cubs in June 1958. Four other Sox—Aparicio, Fox, Lollar, and Wynn—played there in the All-Star Game just two months ago, albeit at night. The Chicagoans' limited experience in the strange stadium would be a challenge.[17]

Since Los Angeles was not a city American League teams visited in the 1950s, the White Sox took full advantage of Tinsel Town's offerings before Sunday's game.[18] Some went to see George Oppenheimer's *A Mighty Man Is He,* not because they knew anything about the playwright but because it starred the comely Nancy Kelly. Dick Donovan took his wife to the Hollywood Brown Derby, while roommates Fox and Pierce accompanied their wives to the early seating at the Cocoanut Grove.

On Sunday, October 4, the biggest crowd in World Series history, 92,394, came to the Coliseum for the first World Series contest west of St. Louis, and the weather was perfect for baseball. The record attendance was 6,100 more than the 86,288 who showed up in Cleveland on October 10, 1948, when the Boston Braves beat the Indians, 11–5, in Game Five of the 1948 Series. Alston and Lopez named Don Drysdale and Dick Donovan as their starters. Drysdale was the rock of the Dodgers pitching staff through early August, going 15–8 up to that point, but had pitched poorly the last six weeks of the season. The tall, blond right-hander with the Hollywood looks had won just two of his last nine decisions to finish the year at 17–13. Drysdale had last pitched a week ago, on Sunday, September 27, in the second playoff game against the Braves. While the Dodgers won that game to clinch the pennant, Drysdale had a rough afternoon. He gave up six hits and four runs in 4⅓ innings, one of the hits being Eddie Mathews' 46th home run of the year. In spite of his two-month slump, the intimidating fireballer led the National League in strikeouts with 242, averaging more than eight per nine innings. He was among the leaders in total innings pitched (270⅔) and had a 3.46 ERA, in spite of the Coliseum's hitter-friendly configuration. Drysdale's sidearm delivery was particularly tough on right-handed hitters. He was never shy about throwing inside and loved to boast about it. His only World Series experience was a two-inning mop-up role in the Dodgers' 6–2 loss in Game Four in 1956 against the Yankees.

Donovan was coming off the worse year in his five seasons with the Sox, after spending many weeks on the disabled list. In spite of his lackluster year, no team relished facing the tall right-hander. He had an odd windup which gave many hitters fits. When Donovan was able to get good movement on his slider and keep his pitches low, he was one of the most effective pitchers in baseball.

Zack Wheat, the 71-year-old Hall of Famer who played for the Dodgers from 1909 to 1927, threw out the first ball. Through the first six innings, neither pitcher allowed a run, but Donovan was having a better outing. The Sox managed seven hits off Drysdale, who also walked four batters during that span, while Donovan surrendered only one safety, an innocent second-inning single by Hodges. Donovan, however, ran into big trouble in the seventh. After Charlie Neal singled for the Dodgers' second hit of the game, Donovan walked Norm Larker. Gil Hodges came up, and the wary and tiring right-hander, pitching too cautiously, walked him as well. Lopez took the frustrated Donovan out and summoned Staley from the bullpen. Alston sent Carl Furillo up to pinch-hit for Don Demeter. Staley got him to hit a grounder to Aparicio that took a terrible hop and got through to center field for a single, driving in two runs.

The White Sox answered the call in the top of the eighth inning. Klus-zewski and Lollar both singled, and Walter Alston hurried to the mound to remove Drysdale. Larry Sherry, who had pitched so well in Game Two, came in to face Goodman. After what seemed like an overly long conference on the mound between Alston and Sherry, Goodman, who already had two solid hits on the afternoon, got in the batter's box. Sherry hit him squarely on the kneecap with a fastball, and Goodman had to be carried off the field. There were grumblings about what Alston's instructions to Sherry might have been; a penny for your thoughts, Mr. Alston. This loaded the bases, but also took the White Sox's most experienced pure hitter out of the game with the lead runs on base. Al Smith came up and grounded into a double play, which scored Kluszewski, but Rivera popped out to Roseboro to end the inning. In the ninth, Sherry struck out Cash and Aparicio, gave up a single to the Fox, and then struck out Landis to end the game. The Sox had left 11 men on base and were hitless the seven times they had runners in scoring position. Dono-van's great outing, one of the better pitched games in World Series history, had gone to waste.

After the game, many had comments about the bad hops in the infield. Aparicio perhaps drew the most attention with his contradictory statements about Furillo's crucial grounder that decided the game. Aparicio first said he got a good jump on it but was handcuffed by the funny hop. He later men-tioned that the white-shirted sea of fans forming the background behind the plate made it hard for him to pick up the ball off the bat. Lopez said it did not matter, that Aparicio had a rare lapse in judgment by trying to get the ball with two hands, and it would have been easier for him to field it cleanly if he had simply leaned over with his glove hand.[19]

The press approached Donovan, one of the hardest losers in the game, very cautiously. To their surprise, the 32-year-old Bostonian, who lit a cigar to help get through the inquiries, was civil, cordial, and not the least bit curt. He deftly wrapped his usual cryptic and humorous statements around what-ever disappointment or anger he had. Donovan admitted that he was nervous about starting a World Series game, even the day before, but once he started to warm up he felt more confident. He praised home plate umpire Ed Hurley for calling a good game. Lollar added that his slider was almost unhittable all afternoon, and Donovan said he was not going to argue with Lopez about coming out of the game because no pitchers *ever* argue with Lopez about coming out of a game. He added "The heat and sun did not get to me, the Dodgers got to me, just once, but that once they got me good." The enigmatic New Englander added that if anyone had any more questions, they could finish up with Staley. "Staley always finishes up for Donovan," he said in closing, deftly adding a footnote to his manager's decision to change pitchers.[20] Nobody in the locker room mentioned anything about Sherry putting the hot-hitting Goodman out of the game—at least on the record.

Sunday, October 4, turned out to be a sad day all the way around for Chicago's South Side. After a great start the week before, the Cardinals fell apart in front of a sparse Soldier Field crowd. Avenging the White Sox's domination of their baseball brethren, the powerful Cleveland Browns turned the Big Red to "little pink" in a 34–7 route.

Game Four

As the White Sox prepared to prevent their backs from going up against the wall on October 5, Walter Alston announced that center fielder Duke Snider would sit out Game Four and Don Demeter would replace him. Snider, who did very little in the first three games of the Series, was getting no relief from the bi-weekly cortisone injections in his injured knee, so Demeter would get the start.[21] Most thought this would help the visiting White Sox. While the 24-year-old Demeter hit 18 home runs in 1959, most of them were short fly balls over the Coliseum's left field wall. He struggled against quality pitching and struck out once every 4.3 times at bat during the season.

Alston also spent some time vehemently denying a report in the media that he had called the Sox a "bunch of second raters." His team had put their foot in their mouth with Podres' ill-advised statements after the second game, and Alston did not want to provide anything else that might become bulletin board material for the White Sox locker room, so he backtracked by saying, "I'd have to be stupid to say that, about a team that beat us 11–0. In all my years in the big leagues, I never talked about any other club and I wouldn't do it now."[22]

While Alston was in the midst of his denials, the White Sox players' wives were complaining about what poor hosts the Dodgers were because of *their* terrible seats. Dodgers general managers Buzzie Bavasi flippantly denied having anything to do with it, dismissing the issue by saying, "We gave the Chicago team 500 good seats and 100 poor ones. They must have given the good ones to other people they considered more important than the wives. The good ones were low, behind third base."[23]

Desperate to put together a lineup with offensive potential, Lopez shuffled his batting order. He put Landis in the leadoff spot, followed by Aparicio, with Fox batting third. Goodman's knee was healed enough for him to get the start at third base, and Rivera, batting eighth, played right field with right-hander Roger Craig on the mound. Since Craig was no puzzle at all for the Sox when Wynn dominated the Dodgers in Game One, the South Siders entered the game feeling more determined than desperate.

In the first inning, things initially looked good for the Sox. After Landis flied out to start the game, Craig walked Aparicio, who promptly stole second. Fox hit a Texas Leaguer and made it to second, pushing Aparicio to third as Kluszewski strode to the plate. Alston signaled to Roseboro to intentionally walk the big slugger, bringing Lollar up. Lollar hit into a double play to end the inning, Wills to Neal to Hodges, leaving the Sox scoreless. The great catcher's one shortcoming—lack of speed—proved to be a detriment for the second time in the Series.

The Dodgers got to Wynn for four runs after two were out in the third inning by stringing together five consecutive singles. Moon, Larker, Hodges, Demeter, and Roseboro all got hits after Wynn had easily retired Gilliam and Neal. Hodges' hit should have been an easy out, but Smith lost the flight of his pop-up in the poor background caused by the huge crowd. Landis committed a throwing error, trying to nail the sliding Moon at third base after Larker's single. Lown closed out the inning, while a disgusted Wynn fumed in the dugout.

In the fourth inning, Pierce came in to pitch for the Chicagoans, and the great lefty threw masterfully for three innings, not allowing a hit, issuing a single walk, and striking out two. In the seventh, after Torgeson grounded out to Neal, Landis singled and reached second on Aparicio's sacrifice bunt. Now, with two away, Fox singled, chasing Landis to third. Even though two were out, Craig was in a jam and he knew it; Kluszewski strode to the plate and Lollar was on-deck. Kluszewski smashed a single to center, scoring Landis. When Lollar unloaded a no-doubt-about-it blast over the Chinese Wall in left field, the Sox had tied the game, 4–4. Suddenly, with one swing of the bat, Sox fans completely forgot about the great catcher's previous misadventures on the bases. Sherry put the Sox down very quietly in the eighth, and all 92,650 in attendance could feel the building tension. Its release came much too soon for the South Siders.

In the bottom of the eighth, Hodges led off against Staley. Hodges made a career out of hitting successfully against a small handful of pitchers, and unfortunately Staley was one of them. They had faced each other 96 times and Hodges had 29 hits, six of them home runs. The seventh turned out to be the biggest hit of his career. The first baseman got ahold of a Staley sinker and put it into the left field bleachers, clearing the odd fence in left and land-ing about ten rows back. What would have been a routine fly ball in every high school baseball field in America put the Dodgers ahead, 5–4. As was his custom, Hodges blew a kiss to his wife as he crossed the plate. In the top of the ninth, Sherry, for the third time, mystified the Sox hitters with his slider. Everyone was on their feet when Kluszewski strode to the plate as the South Side's last hope, since Aparicio and Fox before him had grounded out. The game ended when he flied out to left. Now the South Siders were up against it, and all of Chicago knew it, down 3–1 with one more contest left in Los Angeles.

"Hodges' homer was an easy out anywhere but here. I watched that one all the way, but I couldn't do anything about it," a dejected Al Smith told the assembled media in the Sox's locker room. "We can't blame this park or the bad vision, because they have to put up with the same things," Lopez added, "but we still have a hell of a chance." Landis echoed his sentiments. "They're sweating it out, too. We'll win it if we get [back home]," the center fielder explained. Bob Shaw, designated to start Game Five, exuded a quiet confidence, pointing out that "If I pitch like I can, we'll win. All we need is some runs. If you let the pressure bother you, you're lost. I don't stay awake worrying about my pitching the next day. It's just one more day's work. I can't get anybody out tonight, can I?"[24] Bold words, but it was doubtful if they buoyed the despondent White Sox fandom. The Sox left nine men on base, committed three errors, and had one passed ball during the sad afternoon. They had one more game in this house of horrors which seemed like an impossible place to execute their slick-fielding, run-manufacturing style of play. While Lopez refused to mention the ballpark as a reason for their failures, umpire Ed Hurley made very candid comments about the place. "You know where I picked up the ball? Right here," he said, pointing to a spot about four feet in front of himself. "I'm not exaggerating." Lopez also said nothing about why Pierce, the Sox's best pitcher for more than a decade, was being relegated to a relief role in the team's first World Series in 40 years. Some claimed Lopez was spooked by the Coliseum's close left field fence, but Pierce was not known to give up fly balls, let alone home runs. Relegating one of the best lefties in baseball history to the bench in the World Series became a real head-scratcher.

A different mood prevailed in the Dodgers clubhouse. Thrilled at being one game away from a World Series victory without having to return to chilly Chicago, all eyes were on young Larry Sherry, a mystery man before the World Series who had now mystified Chicago bats for the third straight game. Sherry, a high school teammate of Barry Latman's, had become the reason the Dodgers were still playing baseball this late in the year. He was giving the Sox the same frustrating treatment he gave the Braves in the National League playoffs. Alston described the young phenom to the media, telling them, "We had Sherry up last year and he couldn't get anyone out. The harder he threw, the harder they hit him. This season he was farmed out; when he came back his control was 90 percent improved and he showed us the slider he used today."

Sherry gladly shared his story with the press, telling them,

I signed with the Dodgers a few days before my 18th birthday. Did I regret not going to college? No, I learned more in two seasons in spring training than I ever would have learned in college. In high school I was all-city in basketball. I wasn't anything in baseball. That slider, I developed it during the winter, in Venezuela. I wanted a third pitch, one that would come off the fastball. I couldn't catch on to the overhand change that Podres throws, so some hitters suggested I try the slider. It's a difficult pitch for the batter to pick up.[25]

The 24-year-old Californian had now pitched seven late innings in three consecutive World Series games over a span of only four days, with a flight from Chicago to Los Angeles sandwiched in between, after winning the last playoff game against the Braves. Thus far Sherry's line for the Series was two saves (Games Two and Three) and a victory (Game Four). In his seven innings of work, he had given up one run, one walk, and four hits. Perhaps the best thing going for the White Sox in Game Five was the fact that it was very unlikely that Alston would use him three days in a row.

Dodgers executive Buzzie Bavasi could not handle all the excitement the Dodgers' good fortune had generated. He collapsed after the game, falling to the ground while getting out of a car at his apartment hotel after complaining about being dizzy from the heat.[26] He talked the medical staff out of hospitalizing him. The way Game Five would go for his team, he may have been better off checking in.

Game Five

There was a funereal feeling among the Chicago contingent in Los Angeles on Tuesday, October 6. Few gave the Sox a chance to return to Chicago with anything more than their tails between their legs. Their play in Los Angeles was tentative, lacking the athletic aggression, confidence, and swagger that became their hallmarks during the regular season. The local press became more objective and less optimistic. Edward Prell, in the *Chicago Tribune*'s Tuesday, October 6, edition, pointed out that this 1959 Sox team was on the verge of becoming the eighth Chicago ball club since 1917 to lose a World Series, not the kind of analysis the Sox wanted to read after yesterday's stinging loss. Prell also reminded readers that Lopez's record in World Series games was now one win and seven defeats. The ballplayers turned to superstition to stay alive, discarding the new all-white athletic socks they wore in the first four Series games for their traditional black socks. Lopez also changed the batting order yet again, putting Aparicio back in the leadoff spot, Landis in his customary third spot, and moving Lollar back to cleanup ahead of Kluszewski.

Their opponent in this fifth game was Sandy Koufax, the 24-year-old Brooklyn native who, five weeks earlier on Monday, August 31, tied Bob Feller's record by striking out 18 San Francisco Giants. Alston explained his reasons for going with the young fireballer instead of Podres, candidly pointing out, "I don't like his [Podres'] work with three day's rest. Podres will pitch the first game back in Chicago if we go there. He likes pitching in that park."[27] While he was already one of the fastest pitchers in the majors by the late 1950s, Koufax had not yet put together his eventual Hall of Fame performances. His record since his Dodgers debut in 1955 was 28–27, and he had a 4.15 lifetime ERA. Lack of control impaired his progress. In 516⅔ innings pitched, the slim, swarthy lefty had issued 305 walks, but he also had 486 strikeouts, almost one per inning. If Shaw could approach his previous outing and Koufax could be just a little erratic, there might be some hope for baseball to return to the South Side.

The two young hurlers kept both offenses very quiet until the top of the third inning. Phillips led off and singled, but McAnany followed with a pop out to Hodges at first. Shaw bunted Phillips successfully to second. Aparicio then knocked a shallow single to left field; Phillips could only get to third, and Aparicio was out at second when he tried to advance after the play at third. In the Dodgers' third, after Wills and Koufax grounded out to Aparicio, Junior Gilliam singled to right and Neal singled to left, chasing Gilliam to third. Moon ended the inning with an easy groundout to Fox.

In the fourth, the Sox broke the ice. Fox and Landis started the inning with singles. With men on first and third, Lollar hit a sharp grounder to Neal at second, who opted to turn a double play instead of preventing Fox from scoring, so the Sox took the lead, 1–0. Kluszewski came up and put a scare in Koufax with a tremendous drive deep to center that Demeter hauled down on the run for the third out.

The Dodgers' half of the seventh inning determined the game. After Shaw got Roseboro (who was playing brilliantly behind the plate but hitting only .118) to fly out to Smith, Alston sent Chuck Essegian up to pinch hit for Wills. Shaw, remembering Essegian's power, gave him nothing to hit and walked him. Alston replaced young Essegian with a pinch-runner, veteran Don Zimmer. Duke Snider pinch-hit for Koufax and grounded to Aparicio, and Zimmer was forced out at second. Alston, thinking now or never, sent Johnny Podres in to run for Snider. Jim Gilliam, the Dodgers' leadoff man, came up with two out and singled to left. Lopez played a defensive hunch and took McAnany out of left field, moved Al Smith from right to left, and put Jungle Jim Rivera in right. Red-hot Charlie Neal came up. Shaw unleashed a wild pitch, allowing Podres and Gilliam to move up to second and third. This was the mess the Sox wanted to avoid: a close ballgame, two runners in scoring position, and the Dodgers' best hitter in the Series up. Neal launched a tremendous drive to right-center field. Landis, playing him to pull, was over in left-center, completely out of position to catch it. Over in right field, Rivera streaked for the ball at the moment of impact and made a brilliant, game-saving catch in full sprint. The Sox were still alive, thanks once again to Rivera, one of the greatest defensive outfielders of his era.

Shaw was spent in the eighth inning. Moon started the inning with a single, and Larker flied deep to Rivera in right. Hodges also singled, and when Landis unsuccessfully threw to third to get Moon, Hodges scampered to second base. Suddenly there was one out with the lead run on second. Alston sent Ron Fairly in to pinch-hit for Demeter. Lopez came out, knew he had to make a pitching change, and summoned Billy Pierce from the bullpen, at which time Alston substituted Rip Repulski for Fairly. Lopez did not like the idea of Repulski facing Pierce, so he ordered an intentional walk. The bases were now loaded with Dodgers, there was only one out, and catcher Johnny Roseboro strode to the plate. The managerial chess game continued when Alston called back Roseboro and sent up Carl Furillo to face Pierce. Lopez, out-strategizing Alston, replaced Pierce with Dick Donovan. Donovan pitched brilliantly, getting Furillo to pop out to Phillips at third and Zimmer to make the third out with a lazy fly to left fielder Al Smith. Donovan could not have chosen a better day to throw an unhittable sinker and proceeded to get Sherry, Gilliam, and Neal to end game with three infield grounders in the ninth. Perhaps the most nerve-wracking day in White Sox history ended in triumph, 1–0.

Donovan enjoyed the attention he received from the press after the game. The loquacious hurler pointed out, "I wish I could say I was completely calm, but I've never been in a spot like that. How did I feel? How would you feel? I wasn't exactly whistling 'Yankee Doodle.'"[28]

Thanks to the brilliant efforts of Shaw, a major reason why the Sox were still playing in October, and Donovan, up and down all year but peerless when healthy, the 1959 World Series moved back to Chicago. The disappointment was palpable in the Dodgers' locker room. The last thing any of them wanted to do was take a long flight to Chicago, face the best pitching staff in the majors on cool, clammy autumn afternoons, and try to win a ballgame on the biggest field in the major leagues. The losers were distracted by a throng of television personnel that hurriedly packed up their belongings. They had set up their wiring and cameras about an hour before to televise a victory celebration that, thanks to Donovan, Rivera, and Shaw, was not going to occur.

Dick Donovan casts his doleful gaze toward another unlucky hitter. While he is telegraphing the pitch by showing his grip on the ball, this rarely helped opposing hitters, for when Donovan was on his game he was one of the most difficult pitchers to hit in the major leagues.

Game Six

The White Sox and Dodgers settled back into Chicago, sharing the spotlight but certainly not the sentiment. The Chicagoans were thrilled to be home. Emboldened by the memory that just two days ago they won a game playing "White Sox baseball," and encouraged by the fact that the rest of the

Series would be in their own backyard, they felt confident about coming back and winning it. After all, the Yankees were down three games to one just a year ago, and they roared back to defeat the Braves. The Dodgers, on the other hand, had no interest in leaving their sunny climes and returning to the autumnal, cloudy Midwest. They now had a sense of how good Chicago's pitching really was, since the two games they lost were both shutouts. Also, going into Game Six, the White Sox had six more hits, five more extra-base hits, eight more walks, and eight more runs that the Dodgers—strange statistics for a team down three games to two. If they could somehow come through more consistently with runners on base, the Series would be theirs. The Dodgers also realized that the difficult playing conditions at the Coliseum played a big part in their two West Coast victories. The Sox's fielding was bound to be better in Comiskey Park than it had been in Los Angeles, and they did not want any part of the starting pitchers the White Sox could use in these last two games. Through the sixth game, Wynn had an ERA of 2.79 with one walk and eight strikeouts. Donovan's ERA was 2.19. He had struck out five, walked two, and given up only two hits. Pierce, not given a start by Lopez because of the Coliseum's short left field dimensions, had pitched only three innings in relief, giving up no runs and only two hits. Wynn was starting Game Six, and Lopez had the luxury of choosing between the righty Donovan or the well-rested lefty, Pierce, in Game Seven. Looking at the Series in this light, despite being a game behind, things looked quite encouraging for the Sox and their South Side loyalists. Many South Siders, however, did not agree with Lopez's reasoning. Skeptical Sox fans could not figure out why Pierce was not given the nod to start the critical sixth game. The great Sox lefty had 31⅔ fewer innings under his belt during the season and was seven years younger.

Both teams got in four hours of practice on Wednesday, October 7. Lopez was candid in assessing the White Sox's chances when he spoke with the press, exuding a great deal of confidence when he said,

> Now that we are back home, where we have plenty of playing experience, I think we'll go all the way and win. I'm not making too much of a point about the using it as an alibi; it's the same for both clubs. But there's no doubt the Coliseum is a tough place to play in, and they have had much more experience there than we have. We made some mistakes there that hurt us, and I don't think we'll make them here. Our principal weapon all season has been our defense, and when you move into new surroundings, as we did there, it's not the same.[29]

Wynn also gave the media an earful. Known throughout his career for sometimes being too candid, he unloaded on the West Coast press, criticizing them for not respecting his team, and calling them a "bush league media."

> They make us look like a lousy ball club just because we've had some bad experiences in that circus grounds they call a ball park out there. They have been saying we ought

to try to get into the third major league [the ill-fated and never realized Continental League]. They'd come around and interview you; then you'd look in the paper the next day and couldn't recognize what you had said. One guy asked so many silly questions I wondered if he'd ever been in a ball park before. I told him to go up and sit in the stands and give me his typewriter. I'd write his story for him.[30]

Everyone knew that during the first few years any city had a major league team for the first time, the enthusiasm and bias of the town's press corps could get overwhelming. For all of Los Angeles' urban sophistication, the local writers were not immune from the same condition, but Wynn was oblivious. At this point, he tipped his cap to the opposition but unloaded about the stadium and field conditions, explaining, "The Dodgers are a real good ball club. It's a shame to make them play in that place. Maybe we ought to finish in Soldier Field."[31]

Game Six pre-game ceremonies went smoothly, with no female steeplechases needed to raise the colors and a vocalist who did not butcher the lyrics to the obligatory patriotic songs. The singer herself, however, raised some eyebrows, with some thinking she was a bit too highbrow for the old Comiskey ballyard. Vivienne Della Chiessa, a 45-year-old lyric coloratura soprano, sang the Star Spangled Banner. While nobody could quite see the link between an operatic soprano and a baseball game, Ms. Della Chiessa was in the midst of an engagement at the Drake Hotel and was a true South Sider, a product of East Chicago's Roosevelt High School, and a student at Chicago Musical College.[32] Nobody knew it at the time, but her singing would turn out to be the last thing anybody cheered about at the Baseball Palace of the World for the next six months.

In the team's most important game in 40 years, Early Wynn simply did not have it. He struggled in the first inning, giving up a single to Neal and walking Snider, but managed to keep the Dodgers off the scoreboard. He walked Larker, who led off the second, but then put down Roseboro, Wills, and Podres. With Wally Moon up in the third and two out, Wynn uncharacteristically issued his third walk in three innings. Duke Snider followed and homered deep into left-center to put the Dodgers up, 2–0. Meanwhile, Johnny Podres was having an easy time of it; after the first three frames, the Sox had but one hit, a single by Landis.

The fourth inning was Wynn's last. After Larker singled and was bunted to second by Roseboro, weak-hitting Maury Wills singled to drive in another run, after which the pitcher, Podres, doubled to deep center, scoring Wills. A sense of doom came over the old stadium as Lopez trudged to the mound to remove the despondent Wynn, who had given his team 268⅔ innings for the season, and sadly had nothing left at the end. Donovan, pitching savior for the Sox so far, came in, giving the Sox faithful a little ray of hope, even though their weak-hitting heroes were down, 4–0. Donovan might have saved the Series on the West Coast, but he had just pitched 48 hours ago, and it showed. He walked Gilliam, surrendered a hard-hit double to Neal, and gave up a moon-shot homer deep to left-center by Wally Moon. It was now 8–0, and the angry and crestfallen Donovan gave way to Turk Lown. Why Donovan was called when Pierce had yet to pitch in Comiskey Park was a huge mystery. When the fourth inning ended, the fans were quieter than the patrons at the nearby Bridgeport library. To add insult to injury, in the bottom of the fourth with one away and an 8–0 lead, Podres beaned Jim Landis with a fastball. The pitch hit Landis in the helmet, yet he was cleared to trot down to first base. Some in the crowd started cursing Dodgers manager Alston, and indeed, his team's reputation preceded them. Drysdale spoke freely of willingly throwing inside all through the season; Sherry hit Goodman on the kneecap at a critical juncture after a long mound conference with Alston just a few days ago. Years later the speculation proved to be true when Podres confessed to Landis at a banquet that Alstron screamed at the team between innings not to get complacent, to keep the pressure on, and then told Podres in private to hit Landis when he came to bat.[33]

This outrage was enough to cause commotion and consternation in the Sox dugout. Lollar came up and coaxed a walk out of Podres. Kluszewski crushed a Podres offering deep into the right field seats for his third home run of the Series; suddenly it was Dodgers 8, Sox 3. If anyone on the Sox was going to get to Podres, it would be Kluszewski. Throughout his career, he hit .358 with four home runs and ten RBI off the Dodgers hurler. Torgeson pinch-hit for Lown, and Podres walked him as well. Podres clearly could not regain his composure, and Alston brought in Larry Sherry, who kept the Sox fans' hopes alive when Phillips greeted him with a single. Hopes were soon were dashed, however, when Sherry struck out Goodman and got Aparacio to pop out to Wills. The South Siders might still be alive....

Unfortunately for the Sox, Sherry pitched the rest of the game, and he was just as dominant as he had been in the previous contests. From the fifth through the ninth inning, he surrendered only three hits, a fifth-inning double to Fox, a seventh-inning single to Aparicio, and a ninth-inning double to Kluszewski. Chuck Essegian made it 9–3 when he hit a record-setting second World Series pinch-hit home run off Ray Moore to start the ninth. Nobody seemed to remember that the final score was 9–3, since the game seemed over in the third inning. The greatest season Comiskey Park had seen in 40 years had an empty, hollow ending.

In the disconsolate White Sox locker room, Lopez lamented the fact that the Sox left too many men on base in Los Angeles and had difficulty fielding in the massive football stadium. Veeck praised the team's efforts, but added, "We still need a way to score more runs. We need power, someone to hit the long ball. We went a long, long way with what we had, and we got superlative efforts from a lot of guys. There's no sense in being wrong twice. My biggest regret is only for the White Sox fans, that we got them this far and couldn't quite sneak in."[34]

His last comment was in response to whether the Sox would continue fielding a team like they had in 1959, relying on defense, pitching, and speed. Unfortunately, his solutions to bolster the team's offense would haunt the team for many years to come.

The West Coast had a World Series champion for the first time in history because of the pitching of Larry Sherry, the hitting of Charlie Neal and Gil Hodges, the defensive play of John Roseboro, and the quirky conditions of the Los Angeles Coliseum. Aparicio, Fox, and Kluszewski were the only Chicagoans to produce any offense, and with Roseboro allowing only two stolen bases in six games, the weak offense was inevitable. Lopez's choice to start well-worn Wynn in the sixth game, a pitcher the Dodgers had seen in two previous contests, instead of Pierce, who was used too little in the Series, left many South Siders frustrated and perplexed. In three years, Pierce would get another chance on the big stage, but unfortunately it would be 2,000 miles away from Chicago.

The Series drew 420,784 paying customers for a record $2,626,973 in revenue. A full player's share for the winning Dodgers was $11,231, while the White Sox received $7,257. Larry Doby, Ted Kluszewski, and Harry Simpson were voted half-shares, while Ken McBride got a third and Don Mueller a quarter. Lou Skizas got $250; Camilo Carreon, Joe Hicks, J. C. Martin, and Gary Peters each got $100.[35] *United Press International* named Al Lopez the "Manager of the Year." The Chicago papers *did* report on a championship won by some South Siders that same day, not too far away. In Hyde Park, the University of Chicago beat Cambridge in the world's tiddlywinks championship— on a forfeit.[36]

October 1959 actually turned out to be one of the worst months for sports in Chicago's history. By Halloween, Chicago's NFL record was 2–8, with both the Cardinals and Bears going nowhere, each with one win and four losses that month. The Cards, in spite of the inspired efforts by quarterback King Hill, halfback John David Crow, and receiver Woodley Lewis, looked like the weakest team in football. The Bears, off to one of their worst starts in years, were making dumb mistakes and not playing up to their ability. When the two teams met in late November, the Bears trounced the Big Red soundly, 31–7. Nobody knew at the time that it would be Chicago's last "football city series." Sadly, the Wolfsons gave up trying to make a go of it in the Windy City and moved the franchise to St. Louis for the 1960 campaign; a legendary Chicago institution was lost forever, and George Halas finally was granted his decades-long wish. His cynical public response had its humorous side: "This is the best thing that's happened to St. Louis since Lindbergh."[37]

Chicago's gridiron malaise actually benefited the White Sox. By mid–December, barely two months after the last out of the World Series, ticket manager Thomas Maloney announced that they had over $900,000 in advanced ticket sales for the 1960 season, a 50 percent increase over what they experienced the year before.[38] While the atmosphere in the Hot Stove League was full of optimism, heartbreak would soon follow.

11

The Sadness of Fleeting Success

The issues for the Chicago White Sox at the end of the 1959 season were the same as they were in the beginning. Just five days after their first pennant in 40 years, ownership uncertainty once again grabbed the headlines when Chuck Comiskey announced that he was ready to sell his 46 percent of the team. To take advantage of some generous tax benefits, federal tax law required Veeck's group to control 80 percent of the outstanding shares within one year of their initial purchase. Holding 80 percent by March 1, 1960, would allow for more tax write-offs and a more generous player depreciation schedule, resulting in them saving a whopping $1.6 million in federal taxes. They needed Comiskey to sell at least 26 percent of his holdings to get to 80 percent, but Comiskey's terms were high. He thought the team was now worth $7.4 million, and he was looking for $3.4 million for all his shares. According to Chuck's math, the team's value was almost 50 percent higher than it was the previous March, when Veeck's $2.7 million bought 54 percent of a team worth $5 million. Obviously Veeck was not thrilled with the numbers, in spite of the fact that the Sox had just finished the most lucrative World Series in history. Complicating this for Veeck was the fact that there was a clause in the purchase contract he had with Dorothy Comiskey that said that if Veeck bought any more shares of the team for more than he paid her per share, she must be reimbursed at the same amount. Hence, paying Chuck $3.4 million would also mean forking over $1.2 million to Dorothy—the same amount of federal taxes he would save in the first place.[1] If Comiskey did not hold all the cards in this volley, he certainly held all the important ones: cynics called it "Chuck's Revenge."

Two months later in December, Chuck and Dorothy reached an agreement with the IRS regarding the inheritance taxes due on their mother's estate. Even though Grace had died three years earlier, the estate taxes had not yet been settled. Much to Veeck's chagrin, the court's valuation of the franchise mirrored Chuck's figure of $7.5 million. Veeck and his partners got increasingly nervous about having only three months to save a fortune in taxes, and by mid–December it appeared as though they were ready to give in to Chuck's demands. They convened a meeting and drew up the papers for the sale. The next day Chuck, reportedly on the advice of a family member, pulled out of the deal and refused to sell. Veeck and his fuming associates were thwarted in their bid to save over $1 million in corporate income tax.[2]

Veeck's failed attempts to gain greater control of the franchise, however, did not prevent him from radically changing the identity of the team. Defense, pitching, and speed may have won them a pennant, but Hank Greenberg and Veeck were still obsessed with power. In a four-day span between December 6 and December 9, without discussing the matter with Chuck, Veeck tore the future from the White Sox's pennant flag with two trades that would haunt the team for many years. Norm Cash, John Romano, and Bubba Phillips went to Cleveland for Minnie Minoso, Dick Brown, Don Ferrarese, and Jake Striker. Soon after, Johnny Callison went to the Philadelphia Phillies for veteran third baseman Gene Freese. Four months later in April 1960, Greenberg and Veeck completed the fire sale of the best crop of young players in the majors. Earl Battey and promising young outfielder Don Mincher went to Washington for the aging Roy Sievers, and, in a trade that made little sense, Barry Latman went to Cleveland for Herb Score.

When all this occurred, Sox fans were too excited about the arrival of two power hitters and the return of Minoso to worry about the long-term ramifications of these trades. Like fans everywhere, their most recent memories shaped their level of contentment, and the best season in 40 years was right behind them. Cleveland general manager Frank Lane was just as thrilled to part with the 37-year-old Minoso as Veeck was to have him. Always looking for an edge, the crafty Lane explained, "The Sox already had 40-year-old Wynn, 39-year-old Staley, 38-year-old Rivera, and 36-year-old Torgeson, Lown, Kluszewski, and Lollar. I had to make this deal. I wanted to make sure the White Sox were the oldest club in both leagues."[3]

But in getting Minoso, Freese, and Sievers, Veeck gambled that winning another pennant was more important than being set at catcher, first base, two outfield positions, and a starting pitching slot for the next decade. The golden harvests from Chuck Comiskey's farm system were cast aside for aging stars and sluggers. It looked like a pursuit of one more pennant, and Veeck's critics speculated whether Veeck was interested in the long-term health of the franchise or a short-term spike in its market value. The baseball destinies of the departed White Sox fulfilled their prophesy.

Battey became the anchor of the Senators/Minnesota Twins once he left Chicago, winning three Gold Glove Awards, making four All-Star teams, and leading the Twins to a World Series in 1965. Romano hit 91 home runs in 580 games for the Indians between 1960 and 1964 and twice was named to the American League All-Star team. During those same five seasons, Cam Carreon, Sherm Lollar, and J. C. Martin combined to hit 51 homers as the White Sox's catchers, and none of them during that time period matched Romano's or Battey's defensive play. As a matter of fact, Romano's 91 round-trippers far eclipsed the home run totals that Freese, Minoso, and Sievers put up playing in a White Sox uniform—so much for Veeck's plan to trade for power. Bob Shaw, the only young star on the team to survive this purge of youth, had another explanation for the trades, claiming that Veeck's exploding scoreboard, which was installed for the 1960 season, played a role, pointing out, "It was Veeck's decision to go for power, but the [Comiskey] park wasn't built for power. Another reason he went for the power hitters was to make the new scoreboard go off and draw more fans."[4] Shaw also recalled the penuriousness of general manager Hank Greenberg, who had a history of alienating players over salary issues. During the negotiations for his 1960 contract, Shaw complained, "I made $10,000 in 1959 and went 18–6 with a 2.86 ERA. Greenberg offered me $15,000 and I said 'you've got to be kidding.' I held out until April 4 and got $22,000, but hurt myself by missing spring training."[5]

Callison became one of the most respected outfielders of his era, making three National League All-Star teams, leading the league in doubles once and triples twice. The dramatic pennant chase by the 1964 Phillies would not have occurred without Callison's 32 homers, 104 RBI, and league-leading 19 assists. His career lasted 16 seasons, while Freese played one year at Comiskey Park. Sox fans upset with the lack of compensation for Callison would eventually be even more enraged over the loss of Norm Cash.

After being traded, Cash won the American League batting title in 1961 for Detroit, hitting .361. Playing for 17 seasons, Cash was a four-time All-Star who became one of the most significant power hitters in Detroit history with 377 homers. Mincher made two All-Star teams and hit over 20 home runs five times. Greenberg and Veeck did not know it at the time, but the power hitters they were so desperate to obtain were already in the Sox organization long before these trades were ever consummated. Playing for the Indians, Latman badly outpitched Score, who went 5–10 for the Sox in 1960 and left baseball in 1961 with a grotesque 6.66 ERA.

Even with the influx of power hitters, the 1960 White Sox hit only 15 more homers than the pennant winners of 1959. They finished a poor third, ten games behind the pennant-winning Yankees and two games behind the surprising Orioles and their well-balanced young pitching staff. Yet with advance ticket sales setting all-time records well before the season began, the enthusiasm about Minoso's return, and the opening of the Dan Ryan Expressway making Comiskey Park much more accessible to all Chicagoland, the 1960 White Sox set a new Chicago baseball attendance record. The defending

American League champions drew 1,644,460 fans, breaking the previous Chicago mark set by the pennant-winning 1929 Cubs by more than 150,000.

Things were equally unsettled upstairs in the front office. In January 1960, the Circuit Court threw out Chuck Comiskey's lawsuit to block his sister's sale of the team to Veeck, and four months later the Appellate Court affirmed the ruling. With these last legal setbacks, the grandson of the White Sox's founder was out of options in his seemingly endless bid to gain majority ownership of the team. It seemed like just a matter of time before he would bow out completely. Yet the following June, he surprised everyone by resigning his vice presidency but keeping his ownership.[6]

Greenberg's loyalty to the franchise was called into question when the American League appointed him as its agent to bring a franchise to the West Coast. The *Chicago Tribune's* November 1, 1960, edition reported that Veeck was awaiting Greenberg's report about setting up a franchise in Los Angeles, joining Greenberg in the venture, and recruiting Casey Stengel to manage the team. The article mentioned that there would be a special meeting of the American League in New York on November 17, when Veeck and Greenberg would bid for the new Los Angeles team.[7] While the report was greeted with some skepticism, many thought the story was too elaborate to be completely fictitious. This new development, coupled with Veeck's past ownership issues and previous fascination with the West Coast, raised a lot of questions about his future plans with the White Sox.

Veeck became intrigued with Hollywood and the night club set when he was in Cleveland, before his second marriage.[8] He routinely commuted from Cleveland to New York City, befriending individuals like Skitch Henderson and Frank Sinatra. His attraction to celebrity and the Hollywood lifestyle was such that Henderson even claimed that Veeck thought about getting out of baseball altogether and investing in show business. Veeck issued denials about any interest in being involved with a West Coast team, and a spokesman pointed out that he had just moved to a bigger residence in Chicago.

Veeck's history of not staying in one place too long and eagerness to take on new challenges, however, left many people skeptical. His ownership of the Indians ended prematurely, complicated by the divorce settlement from his first marriage, but the logic behind the timing of that sale was valid. Veeck claimed the divorce cost him $375,000, but court records put the figure at least $100,000 less. Since federal tax rates in 1949 were 25 percent on capital gains but ranged from 52 to 87 percent for incomes over $25,000, the only logical way he could meet this obligation was to sell the Indians.[9] After Veeck bought the Browns in 1951, he sold the team within only 30 months after he was unsuccessful in his attempts to move them to Milwaukee and Baltimore. The sale of the Browns in 1953 netted him a handsome 38 percent profit for the worst-performing franchise in the majors. With the White Sox value at an all-time high, and Comiskey refusing help Veeck save taxes by not selling his shares, could Veeck be considering this to be the perfect time to unload?

The variable nobody took into consideration which limited all of Veeck's options was his poor health.[10] He was extremely ill at the start of the 1961 season, and Greenberg ran most of the team's day-to-day activities. A heavy smoker throughout his life, Veeck was having uncontrolled coughing spells which triggered frequent blackouts. The initial diagnosis was a brain tumor. He went to the Mayo Clinic, where specialists determined that instead of having a tumor, his incessant smoker's cough had damaged blood vessels in his brain, causing him to pass out. He was told to get out of baseball.[11] Just like his purchase of the Sox, this sale had plenty of drama.

In June 1961, Bernard Epton, a 39-year-old LaSalle Street attorney and long-time Comiskey acquaintance, offered Veeck's group a generous $4.8 million for their 54 percent of the team, an amount that put the franchise's value at almost $8.9 million. Epton had formed a partnership with comedian and television star Danny Thomas.[12] Veeck and Greenberg put off Epton and Thomas until June 6, when they rejected the offer, citing a lack of confidence in Epton's and Thomas' financial capabilities and having some suspicion that Epton had an alliance with Comiskey. Veeck then did what Dorothy Comiskey did two years before, accepting a significantly lower offer than Chuck's and sealing the deal. Arthur Cecil Allyn, Jr., who with his brother John had just inherited the family's Artnell Investment Group following the death of their father (and original Veeck partner) Arthur Allyn, Sr., bought Veeck's 54 percent for $3.25 million.[13] The Veeck Syndicate's after-tax profit for 27 months of White Sox ownership was $370,000. Veeck left Chicago soon after, moving to an 18-acre estate on the eastern shore of Maryland that he named "Tranquility." At the time he purchased the White Sox, Allyn Jr., had been to two baseball games in his life.[14] Chicagoans did not hear about Bernard Epton until 20 years later, when he ran for mayor and lost to Harold Washington.

Greenberg resigned as general manager in August 1961. Allyn promoted Ed Short, who had been the White Sox's publicity director since 1950, to become the general manager. By late 1961 it became obvious that trading promising youth for aging sluggers had been a mistake. The Sox won only one less game in 1961 than they did in 1960 but finished a distant fourth, 23 games behind the Yankees. They also slipped from third to fourth because of the continued rise of Baltimore and Detroit, two youthful, aggressive squads with their best years in front of them. The Sox had become an old, slow team that had gambled on a group of aging veterans putting together a few more good years. Unfortunately for Sox fans, the architects of this failed master plan were long gone, with their profits in hand, before the scope of the failure was realized.

Chuck Comiskey finally sold his 46 percent to a group of 11 investors for $3.3 million on December 15, 1961.[15] Nobody would have predicted he would still be an owner after Veeck and Greenberg sold out, even if he outlasted them by only six months. This marked the first time in history that a Comiskey did not own part of the Sox. The buyers were three Chicago-area investors: William Bartholomay, a Chicago area insurance executive; Thomas A. Reynolds, Jr.; and Bryan S. Reid. Chuck Comiskey hoped that the Bartholomay group would eventually buy out Allyn, setting the stage for his return and control of the team, but it never happened. The new owners' relationship with the Allyn brothers was as distant and remote as Chuck's had been. Within five months, they realized that the situation was not about to change, so Bartholomay and his group sold out to the Allyns, finalizing the deal in May 1962.[16] Six months later, the Bartholomay group bought the Milwaukee Braves. Continuing the huckster legacy that baseball owners started with all the franchise moves of the 1950s, Bartholomay, after repeated denials up until the last minute about his plans, moved Milwaukee's beloved team to Atlanta. For all the hand-wringing and civic sadness that the departure of the Boston Braves, Philadelphia Athletics, St. Louis Browns, Brooklyn Dodgers, and New York Giants created in their home cities, Bartholomay's move of the Braves to Atlanta is right up there among the most heartless franchise moves in sports history.

Like 1919, history repeated itself and hard times befell the Sox as the pennant of 1959 became a distant memory. By 1967, when civil unrest and racial tensions gripped the nation, attendance at Comiskey Park plummeted, and from 1966 through 1971 the Sox were one of the worst draws and least competitive teams in baseball. The front office became so desperate for revenue that they played eight home games in Milwaukee in 1968 and 1969. Long-suffering Sox fans suffered other indignities: the rise of the Chicago Cubs as the dominant team Chicago; Comiskey Park's grotesque artificial turf infield and natural grass outfield, compliments of the Allyn brothers; and a 106-loss season in 1970. It took many decades, but the fans, some of the most fervent, resilient in the country, would say their undying loyalty paid off when their heroes, America's last neighborhood team, capped one of the greatest post-seasons in history and brought a World Series championship to 35th and Shields in 2005. Yet in spite of falling short of a world's championship, the 1959 White Sox remain indelibly etched in the memory of thousands of fans, justifiably filed away as their favorite baseball heroes.

Chapter Notes

Chapter 1

1. "For 1957, Sox Net: $396,036," *Chicago Tribune,* February 8, 1959.
2. John Snyder, *White Sox Journal* (Cincinnati: Clerisy Press, 2009), 253.
3. Bill Veeck with Ed Linn, *Veeck as in Wreck* (Chicago: University of Chicago Press, 2001), 84.
4. Richard C. Lindberg, *Stealing First in a Two-Team Town* (Champaign, IL: Sagamore, 1994), 124.
5. Snyder, *White Sox Journal,* 255.
6. Lindberg, *Stealing First,* 127.
7. *Ibid.,* 128.
8. *Ibid.,* 124–125.
9. "Grace Comiskey Says Sox Will Be Back," *Chicago Tribune,* December 17, 1950.
10. Snyder, *White Sox Journal,* 284.
11. Bob Vanderberg, *SOX: From Lane and Fain to Zisk and Fisk* (Chicago: Chicago Review Press, 1982), 67.
12. Vanderberg, *SOX,* 14.
13. "For 1957, Sox Net: $396,936," *Chicago Tribune,* February 8, 1959.
14. "Sox Big Story," *Chicago American,* July 2, 1958.
15. Vanderberg, *SOX,* 9.
16. "Outbid All for Sox Control, Says Chuck Comiskey," *Chicago Tribune,* February 15, 1959.
17. "Pay Cuts Retard Signing of Major League Players," *Chicago Tribune,* February 5, 1959.
18. "Landis Signs New Contract," *Chicago Tribune,* February 6, 1959.
19. "Sox Notes," *The Sporting News,* February 11, 1959.
20. *Ibid.*
21. "Outbid All for Sox Control: Chuck Comiskey," *Chicago Tribune,* February 15, 1959.
22. "39 White Sox Begin Spring Drills," *Chicago Tribune,* February 15, 1959.
23. "Sox Notes," *The Sporting News,* February 11, 1959.
24. "Veeck Buys Sox Control, Woos Chuck," *Chicago Tribune,* February 18, 1959.
25. "Comiskey 59-Year Rule Ends," *Chicago Daily News,* March 3, 1959.
26. "Veeck Buys Sox Control," *Chicago Tribune,* February 18, 1959.
27. *Ibid.*
28. Lindberg, *Stealing First,* 135.
29. "Cards Seek to Use Lake Front Field," *Chicago Tribune,* February 27, 1959.

Chapter 2

1. "Good Catching Plentiful on Sox," *Chicago Tribune,* March 1, 1959.
2. Don Zminda, Editor, *Go-Go to Glory* (Skokie, IL: ACTA, 2009), 58.
3. *Ibid.,* 164–166.
4. *Ibid.,* 65–67.
5. Both Cantwell quotations in Lindberg, *Stealing First,* 137–138.
6. "Chuck Loses Plea to Halt Sale," *Chicago Tribune,* March 6, 1959.
7. *Ibid.*
8. "End of a Baseball Dynasty," *Chicago Daily News,* March 5, 1959.
9. "Gimmicks & Gadgets," *Chicago Tribune,* March 1, 1959.
10. Zminda, *Go-Go to Glory,* 87–88.
11. "Veeck Sees Sox Lose, 7–5," *Chicago Tribune,* March 22, 1959.
12. "Finally! Veeck Meets Chuck," *Chicago Tribune,* March 23, 1959.
13. "Cards to Move to Soldier Field," *Chicago Tribune,* March 19, 1959.
14. "Bell Hears Bear-Cardinal Dispute," *Chicago Tribune,* January 21, 1959.
15. *Ibid.*
16. "Bell Vetoes Cards' Shift to Evanston," *Chicago Tribune,* January 23, 1959.
17. Jeff Davis, *Papa Bear: The Life and Legacy of George Halas* (New York: McGraw-Hill, 2005), 361.
18. Liam Ford, *Soldier Field: A Stadium and Its City* (Chicago: University of Chicago Press, 2009), 184.
19. "Chuck Loses Again in Stock Fight," *Chicago Tribune,* March 18, 1959.

Chapter 3

1. "Tampa Not Big Enough for Sox, Reds, Latter Say," *Chicago Tribune,* April 3, 1959.
2. "Indians Set Up Plan for Combating TV," *Chicago Tribune,* February 8, 1959.
3. *Ibid.*
4. "White Sox Owner Dispute Continues," *The Sporting News,* April 3, 1959.
5. "Comiskey Suit Decree: Chuck to Handle Tax," *Chicago Tribune,* April 9, 1959.
6. "Sox in Detroit, Cubs Meet Dodgers," *Chicago Tribune,* April 10, 1959.
7. "Heavenly Days Are Here Again," *Chicago Daily News,* April 9, 1959.
8. Dennis Purdy, *The Team-by-Team Encyclopedia of Major League Baseball* (New York: Workman, 2006), 380–381.
9. "1959 Detroit Tigers," n.d., http://Baseball-Reference.Com/DetroitTigers.Html (accessed May 15, 2018). *NOTE:* Kaline played a majority of his games in center field in 1959 and played there exclusively in 1960, moving back to right field when the Tigers traded Harvey Kuenn for Rocky Colavito.
10. "Cops Away, Fans Play," *Chicago Tribune,* April 11, 1959.
11. "Sox Home Given Thorough Scouring," *Chicago Tribune,* April 8, 1959.
12. "Sox Invite Castro to Opener," *Chicago Daily News,* April 9, 1959.
13. "In the Wake of the News," *Chicago Tribune,* April 9, 1959.
14. "Jack Eigen Speaking," *Chicago Tribune,* March 21, 1959.
15. "Jack Eigen Speaking," *Chicago Tribune,* April 4, 1959.
16. "Comiskey Suit Decree: Chuck to Handle Tax," *Chicago Tribune,* April 9, 1959.
17. Charles C. Alexander, *Breaking the Slump: Baseball in the Depression Era* (New York: Columbia University Press, 2002). In 1932, before the FDIC was established the following year, Mack supposedly had $80,000 equally deposited at four banks, and three of them went under.
18. Purdy, *Team-By-Team Encyclopedia,* 751–752.
19. *Ibid.,* 314–316.
20. Charles N. Billington, *Wrigley Field's Last World Series* (Chicago: Lake Claremont Press, 2005), 90.

21. Purdy, *Team-By-Team Encyclopedia*, 700–701.
22. "Judge Rules for Dorothy in Sox Fight," *Chicago Tribune*, April 30, 1959.

Chapter 4

1. Card #179 Don Rudolph, Series 1959, #179 (New York: Topps Chewing Gum, Inc., One Whitehall Street, Lower Manhattan, New York City).
2. Snyder, *White Sox Journal*, 328.
3. Zminda, *Go-Go to Glory*, 168–170.
4. Purdy, *Team-By-Team Encyclopedia*, 168–170.
5. "Pay Cuts Retard Signing of Major League Players," *Chicago Tribune*, February 5, 1959.
6. *The Baseball Register: The Game's 400, 1953 Edition* (St. Louis: The Sporting News Press, 1953), 85.
7. Zminda, *Go-Go to Glory*, 200–202.
8. Hank Greenberg, *The Story of My Life* (New York: Times Books, 1989), 212–213.
9. Zminda, *Go-Go to Glory*, 175–178.
10. Purdy, *Team-By-Team Encyclopedia*, 67–68.
11. *Ibid.*, 622–624.
12. "And to Complete the Report," *Chicago Tribune*, May 5, 1959.
13. "Veeck Announces New Administrative Table," *Chicago Tribune*, May 8, 1959.
14. "The Tower Ticker," *Chicago Tribune*, May 9, 1959.
15. Greenberg, *The Story of My Life*, 213.
16. *Ibid.*, 226–228.
17. Veeck, *Veeck as in Wreck*, 176.
18. Snyder, *White Sox Journal*, 329.
19. Veeck, *Veeck as in Wreck*, 12.
20. Thurber, James, "You Can Look It Up," *Saturday Evening Post*, April 5, 1941.

Chapter 5

1. "Comiskey Invites Breach in Return to Court—Veeck," *Chicago Tribune*, June 1, 1959.
2. "Chuck Bids to Set Aside Court Ruling," *Chicago Tribune*, June 2, 1959.
3. "Sox and Bugs Bomb Wilhelm," *Chicago Tribune*, June 3, 1959; Snyder, *White Sox Journal*, 345.
4. Neal Samors and Michael Williams, *Old Chicago Neighborhood* (Chicago: Chicago's Neighborhoods, 2000), 161.
5. Pierce statement to Vandenberg and Lane comments on Pierce are from Vanderberg, *SOX*, 16.
6. Samors and Williams, *Old Chicago Neighborhood*, 161.
7. "Sox Notes," *The Sporting News*, February 11, 1959.
8. "Veeck's 11th Hour $500,000 Deal Fails," *Chicago Tribune*, June 16, 1959.
9. Zminda, *Go-Go to Glory*, 116–118.
10. *Ibid.*, 117.
11. Vanderberg, *Sox*, 116.
12. *Ibid.*
13. "Sox Grand Slam Yanks: Simpson's 4 Run Homer," *Chicago Tribune*, June 28, 1959.
14. "Callison Sent Down by Sox for McAnany," *Chicago Tribune*, June 28, 1959.

Chapter 6

1. Zminda, *Go-Go to Glory*, 112–113.
2. "In the Wake of the News," *Chicago Tribune*, August 22, 1959.

3. "Sox Rap A's Slow Track," *Chicago Tribune,* July 5, 1959.
4. Zminda, *Go-Go to Glory,* 147–148.
5. "The Tower Ticker," *Chicago Tribune,* July 10, 1959.
6. "Spectacles with Curves Put McAnany in Majors," *Chicago Tribune,* July 16, 1959.
7. Peter Golenbock, *Wrigleyville* (New York: St. Martin's Press, 1996), 231–233; Alexander, *Breaking the Slump,* 54–56. Jurges was well-known to Chicagoans as a three- time All-Star shortstop starting on three pennant-winning Chicago Cubs teams in the 1930s. His career almost came to an end July 6, 1932, when love-sick Violet Popovich burst into Room 509 at the Carlos Hotel (two blocks north of Wrigley Field) and shot him in a jealous rage; miraculously, Jurges returned that season. He refused to prosecute the woman who became a Chicagoland nightclub singer, billing herself as "Violet Valli, the Girl That Did It for Love."
8. "Meet Boston, Then Yankees," *Chicago Tribune,* July 14, 1959.
9. Zminda, *Go-Go to Glory,* 123–125.
10. *Ibid.*
11. "Sox Notes," *The Sporting News,* May 14, 1959.
12. *Ibid.*

Chapter 7

1. Zminda, *Go-Go to Glory,* 137–139.
2. "The Tower Ticker," *Chicago Tribune,* August 2, 1959.
3. "Lane Blasts Stengel Again," *Chicago Tribune,* August 5, 1959.
4. "Wynn, Shaw Hold Up Sox," *Chicago Tribune,* August 18, 1959.
5. Zminda, *Go-Go to Glory,* 96–99.
6. Cover photograph, *Sports Illustrated,* August 10, 1959.
7. Zminda, *Go-Go to Glory,* 119–122.
8. Billington, *Wrigley Field's Last World Series,* 13.
9. "Sherm Lollar to the Top," *Saturday Evening Post,* July 21, 1959.
10. "TV Listings," *Chicago Tribune,* August 15, 1959.
11. "Wynn, Shaw Hold Up Sox," *Chicago Tribune,* August 18, 1959.
12. "In the Wake of the News," *Chicago Tribune,* August 21, 1959.
13. *Ibid.,* August 29, 1959.
14. *Ibid.*
15. Billington, *Wrigley Field's Last World Series,* 111.
16. Kluszewski averaged over 38 home runs and only 34 strikeouts over five seasons from 1952 to 1956. Only six other players in history have had more than 30 homers in a season with fewer strikeouts than round-trippers, and Kluszewski was the last to accomplish this incredible feat. The only other player to achieve this since 1950 was Andy Pafko, who hit 36 home runs and struck out only 32 times (in 514 at-bats) in 1950 for the Chicago Cubs.
17. Zminda, *Go-Go to Glory,* 108–110.
18. "Secret Formula to Slow Looie," *Chicago Tribune,* August 28, 1959.

Chapter 8

1. "In the Wake of the News," *Chicago Tribune,* August 29, 1959.
2. *Ibid.*
3. "Sox Hold Up Printing World Series Tickets," *Chicago Tribune,* September 9, 1959.
4. "In the Wake of the News," *Chicago Tribune,* September 7, 1959.
5. *Ibid.*
6. *Ibid.*
7. "Lopez Calls Landis Great—Getting Better," *Chicago Tribune,* September 8, 1959.
8. *Ibid.*

9. "Durocher Concedes Flag to White Sox, Lopez," *Chicago Tribune,* September 6, 1959.

10. "Sox Hold Up Printing World Series Tickets," *Chicago Tribune,* September 9, 1959.

11. "Donovan Hit on Foot by Batted Ball," *Chicago Tribune,* September 6, 1959.

12. "Nellie's Right, Orioles Prove Too Tough," *Chicago Tribune,* September 12, 1959.

13. "Old Timers Get Break in Series Tickets," *Chicago Tribune,* September 12, 1959.

14. "Committee to Draw Series Ticket Mail," *Chicago Tribune,* September 14, 1959.

15. Advertisement, *Chicago Tribune,* September 17, 1959, Section I, 6.

16. "Here's How the Chicago City Council Passed a Resolution," *Chicago Tribune,* September 17, 1959.

17. *Ibid.*

18. "Leo to Manage Indians?," *Chicago Tribune,* September 18, 1959.

19. "Lopez Talks of '54 and '56 Title Races," *Chicago Tribune,* September 21, 1959.

20. "May Go to Last Game!," *Chicago Tribune,* August 29, 1959.

21. "WGN-TV Game Viewed by a Peak Audience," *Chicago Tribune,* September 22, 1959.

22. Adam Cohen and Elizabeth Taylor, *American Pharaoh: Mayor Richard J. Daley* (Boston: Little, Brown, 2000), 148–149.

23. *Ibid.*

24. "Files Formal Protest Over Sirens for Sox," *Chicago Tribune,* September 25, 1959.

25. All quotations are from "Letters to the Editor," *Chicago Tribune,* September 26, 1959.

26. "25,000 Jam Airports to Greet Team," *Chicago Tribune,* September 23, 1959.

27. "Mrs. Veeck Savors Memories of Husband, Sox in '59 Series," *Chicago Sun Times,* October 20, 2005.

28. "The Tower Ticker," *Chicago Tribune,* September 25, 1959.

29. *Ibid.*

30. All quotations about and by Frank Lane are from "In the Wake of the News," *Chicago Tribune,* September 23, 1959.

31. "Harder Takes Gordon's Job with Indians," *Chicago Tribune,* September 23, 1959.

32. "Dykes Recalls White Sox Lean Years," *Chicago Tribune,* September 2, 1959.

33. "In the Wake of the News," *Chicago Tribune,* September 4, 1959.

34. All quotations about the Chicago Cardinals, "In the Wake of the News," *Chicago Tribune,* September 27, 1959.

Chapter 9

1. "There's More to a World Series than Winning a Pennant," *Chicago Tribune,* October 1, 1959.

2. "Don't Be Taken In," *Chicago Tribune,* September 29, 1959.

3. "Could Sell 25 Times Park's Seats—Chuck," *Chicago Tribune,* October 1, 1959.

4. "Long, Loyal Fans Hail the Surge of White Sox," *Chicago Tribune,* September 23, 1959.

5. *Ibid.*

6. Zminda, *Go-Go to Glory,* 229.

7. *Ibid.,* 230.

8. *Ibid.*

9. *Ibid.,* 231.

10. "After 40 Years," *Chicago Tribune,* October 1, 1959.

11. "In the Wake of the News," *Chicago Tribune,* October 1, 1959.

12. *Ibid.*

13. *Ibid.*

14. "Lopez Signs to Manage Sox in 1960," *Chicago Tribune,* September 30, 1959.

15. "Series Expected to Bring 10 Million Dollars to City," *Chicago Tribune,* September 24, 1959.

16. "That's All Right, Mr. Alston, Our Sox Were Very Different, Too," *Chicago Tribune,* October 3, 1959.

17. Cobb and Lopez quotes from "Ty Cobb Picks Sox to Take Series," *Chicago Tribune,* September 22, 1959.

Chapter 10

1. "Patient Tony Bargains for Trouble," *Chicago Tribune,* October 2, 1959.
2. "Veeck Gets Even with Perini," *Chicago Tribune,* October 2, 1959.
3. Condon, Dave, *The Go-Go Chicago White Sox* (New York: Coward-McCann, 1960), 190.
4. *Ibid.*
5. "Young Mother Holds Daring Series Role," *Chicago Tribune,* October 3, 1959.
6. Zminda, *Go-Go To Glory,* 268.
7. Snyder, *White Sox Journal,* 334. Oil company executive Melvin Piehl was the subject of one of the most famous pictures in World Series history when he reached over for Neal's homer and spilled a full beer on the hapless Smith. Up in the press box 500 feet away, Ray Gora, a Chicago newspaper photographer, captured the image with a state-of-the-art camera developed by the government that was to be used only for space launches at Cape Canaveral.
8. Condon, *The Go-Go Chicago White Sox,* 193–194.
9. "Cuccinello Signaled Lollar, All the Way," *Chicago Tribune,* October 3, 1959.
10. *Ibid.*
11. "That's All Right, Mr. Alston, Our Sox Were Very Different, Too," *Chicago Tribune,* October 3, 1959.
12. "Podres Isn't Impressed by White Sox," *Chicago Tribune,* October 3, 1959.
13. "Record Air Lift for Ball Fans," *Chicago Tribune,* October 3, 1959.
14. Condon, *The Go-Go Chicago White Sox,* 194.
15. "White Sox Inspect Coliseum and Begin to Wonder," *Chicago Tribune,* October 4, 1959.
16. *Ibid.*
17. *Ibid.*
18. Condon, *The Go-Go Chicago White Sox,* 194.
19. "Did Luis React Slowly on Furillo's Drive?," *Chicago Tribune,* October 5, 1959.
20. "In the Wake of the News," *Chicago Tribune,* October 5, 1959.
21. *Ibid.* Cortisone usage was vastly different in 1959 than it is today. Bi-weekly cortisone injections, unheard-of today, were commonplace. Snider's Hall of Fame teammate Sandy Koufax, at the end of his career, was getting cortisone injections in his pitching elbow almost every time he pitched, as the risks of cortisone overuse had not yet been established.
22. "It's Wynn Vs. Craig," *Chicago Tribune,* October 6, 1959.
23. *Ibid.*
24. Smith, Lopez and Shaw quotations all from "Winning Hits Not Genuine, Says Smith," *Chicago Tribune,* October 6, 1959.
25. Alston and Sherry quotations from "In the Wake of the News," *Chicago Tribune,* September 29, 1959.
26. "Dodgers' Bavasi Collapses," *Chicago Tribune,* October 6, 1959.
27. "In the Wake of the News," *Chicago Tribune,* October 7, 1959.
28. *Ibid.*
29. "We're Going to Win It, Says," *Chicago Tribune,* October 7, 1959.
30. "Wynn Lets Off Steam and Tosses Curves to West Coast Reporters," *Chicago Tribune,* October 7, 1959.
31. *Ibid.*
32. Condon, *The Go-Go Chicago White Sox,* 203.
33. Mark Liptak, "Interview with Jim Landis," http://www.Flyingsock.Com (Accessed May 15, 2018).
34. Condon, the *Go-Go Chicago White Sox,* 217.

35. "Dodgers Received $11,231 for a Full Share," *Chicago Tribune,* October 16, 1959.
36. "Well, Anyway, We Have One World Champ!" *Chicago Tribune,* October 10, 1959.
37. Ford, *Soldier Field: A Stadium and Its City,* 186.
38. "Sox Ring Up $900,000 on Tickets," *Chicago Tribune,* December 19, 1959.

Chapter 11

1. "Comiskey Gets New Veeck Bid Today," *Chicago Tribune,* October 13, 1959.
2. "Big Demands Fail Veeck in Sox Bid," *Chicago Tribune,* December 1, 1959.
3. Vanderberg, *SOX,* 10.
4. *Ibid.,* 214.
5. *Ibid.*
6. "Comiskey Quits Sox Vice Presidency," *Chicago Tribune,* June 9, 1960.
7. "Is Veeck Selling Sox to Get L.A.?" *Chicago Tribune,* November 1, 1960.
8. Gerald Eskenazi, *Bill Veeck: A Baseball Legend* (New York: McGraw-Hill, 1988), 73–77.
9. *Ibid.,* 80–82.
10. *Ibid.,* 6, and "Sox Notes," *The Sporting News,* June 3, 1959. As an adolescent, Veeck suffered from severe eczema, aggravated by an asthmatic condition, and was sent to the Ranch School in Los Alamos, New Mexico. Climate and air quality were big selling points of Ranch School, and his experiences there contributed to his social ease in the company of wealthy individuals. The annual tuition was $2,000 when Harvard's was $500. Eskenazi points out that Gore Vidal, William Burroughs, Antonio Taylor (First Lady Ladybird Johnson's brother), and the future corporate heads of American Motors, Quaker Oats, and Sears all attended the Ranch School.
11. Eskenazi, *Bill Veeck,* 134.
12. "Epton Group Bids for Sox Control," *Chicago Tribune,* June 2, 1961.
13. "Veeck & Greenberg Sell Sox," *Chicago Tribune,* June 11, 1959.
14. Snyder, *White Sox Journal,* 347–348; Lindberg, *Stealing First,* 144–146.
15. Snyder, *White Sox Journal,* 351.
16. *Ibid.;* Lindberg, *Stealing First,* 149.

Bibliography

Books

Alexander, Charles C. *Breaking the Slump: Baseball in the Depression Era*. New York: Columbia University Press, 2002.

Billington, Charles N. *Wrigley Field's Last World Series: The Wartime Chicago Cubs and the Pennant of 1945*. Chicago: Lake Claremont, 2005.

Carney, Gene. *Burying the Black Sox*. Dulles, VA: Potomac, 2006.

Cohen, Adam, and Elizabeth Taylor. *American Pharaoh: Mayor Richard J. Daley*. Boston: Little, Brown, 2000.

Condon, Dave. *The Go-Go Chicago White Sox*. New York: Coward-McCann, 1960.

Cowan, David, and John Kuenstler. *To Sleep with Angels: The Story of a Fire*. Chicago: Ivan R. Dee, 1996.

Cramer, Richard Ben. *Joe DiMaggio: The Hero's Life*. New York: Simon & Schuster, 2000.

Davis, Jeff. *Papa Bear: The Life and Legacy of George Halas*. New York: McGraw-Hill, 2005.

Eig, Jonathan. *Luckiest Man: The Life and Death of Lou Gehrig*. New York: Simon & Schuster, 2005.

_____. *Opening Day: Jackie Robinson's First Season*. New York: Simon & Schuster, 2007.

Eskenazi, Gerald. *Bill Veeck: A Baseball Legend*. New York: McGraw-Hill, 1988.

Ford, Liam. *Soldier Field: A Stadium and Its City*. Chicago: University of Chicago Press, 2009.

Gilbert, James. *They Also Served: Baseball and the Home Front*. New York: Crown Books, 1992.

Goldstein, Richard. *Spartan Seasons*. New York: Macmillan, 1980.

Golenbock, Peter. *Wrigleyville*. New York: St. Martin's Press, 1996.

Greenberg, Hank. *The Story of My Life*. New York: Times Books, 1989.

Grossman, James R. et al, editors. *The Encyclopedia of Chicago*. Chicago: University of Chicago Press, 2004.

Higbe, Kirby. *The High Hard One*. New York: Viking, 1960.

Hirsch, James S. *Willie Mays: The Life, the Legend*. New York: Scribner's, 2010.

James, Bill. *The New Bill James Historical Baseball Abstract*. New York: Free Press, 2003.

Katz, Lawrence. *Baseball in 1939: The Watershed Season of the National Pastime*. Jefferson, NC: Banner Books, 1991.

Leavy, Jane. *The Last Boy: Mickey Mantle*. New York: HarperCollins, 2010.

Leventhal, Josh. *Take Me Out to the Ballpark*. New York: Black Dog & Leventhal, 2000.

Lindberg, Richard C. *Stealing First in a Two-Team Town*. Champaign, IL: Sagamore, 1994.

_____. *White Sox Encyclopedia*. Philadelphia: Temple University Press, 1997.

_____. *Who's on 3rd? The Chicago White Sox Story*. South Bend: Icarus Press, 1983.

Mead, William B. *Even the Browns*. Chicago: Contemporary, 1978.

Nemec, David, et al. *The Baseball Chronicle*. Lincolnwood, IL: Publications International, 2001.

Purdy, Dennis. *The Team-By-Team Encyclopedia of Major League Baseball*. New York: Workman, 2006.

Samors, Neal, and Michael Williams. *Chicago in the Fifties*. Chicago: Chicago's Neighborhoods, 2005.

_____. *The Old Chicago Neighborhood*. Chicago: Chicago's Neighborhoods, 2000.

Scheinin, Richard. *Field of Screams*. New York: W. W. Norton, 1994.

Snyder, John. *White Sox Journal*. Cincinnati: Clerisy, 2009.

Spink, J. G. Taylor. *Baseball Register, 1953 Edition*. St. Louis: C. C. Spink & Son, 1953.

Sugar, Bert Randolph. *The Baseball Maniac's Almanac*. New York: Skyhorse, 2010.

Thorn, John. *Total Baseball*. New York: Total Sports, 2000.

Tofel, Peter. *A Legend in the Making*. Chicago: Ivan R. Dee, 2000.

Tygiel, Jules. *Past Time: Baseball as History*. New York: Oxford University Press, 2000.

Vanderberg, Bob. *SOX: From Lane and Fain to Zisk and Fisk*. Chicago: Chicago Review Press, 1982.

Veeck, Bill, with Ed Linn. *Veeck as in Wreck*. Chicago: University of Chicago Press, 2001.

Wolff, Rick. *The Baseball Encyclopedia*. New York: Macmillan, 1990.

Zimbalist, Andrew. *Baseball and Billions*. New York: Basic Books, 1996.

Zirin, David. *Bad Sports: How Owners Are Ruining the Games We Love*. New York: Scribner's, 2010.

Zminda, Don, editor. *Go-Go to Glory*. Skokie, IL: ACTA, 2009.

Government Publications

United States House of Representatives, 82nd Congress, First Session, Part 6. *Hearings Before the Subcommittee on the Study of Monopoly Power of the Committee on the Judiciary*. United States Government Printing Office: Washington, D.C., 1951.

Internet Sites

BaseballAlmanac.com

Baseball-Reference.com

FlyingSox.com

Pro-Football-Reference.com

St. Louis Browns Historical Society: www.thestlbrowns.com

Newspapers and Magazines

Chicago Daily Tribune, September 29, 1952, through June 2, 1961.

Chicago Sun Times, April 1 through April 9, 1959.

The Saturday Evening Post, April 5, 1941, and July 21, 1947.

The Sporting News, February 5 through December 16, 1959.

Sports Illustrated, August 10, 1959.

Index